OXFORD MONOGRAPHS ON MUSIC

UNPREMEDITATED ART

UNPREMEDITATED ART

THE CADENZA
IN THE
CLASSICAL KEYBOARD CONCERTO

PHILIP WHITMORE

CLARENDON PRESS · OXFORD
1991

Oxford University Press, Walton Street, Oxford OX2 6DP
Oxford New York Toronto
Delhi Bombay Calcutta Madras Karachi
Petaling Jaya Singapore Hong Kong Tokyo
Nairobi Dar es Salaam Cape Town
Melbourne Auckland
and associated companies in
Berlin Ibadan

Oxford is a trade mark of Oxford University Press

Published in the United States
by Oxford University Press, New York

British Library Cataloguing in Publication Data
Whitmore, Philip J.
Unpremeditated art: the cadenza in the classical
keyboard concerto – (Oxford monographs on music)
1. Music. Composition
I. Title II. Series
781.61
ISBN 0-19-315263-0

Library of Congress Cataloging in Publication Data
Whitmore, Philip.
Unpremeditated art: the cadenza in the classical keyboard
concerto/Philip Whitmore.
(Oxford monographs on music)
Includes bibliographical references and index.
1. Concertos (Piano)—18th century—Cadenzas—History and
criticism. 2. Improvisation (Music) I. Title. II. Series.
ML1263.W55 1991
784.2'62'09033—dc 20   90-7831
ISBN 0-19-315263-0

Photoset by Rowland Phototypesetting Ltd
Bury St Edmunds, Suffolk
Printed in Great Britain by
Bookcraft (Bath) Ltd
Midsomer Norton, Avon

Hail to thee, blithe spirit!
        Bird thou never wert—
That from heaven or near it
        Pourest thy full heart
In profuse strains of unpremeditated art.
                        (Shelley)

To my mother

Preface

⟨∾≭∾⟩

A SOLOIST seeking to provide a cadenza for a classical concerto is faced with an aesthetic dilemma: the composer would have expected him to improvise in his own personal style, rather than that of the composer of the concerto, yet how is it possible for a twentieth-century performer to do so in an eighteenth-century work without stylistic incongruity? In an age as sensitive as our own to 'authentic' performing practice it would scarcely be acceptable to insert a cadenza in a modern idiom, although it should be remembered that Mozart and Beethoven had no hesitation in doing precisely that when performing concertos from an earlier generation. We should bear this in mind before condemning too loudly the cadenzas written by soloists from the nineteenth and early twentieth centuries for the concertos of the classical masters. In today's more historically conscious climate, however, what is the soloist to do? Many now strive to imitate as closely as possible the style of the composer of the concerto, and they utilize original cadenzas by the composer whenever these are available. While this approach seems to satisfy the present-day demand for recreating the 'original' conditions of performance, it unfortunately introduces a wholly foreign element of fixity into a convention that was intended to leave room for a great variety of expression. It was far from Mozart's intention that other performers should write cadenzas in his personal style. Yet it is idle to speculate on what he would have expected a present-day soloist to play, in so far as he could have imagined that his concertos would continue to be performed two hundred years after his death; it must be admitted that no solution to the problem can be entirely satisfactory.

The purpose of this book is not to suggest to present-day performers how they should solve the cadenza problem posed by the classical concerto repertoire. Rather, it is to offer a history of the cadenza in the classical keyboard concerto, in the hope of contributing towards a better understanding of its changing nature and function during the period under consideration. The origins, the growth, and the eventual decline of the convention are all examined, and the contributions of such major composers as C. P. E. Bach, Mozart, and Beethoven to this process are placed in a context which, it is hoped, will shed some light upon their intentions and expectations regarding ad libitum cadenzas.

While the principal focus of attention here is the keyboard concerto cadenza, some consideration must also be given to other types. Keyboard cadenzas are found in works that are not concertos, and these too have occasionally been brought into the discussion. Besides, the origins of the cadenza lie outside the keyboard repertoire altogether, and so some treatment of cadenzas for other instruments and for the voice is needed if certain developments in the history of the keyboard cadenza are to be adequately explained. The particular study of keyboard cadenzas in Part II needs to be placed in the context of a more general history of the cadenza from its origins to its decline, and it is this which forms the subject-matter of Part I. In the course of this general history a definition is proposed, and a summary of the recommendations made in eighteenth-century treatises on performing practice is provided.

The principal focus of attention in Part II is the contribution made to the development of the keyboard concerto cadenza by individual composers from J. S. Bach to Beethoven. Relatively brief treatment is accorded to regional 'schools'. For all but the most specialized reader, this should suffice. Any reader in search of greater detail concering the role of minor composers should refer to my D.Phil. thesis, 'The Cadenza in the Classical Keyboard Concerto' (University of Oxford, 1986), on which the present book is based.

At least as much attention is given to the context of cadenzas as to their content; the latter is frequently an unknown variable, whereas a great deal of information is available concerning the former. Our study of individual composers, then, will be concerned with such questions as how frequently they invite cadenzas, in what type of work or in which movements, at what point in the structure thereof, and how the cadenzas are approached and quitted, in addition to more obvious questions about what the cadenzas themselves were like. Surviving written-out cadenzas, in any case, reveal more about those who wrote them than about the composers for whose concertos they were intended. Hence, for example, discussion of Beethoven's cadenzas for Mozart's D minor Concerto belongs properly in the chapter devoted to Beethoven, and not in the chapter devoted to Mozart. When the authorship of a cadenza is unknown, however, it is discussed together with the concerto to which it belongs.

Finally, mention should be made of the problem of definition. A great deal of confusion can arise when the comments of an eighteenth-century writer about the cadenza are applied indiscriminately to other types of improvised or improvisatory interpolations, and vice versa; it is necessary to distinguish carefully between the fermata, the *Eingang*, the perfidia, and the capriccio (see Chapter 3). Contemporary accounts and definitions of the cadenza, while invaluable as documentary evidence, need to be evaluated critically and placed in their context. Unfortunately the terminology used by eighteenth-century composers and writers was inconsistent, and needs to be modified in a history such as this. Nor have present-day commentators adopted a uniform set of terms, and it is inevitable that the usage adopted and the conclusions reached here will conflict with those of some recent studies as a result.

The approach used in the present work has been to adopt as a starting-point the mature classical keyboard cadenza, as exemplified in the works of Mozart, and to trace the history of this phenomenon from its earliest manifestations as far as its disappearance, or rather metamorphosis, in the early nineteenth century. The so-called biographical model,[1] by which the history of a phenomenon is described in terms of its antecedents, its birth, growth, prime, decline, and death, may be unfashionable, but is adopted here without apology, as it seems the model best suited to charting the development of this particular phenomenon.

Some form of definition is needed before the origins of the cadenza can be discussed, in order to distinguish between anticipations and early manifestations. On the other hand, before a satisfactory definition can be given, it is necessary to consider as many different manifestations of the phenomenon as possible from all periods of its history, in order that the definition may be expressed in terms sufficiently broad to embrace all existing types. A degree of circularity is thus unavoidable given an approach of this kind, and it must be accepted that the criteria for definition might be thought somewhat subjective. In the first place, great emphasis is placed upon harmonic context; this seems justified by the etymology of the word 'cadenza', it is consonant with current ways of thinking about the fundamental processes of tonal music, and it seems to match the evidence provided by a wide sample of eighteenth-century music, in which particular methods of articulation are developed for important cadences. The emphasis placed upon clarity of articulation at the beginning may be more controversial, but once again it is consonant with current methods of analysing the listener's experience of music, in particular with Leonard Meyer's work, and it too seems to match the evidence.

In the musical examples beaming and clefs have been modernized where necessary, and editorial suggestions concerning accidentals and cadential trills have been added in some places. The glossary gives a summary of the definitions used in the book.

Translations of extracts from works originally written in French, German, or Italian have in most cases been quoted from standard translations, where these exist. Details of such translations are in all cases to be found in the footnotes or the Bibliography, and references to page numbers or to chapter and paragraph numbers are given in footnotes. In the case of the Rousseau passage appearing in Chapter 10 and the quotations from C. P. E. Bach's *Versuch*, however, the translations are by the author.

Finally I should like to express my gratitude for all the valuable help and advice received from Dr D. E. Olleson and from Dr S. L. F. Wollenberg, who supervised this research, and for the patient assistance supplied by the staffs of the Bodleian Library, Oxford, the British Library, London, and many

---

[1] This approach to musical historiography is discussed in C. Dahlhaus, trans. J. B. Robinson, *Foundations of Music History* (Cambridge, etc., 1983), 44 f.

other libraries in Europe. I would like to thank in particular the music section of the Österreichische Nationalbibliothek and the Gesellschaft der Musik-freunde in Vienna for permission to reproduce Exx. 40 and 41 respectively. The figure on pages 41–3 is reproduced by kind permission of the Provost and Fellows of King's College, Cambridge. Dr H. D. Johnstone has provided many useful suggestions and ideas relating to the revision of my doctoral thesis for publication. Financial support from the governments of the United Kingdom, Austria, and the Federal Republic of Germany, and from Merton and Magdalen Colleges Oxford, is gratefully acknowledged, as is also the generous help and advice of innumerable friends and colleagues at every stage in the preparation of the book.

P.J.W.

January 1989
Palazzola
AMDG

Contents

∽ɷ∾

List of illustrations   xii
List of tables   xv
Abbreviations   xvi
Notes on Reference Style   xix

PART I   1
1. What is a Cadenza?   3
2. On the Performance of Cadenzas   20
3. When is a Cadenza not a Cadenza?   35
4. Growth and Decline   47

PART II   63
5. Late Baroque Cadenzas   65
6. C. P. E. Bach and the Cadenza   77
7. Other Composers in Germany and Austria   98
8. Mozart and the Cadenza   119
9. Haydn and the Cadenza   149
10. Outside Germany and Austria   154
11. Viotti and the Cadenza   171
12. Beethoven and the Cadenza   181
13. The Virtuoso Concerto   204
Bibliography   214
Glossary of terms   219
General index   221

List of Illustrations

༺✦༻

EXAMPLES

1. A. Corelli, Sonata, Op. 5 No. 11, first movement: (*a*) Corelli's original version, (*b*) the version given in 'Walsh Anonymous' 8
2. W. A. Mozart, Sonata in F, K. 533, finale 13
3. W. A. Mozart, Sonata in F, K. 332, finale 14
4. J. Haydn, Concerto in G, Hob. XVIII: 4, finale 16–18
5. J. A. Hiller, example of a cadenza from *Anweisung* 25
6. G. Tartini, example of a cadenza from *Traité* 27
7. C. P. E. Bach, example from *Versuch* 28
8. C. P. E. Bach, example from *Versuch* 29
9. C. P. E. Bach, example from *Versuch* 29
10. J. J. Quantz, *Versuch*: (*a*) example of a plain *halbe Kadenz*, (*b*) example of an embellished *halbe Kadenz* 36
11. J. J. Quantz, *Versuch*, examples of initial vocal entries (*a*) unembellished, (*b*) embellished 36
12. C. P. E. Bach, example of an embellished fermata from *Versuch* 37
13. G. Torelli, openings of perfidias, TV 65 and TV 66 40
14. A. Corelli, Sonata, Op. 5 No. 3, second movement 40
15. G. Tartini, Capriccio from Concerto, D. 103, finale 45
16. Examples of vocal cadences in which the last few words are repeated after a rest: (*a*) G. F. Handel, *Messiah*, 'But Who May Abide', (*b*) A. Scarlatti, *Griselda*, 'Quella tiranna' 51
17. Example of a pre-tutti cadenza: G. A. Benda, Concerto in F minor, second movement 55
18. Example of simple tutti reinforcement of cadence: C. P. E. Bach, Concerto in D, H. 433, second movement 55
19. Examples of extended cadences, with and without interruption: (*a*) J. Haydn, Concerto in D, Hob. XVIII: 11, second movement, (*b*) J. B. Vanhal, Concerto in C, second movement 56
20. Example of an inserted cadenza: W. A. Mozart, Concerto in G, K. 107 No. 2, first movement 57
21. Harmonic schemes of first-movement cadenzas in (*a*) Schumann's Piano Concerto and (*b*) Rachmaninov's First Piano Concerto 60
22. G. F. Handel, Organ Concerto, Op. 4 No. 2, second movement 66
23. G. F. Handel, Organ Concerto, Op. 4 No. 4, first movement 66
24. J. S. Bach, E major Violin Concerto, BWV 1042, first-movement

cadenza (*a*) with harmonization borrowed from Bach's
harpsichord arrangement, BWV 1054, and (*b*) with simpler
harmonization   71
25. (*a*) Two cadenzas for an aria from Handel's *Poro*; (*b*) the cadence
    at which the above cadenzas were inserted   75
26. C. P. E. Bach, Sonata, H. 25, second movement   77
27. C. P. E. Bach, Concerto, H. 430, first movement   81
28. C. P. E. Bach, Concerto, H. 441, first movement   81
29. C. P. E. Bach, (*a*) 'Einfall' from H. 264, and (*b*) Concerto,
    H. 434, first movement, closing bars   87
30. C. P. E. Bach, (*a*) cadenza 18 from H. 264, and (*b*) Concerto,
    H. 430, first movement, opening   89
31. C. P. E. Bach, beginning of cadenza 1, H. 264   90
32. C. P. E. Bach, cadenza 33 from H. 264   92
33. (*a*) C. P. E. Bach, Concerto, H. 473, first movement; (*b*) C. P. E.
    Bach, Concerto, H. 475, first movement   94
34. C. P. E. Bach, Concerto, H. 476, first movement   95
35. C. P. E. Bach, Concerto, H. 474, 'Finale'   96
36. J. C. Bach, Concerto, Op. 13 No. 4, second movement, cadenza
    from Sieber edn.   104
37. J. C. F. Bach, Concerto in E major, first movement   105
38. G. J. Vogler, Concerto, Op. 2 No. 1, first-movement cadenza   107
39. J. M. Steinbacher, Concerto in F: (*a*) first-movement cadenza, (*b*)
    second-movement cadenza, (*c*) finale cadenza   109
40. A. Salieri, Concerto in B flat, first-movement cadenza (from A-Wn
    Mus. Hs. 3728)   112–14
41. L. Kozeluch, Concerto in C, P. IV: 17, cadenza from A-Wgm
    Q 16250 (VII 12281)   115–18
42. W. A. Mozart, Concerto in F, K. 459, first movement   122
43. W. A. Mozart, cadenza 58   123
44. W. A. Mozart, Musical Joke, K. 522, third movement   127
45. W. A. Mozart, cadenza 62   130–2
46. W. A. Mozart, cadenza 17   139
47. W. A. Mozart, (*a*) cadenza 61, (*b*) Concerto in A, K. 488, first
    movement, (*c*) cadenza 27   141
48. T. S. Dupuis, Concerto, Op. 1 No. 6, fourth movement   156
49. W. Hayes, Concerto in G major, second-movement cadenza   158
50. J. Stanley, Organ Voluntary, Op. 7 No. 3   159
51. J.-B. Davaux, Symphonie concertante No. 2, arranged as a trio,
    first-movement cadenza   166–8
52. H.-J. Rigel, Concerto Concertant, Op. 20, first-movement
    cadenza   169
53. G. B. Viotti, Concerto Wh. I: 22, finale cadenza (solo violin
    part only)   173–4

54. G. B. Viotti, Concerto Wh. I: 27, finale cadenza   176
55. L. van Beethoven, Piano Concerto No. 2, second movement   183
56. L. van Beethoven, Piano Concerto No. 4, second movement   184
57. J. L. Dussek, Piano Concerto, Op. 27, C. 104, finale cadenza
    (from 1st edn.)   205
58. M. Clementi, 'Cadenza alla Haydn', Op. 19   209
59. M. Clementi, 'Cadenza alla Clementi', Op. 19   209

FIGURE

P. A. Locatelli, Violin Concerto, Op. 3 No. 8, finale, conclusion
(solo violin part only)   41–3

List of Tables

1. The cadenzas by C. P. E. Bach contained in H. 264   85–6
2. Cadenzas by Mozart for use in his mature concertos   120–1
3. Cadenzas by Mozart for use in concertos by other composers and in his early concerto arrangements   121
4. Alterations in the distribution of cadenzas/cadential fermatas in the piano concerto arrangements of Viotti's violin concertos   178
5. Structural overview of Cramer's arrangement (Wh. Ia: 13) of the finale of Viotti's Violin Concerto No. 27 (Wh. I: 27)   179
6. The incidence of cadenzas and cadential fermatas in Beethoven's piano concertos (not including *Eingänge*)   182
7. Cadenzas by Beethoven   194
8. Craw's list of piano concertos by Dussek   204

Abbreviations

1. LIBRARY SIGLA

The sigla given here are those used in the publications of Répertoire international des sources musicales (RISM), except that the national sigillum 'D' is used without further qualification to indicate both the former Federal Republic and the former Democratic Republic of Germany, and 'Lbl' has replaced 'Lbm' as the sigillum for the British Library, formerly the British Museum.

Austria

A-M   Benediktiner-Stift Melk
A-Wgm Vienna, Gesellschaft der Musikfreunde
A-Wn   Vienna, Österreichische Nationalbibliothek, Musiksammlung

Belgium

B-Bc   Brussels, Conservatoire Royal de Musique
B-Br   Brussels, Bibliothèque Royale Albert 1er

France

F-Pn   Paris, Bibliothèque Nationale (including the collection formerly housed in the Conservatoire National de Musique and indicated in RISM by the sigillum F-Pc)

Germany

D-B   West Berlin, Staatsbibliothek Preussischer Kulturbesitz
D-Bds   East Berlin, Deutsche Staatsbibliothek
D-Dlb   Dresden, Sächsische Landesbibliothek
D-Rtt   Regensburg, Fürstliche Thurn und Taxis'sche Hofbibliothek
D-SW1 Schwerin, Wissenschaftliche Allgemeinbibliothek des Bezirkes Schwerin

Great Britain

GB-Ckc Rowe Music Library, King's College, Cambridge
GB-Lbl   London, British Library
GB-Lcm London, Royal College of Music
GB-Ob   Oxford, Bodleian Library

Italy

I-Tn   Turin, Biblioteca Nazionale Universitaria

2. REFERENCES TO THEMATIC CATALOGUES

BWV W. Schmieder, *Thematisch-systematisches Verzeichnis der musikalischen Werke Johann Sebastian Bachs*, 3rd edn. (Leipzig, 1966).

C. H. A. Craw, 'A Biography and Thematic Catalog of the Works of J. L. Dussek (1760–1812)' (diss., Univ. of Southern California, 1964).

D. M. Dounias, *Die Violinkonzerte Giuseppe Tartinis* (Wolfenbüttel, 1935).

F. M. Falck, *Wilhelm Friedemann Bach* (Leipzig, 1913).

H. E. E. Helm, *Thematic Catalogue of the Works of Carl Philipp Emanuel Bach* (New Haven, Conn., and London, 1989).

Hob. A. van Hoboken, *Joseph Haydn: Thematisch-bibliographisches Werkverzeichnis*, 2 vols. (Mainz, 1957–71).

K. L. von Köchel, *Chronologisch-thematisches Verzeichnis sämtlicher Tonwerke Wolfgang Amade Mozarts*, 6th edn., ed. F. Giegling, A. Weinmann, and G. Sievers (Leipzig, 1964). (Superscript figures 1, 3, or 6 appearing after K refer specifically to the 1st, 3rd, or 6th edn. respectively.)

P. M. Poštolka, *Leopold Koželuh* (Prague, 1964).

RV P. Ryom, *Verzeichnis der Werke Antonio Vivaldis: Kleine Ausgabe* (Leipzig, 1974; suppl., Poitiers, 1979).

SM H. Scholz-Michelitsch, *Das Orchester- und Kammermusikwerk von G. C. Wagenseil: Thematischer Katalog* (Vienna, 1972).

TV F. Giegling, *Giuseppe Torelli: Ein Beitrag zur Entwicklungsgeschichte des italienischen Konzerts* (Kassel and Basle, 1949).

Wh. C. White, *Giovanni Battista Viotti (1755–1824): A Thematic Catalogue of His Works* (New York, 1985).

WoO G. Kinsky and H. Halm, *Das Werk Beethovens: thematisch-bibliographisches Verzeichnis seiner sämtlichen vollendeten Kompositionen* (Munich and Duisburg, 1955). (WoO = Werke ohne Opuszahl = works with no opus number.)

Wq. A. Wotquenne, *Thematisches Verzeichnis der Werke von Carl Philipp Emanuel Bach (1714–1788)* (Leipzig, 1905; repr. 1964).

3. JOURNALS AND REFERENCE WORKS

AMZ *Allgemeine musikalische Zeitung*
B-Jb *Bach-Jahrbuch*
DAM *Dansk Aarbog for Musikforskning*
Grove S. Sadie (ed.), *The New Grove Dictionary of Music and Musicians*, 20 vols. (London, 1980).
JAMS *Journal of the American Musicological Society*
JRMA *Journal of the Royal Musical Association*
MGG F. Blume (ed.), *Die Musik in Geschichte und Gegenwart*, 17 vols. (Kassel and Basle, 1949–68; suppl. 1973–9).
M-Jb *Mozart-Jahrbuch*
MQ *The Musical Quarterly*
NOHM E. Wellesz, J. A. Westrup, and G. Abraham (eds.), *The New Oxford History of Music*, 10 vols. (London, 1954–).
SIMG *Sammelbände der internationalen Musikgesellschaft*

4. EDITIONS

AMA *Alte Mozart Ausgabe = W.A. Mozarts Werke*, ed. L. von Köchel etc. (Leipzig, 1877–83, suppls. 1877–1910).

BG *J. S. Bach: Werke*, ed. Bach-Gesellschaft (Leipzig, 1851–99; repr. 1947).

BW *L. van Beethoven: Werke: Neue Ausgabe sämtlicher Werke*, ed. J. Schmidt-Görg etc. (Munich and Duisburg, 1961–).

DTÖ *Denkmäler der Tonkunst in Österreich*, ed. G. Adler, vols. i–lxxxiii, and E. Schenk, vols. lxxxiv– (Vienna, Leipzig, and Graz, 1894–).

HG Händel-Gesellschaft = *G. F. Händels Werke*, ed. F. W. Chrysander (Leipzig and Bergedorf, 1858–1902; repr. 1965).

HHA *Hallische Händel Ausgabe*, ed. M. Schneider and R. Steglich etc. (Kassel and Basle, 1955–).

JHW *Joseph Haydns Werke*, ed. J. P. Larsen and G. Feder (Munich and Duisburg, 1958–).

NBA *Neue Bach Ausgabe = Neue Ausgabe sämtlicher Werke*, ed. Johann-Sebastian-Bach-Institut, Göttingen, and Bach-Archiv, Leipzig (Kassel and Basle, 1954–).

NMA *Neue Mozart Ausgabe = Neue Ausgabe sämtlicher Werke*, ed. E. F. Schmid, W. Plath, and W. Rehm (Kassel etc., 1955–).

Notes on Reference Style

❧

References to works by C. P. E. Bach use Helm numbers; in some instances, the older Wotquenne numbers have been supplied in brackets, but in all instances the Wotquenne number is given after the Helm number in the index. References to the works of Mozart use K^1 numbers, although the K^6 (i.e. 6th edition) number, if different, is given in brackets in the index, and after at least the first reference to the work in question in the text. The only exception to this rule concerns Mozart's concerto cadenzas, where the K^6 numeration is used invariably. This is always indicated in the text. The numeration of C. P. E. Bach's cadenzas, H. 264, is taken from the order in which they appear in the manuscript B-Bc 5871. The numeration of Beethoven's cadenzas is taken from the cadenza volume of the complete edition, *BW* VII: 7.

For ease of reference to particular movements, lower-case Roman numerals have been used after a catalogue number, e.g. K. 488/i refers to the first movement of Mozart's A major Concerto, K. 488; H. 476/iii refers to the third movement of C. P. E. Bach's C Major Concerto, H. 476.

PART I

1

What is a Cadenza?

Some Preliminary Definitions

IT is useful to begin by quoting some of the remarks made by Johann Joachim Quantz in his *Versuch einer Anweisung die Flöte traversiere zu spielen* (1752), one of the earliest treatises on performing practice to devote a chapter to the subject of the improvisation of cadenzas.[1]

> By the word cadenza I understand here neither the closes and stops in a melody, nor the shakes which some Frenchmen call *cadence*. I treat here of that extempore embellishment created, according to the fancy and pleasure of the performer, by a concertante part at the close of a piece on the penultimate note of the bass, that is, the fifth of the key of the piece.

'. . . neither the closes and stops in a melody, nor the shakes which some Frenchmen call *cadence* . . .'

At no stage in its history has the word 'cadenza' been used consistently. Quantz found it necessary to preface his discussion of the cadenza by excluding from consideration certain types of passage to which the label was sometimes applied, and the same necessity obtains here. The word is used in Italian to describe both the harmonic event (the 'closes and stops' mentioned by Quantz, in modern English usage 'cadence') and its improvised embellishment (in modern English, 'cadenza'). Rousseau in 1768 appears to have been the first writer to apply different meanings to these two forms of the word,[2] though his usage never became standard in the French language,[3] and modern English is still the only major European language in which such a terminological distinction can be made.[4] Hence confusion can sometimes arise

---

[1] Berlin, 1752, ch. xv, par. 1. Henceforth abbreviated to *Versuch*. A facsimile repr. of the 3rd edn., 1789, has been edited by H.-P. Schmitz (Kassel and Basle, 1953), and there exists also an English trans. by E. R. Reilly as *On Playing the Flute* (London, 1966; 2nd edn., 1985). All refs. here are made by chapter and paragraph, to facilitate the consultation of different versions of the text.

[2] See the entries 'Cadence' and 'Cadenza' in J.-J. Rousseau, *Dictionnaire de musique* (Paris, 1768).

[3] The French more often made the distinction in a different way, by using the term 'point d'orgue' to describe what Rousseau called a 'cadenza'.

[4] 18th-cent. English knew no such distinction; e.g. Burney refers to 'closes' and 'cadences', but only the context can provide a clue as to whether he means 'cadenzas' or 'cadences'.

between the harmonic cadence and the cadenza which served to articulate it. Quantz also refers to a usage common in France, where *cadence* could mean 'trill'. This too is an instance of synecdoche: the word describing the whole (the harmonic cadence) is used to refer to a part of the whole (the trills with which the French decorated their cadences; they did not at this stage improvise cadenzas).[5] Quantz's restriction of the meaning of the word 'cadenza', as reflected in modern English usage, is to be preferred.

More serious confusion arises when the word 'cadenza' is used to describe other forms of improvised embellishment, not actually occurring at a cadence. The most common instance of this is found when the improvised transitions between a pause chord and a new section, perhaps the return of a rondo theme, are so labelled. Again, an embellished fermata occurring at or soon after the first vocal entry in an aria may be so described. These usages depart still further from the original meaning of the word 'cadenza', which has clearly evolved through a number of stages. For present purposes, the word 'cadenza' is restricted to genuinely cadential embellishments, as befits its etymology, and is not used to describe these other forms of improvisation. It applies, moreover, to embellishments made over the penultimate bass-note of a cadence, and not over the final, in accordance with Quantz's definition. A cadence involves movement from one harmony to another, and it is this progression which is articulated by the cadenza. Embellishments applied to the final chord are of an altogether different kind, for they articulate not movement but stasis, like certain types of embellished fermata (see Chapter 3).[6] Improvisations occurring at transitions between a pause chord and a new section are known as *Eingänge*, following Mozart's usage. Other improvisations on pause chords are termed 'embellished fermatas'. See Chapter 3 for further discussion of these types of improvisation.

'. . . that extempore embellishment created, according to the fancy and pleasure of the performer'

From Quantz's definition it would appear that cadenzas were improvised by the performer or performers. Frequently, however, cadenzas were written down, sometimes separately from concerto sources,[7] sometimes squeezed onto empty staves in a manuscript source of a concerto, perhaps at the end, and sometimes written into the source at the point where they were to be performed. It is not always clear whether the cadenzas which have survived

---

[5] See Quantz, *Versuch*, Ch. xv, par. 2; see also Rousseau, 'Cadenza', *Dictionnaire*, quoted in Ch. 10 below.

[6] Embellishments made over the final bass-note of a cadence are discussed briefly by Heinrich Knödt, who calls them 'tonische Kadenzen' ('Zur Entwicklungsgeschichte der Kadenzen im Instrumentalkonzert', *SIMG* 15 (1913–14), 380).

[7] Not infrequently such separately preserved cadenzas are written on pieces of manuscript inserted within the printed source of a concerto, and in most cases these cadenzas are of later origin than the printed source.

are by the composer or by performers. Certainly the appearance of a cadenza written into the source at the point where it should be performed suggests that the composer has written it, but this is not always so; such sources are sometimes late copies to which a cadenza has been added by the copyist, or arrangements in which the cadenza has been added by the arranger. And while an anonymous, separately preserved cadenza is less likely to be by the composer of the concerto, the possibility that it is cannot be ruled out altogether.

There are several reasons why a composer might have written cadenzas for concertos of his own. In the first instance, he may have been a performer himself, and perhaps wrote the cadenzas for himself to play. He may or may not have expected other performers to use his cadenzas. Mozart is an example of a composer who did not; while cadenzas written by him are extant for all but six of his original piano concertos, only two are included in the autographs of the concertos. Until recently, performers did not generally use Mozart's cadenzas, and many still do not. Such cadenzas may be described as 'ad libitum', meaning that other cadenzas might equally well be substituted for them.[8] On the other hand, composers sometimes wrote what are here termed 'obbligato cadenzas', meaning that the performer was not at liberty to substitute another cadenza, but was obliged to perform the one provided by the composer.[9] Examples of this type are contained in C. P. E. Bach's set of six concertos, H. 471–6 (Wq. 43). In this case it was for didactic reasons that Bach wrote out the cadenzas, these concertos being aimed at the amateur market—only a professional performer could be expected to possess the expertise necessary to improvise a keyboard cadenza. In other instances it would be on account of the difficulty of simultaneous improvisation in a concerto for more than one solo instrument that a composer would write a cadenza; such concertos contain a high incidence of obbligato cadenzas.

Quantz's definition, however, makes no allowance for the possibility of an obbligato cadenza; improvisation by the soloist appears from the quotation above to have been an essential aspect of the cadenza according to his understanding. And yet elsewhere we read that Quantz was prepared to tolerate the use of cadenzas that had been prepared in advance, especially when there was more than one soloist playing.[10] What really mattered was that the effect of an improvisation should be achieved in performance, even if the cadenza had in fact been worked out and rehearsed beforehand. This is true

[8] Cadenzas written by performers for use in concertos not written by themselves are necessarily 'ad libitum'.

[9] Obbligato cadenzas are always written into the source of a concerto at the point where they are to be performed. Not every cadenza found at this point, however, can be assumed to be obbligato. It is usually safe to assume that such a cadenza is obbligato if it appears in the autograph or in all available sources, or if the orchestral instruments are given a specified number of bars' rest to count for its entire duration. If the accompanying instruments participate in a cadenza that appears in the score, then it is unquestionably obbligato.

[10] Quantz, *Versuch*, Ch. xv, pars. 19, 22.

not only of cadenzas prepared in advance by the performer, but also of obbligato cadenzas written by the composer.

Obbligato cadenzas are sometimes labelled 'cadenza in tempo' in the sources;[11] in such cases they are generally written with bar-lines throughout, and contain little or no rhapsodic writing. The term is one which is used frequently in the present survey. There may or may not be a corresponding indication in the accompanying parts of the actual number of bars' rest to be counted while the cadenza is being played. Obbligato cadenzas may equally well be rhapsodic, in whole or in part. If this is the case, the indication given to the accompanying parts is likely to take the form of a short rest, much shorter in fact than the actual duration of the cadenza, with a fermata placed above it.

'. . . at the close of a piece on the penultimate note of the bass'

Here Quantz is somewhat misleading. While it is true that in chamber music and solo keyboard music a cadenza is often found at the very end of a movement, this is seldom the case in an aria or a concerto movement, the genres which were destined to be more important historically for the development of the cadenza. Here the usual location is at a cadence leading from a solo section into a ritornello, most frequently at the one leading from the final solo section into the final ritornello, which is described hereafter as the 'final solo cadence'.

Yet it was not only the final solo cadences which were so embellished; while these were to become by far the most frequent, and in many cases the sole locations for cadential improvisation, there is plenty of evidence for the practice of introducing cadenzas at subsidiary cadences in keys other than the tonic in the course of a piece or movement. These are termed 'subsidiary cadenzas', while those which occur at the final solo cadence or literally 'at the close of a piece' are termed 'final cadenzas'.

It was customary for cadenzas to conclude with a trill, as is clear from all of Quantz's examples, and this trill is termed a 'cadential trill'. It is pointed out in Chapter 4 below that the cadenza is sometimes delayed until after the final solo cadence. When this happens, a long trill is frequently introduced in the solo part at the final solo cadence, before the cadenza in other words. To avoid confusion, such trills are always described here as 'the trill at the final solo cadence' and never as 'the cadential trill'.

The term 'cadential fermata' is used to refer to the sign ⌒ placed over the penultimate note of a cadence in order to indicate that a cadenza might be introduced at this point. In those instances where no such sign is present, but the effect of a cadential fermata is obtained by writing out the duration of the chord in full at this point, the term 'composed fermata' is used instead. The

---

[11] The cadenza in the finale of Mozart's Quintet for Piano and Wind, K. 452, is a case in point.

chord (or unison or octave) over which a cadential fermata is placed (or to which a 'composed fermata' is applied) is called the 'penultimate'. These same terms are used in the case of obbligato cadenzas;[12] so the cadential fermata and the penultimate indicate either the point where a cadenza might be introduced, or else the point where an obbligato cadenza begins.

'. . . that is, the fifth of the key of the piece'

It is true that the penultimate is almost invariably the 'fifth of the key of the piece' in a final cadenza. Yet in a subsidiary cadenza it is almost invariably the fifth of whichever key is being established by the cadence. While exceptions are extremely rare, they do occur, and examples are found in which the cadenza begins over a bass-note other than the dominant, perhaps the sixth or the sharpened fourth.

The Origins of the Cadenza

Perhaps the surest account which can be given of the origin of cadenzas is that several years before the end of the previous century, and in the first ten years of the present one, the close of a concertante part was made with a little passage over a moving bass, to which a good shake was attached; between 1710 and 1716, or thereabouts, the cadenzas customary at present in which the bass must pause, became the mode.[13]

'. . . the cadenzas customary at present, in which the bass must pause'

The reference to a pausing bass is of great significance. The concentration of ornaments around cadences was not a new development at all; examples can be found, not only in earlier music but also in much eighteenth-century and later music, of cadential embellishments, improvised or otherwise, which do not prolong the cadences beyond their natural length; the implication of the term 'division', by which this procedure is frequently known, is that longer note-values are split up into shorter ones, while the total duration remains unchanged.[14] Cadences embellished by divisions in this way are known as *cadenze fiorite*.[15] The moment when the ornamentation of cadences began to require the bass to pause, however, may be regarded as the birth of the

---

[12] This in spite of the fact that the 'penultimate' is often not literally the penultimate bass-note in an obbligato cadenza, and that the cadential fermata has an entirely different meaning here—it is not an invitation to insert an improvisation.

[13] Quantz, *Versuch*, Ch. xv, par. 2.

[14] The many written-out cadential embellishments included in J. A. Herbst, *Musica Moderna Prattica* (Frankfurt, 1653), are of this kind.

[15] The term 'Cadenza fiorita' appears in S. de Brossard, *Dictionnaire de musique* (Paris, 1703), under the heading 'Fiorito', where it is defined as a 'cadence in which the penultimate is divided or diminished [*diminuée*] into several little notes'. For a modern English trans. see *Sébastien de Brossard: Dictionary of Music*, trans. and ed. A. Gruber (Henryville, etc., 1982).

cadenza. The kinds of cadenza which Quantz has in mind are those in which the bass proceeds in strict time until the penultimate, when it simply stops, with at the most a very slight rallentando just beforehand. Such were the cadenzas of the eighteenth century after the convention of a pausing bass had become established. Yet conventions of this kind do not establish themselves overnight. A clue to the kind of ornamentation which may have preceded the 'birth' of the cadenza is provided by an ornamented version, discovered by David Boyden,[16] of Corelli's solo Violin Sonata, Op. 5 No. 11.

Ex. 1.   *A. Corelli, Sonata, Op. 5 No. 11, first movement: (a) Corelli's original version, (b) the version given in 'Walsh Anonymous'*

One of the numerous ornamented sources of Corelli's Op. 5 sonatas is an anonymous manuscript, probably dating from the 1720s and labelled 'Walsh Anonymous' by Boyden; it gives the version shown in Ex. 1*b* for the passage in the first movement of the eleventh sonata corresponding to Ex. 1*a* in Corelli's original. The animation of the added ornamentation is gradually increased, suggesting more a rallentando than a pause in the accompaniment.

Three-quarters of a century before the date to which Quantz assigns the

[16] See D. D. Boyden, 'The Corelli "Solo" Sonatas and Their Ornamental Additions by Corelli, Geminiani, Dubourg, Tartini and the "Walsh Anonymous"', *Musica Antiqua Europae Orientalis*, 3 (Bydgoszcz, 1972), 596 f. and 603.

birth of the cadenza, Frescobaldi had written: '[As for] *cadenze*, even though they may be written in fast notes, it is best to play them quite slowly; and in the approach to the end of [an embellished] passage or *cadenza*, the tempo should be slower still.'[17] Frescobaldi seems to imply that even in 1637 cadential embellishments were at times so extensive as to require a rallentando, such that by the time the cadence itself was reached, the beat had become particularly slow. A limited number of examples of this type of cadential embellishment, or 'rallentando cadenza', has been found in music written at various stages during the eighteenth century. It requires little reflection to realize that a rallentando of this kind presents great difficulties for ensemble playing. In solo keyboard works, like those contained in Frescobaldi's 1637 publication, there is no such problem. On the other hand, a close rapport was needed between the violinist who performed the anonymous version of the Corelli Op. 5 sonatas and his continuo player, and such a rapport would be much harder to achieve between a singer on stage and a whole orchestra positioned in front of the stage.[18] Once the level of improvised ornamentation had become such as to oblige the accompanying forces to slow down, it may readily be imagined that the requirements of ensemble playing favoured the establishment of a convention whereby they simply stopped and waited.

'. . . between 1710 and 1716, or thereabouts'

The dates which Quantz suggests for the birth of the cadenza reappear in numerous treatises from the later eighteenth century, but in each case it seems that the author has simply taken them on Quantz's authority. The only hint which may explain Quantz's choice of *terminus post quem* is the following: 'It is . . . probable that cadenzas first came into use after the time *Corelli* published his twelve solos for the violin, engraved in copper.'[19] The first edition of the solo sonatas in question (Op. 5) appeared in 1700. In a footnote attached to this paragraph, Quantz goes on to discuss two ornamented versions of these sonatas; he mentions Corelli's own ornamented version and that by Nicola Matteis (now lost), adding that neither of these versions contained pausing-bass cadenzas. The Corelli version appeared *c.*1710, and

---

[17] G. Frescobaldi, *Toccate d'intavolatura di cimbalo et organo . . . libro primo* (1637), Preface. The word *cadenza* has been left untranslated advisedly, since Frescobaldi was using the Italian word for cadence, and was not referring to something that might now be recognized as a cadenza.

[18] C. P. E. Bach explains a refinement in the art of accompaniment as follows, admittedly in the context of embellished fermatas, although the comment applies equally well to cadenzas: 'When the principal part broadens before entering a fermata, the accompanist must do likewise . . .', *Versuch über die wahre Art das Clavier zu spielen* (Berlin, 1753–62), ii. 267; trans. W. J. Mitchell as *Essay on the True Art of Playing Keyboard Instruments* (New York and London, 1949), 385. Henceforth the original German title will be abbreviated to *Versuch*, and the English translation to *Essay*. Since the numbering of chapters differs between the two, page refs. will normally be given for both.

[19] Quantz, *Versuch*, Ch. xv, par. 2.

the other, according to Quantz, 'a short time later'. Quantz seems to conclude that these two ornamented versions must predate the birth of the cadenza: otherwise he would have expected them to contain cadenzas.

It is harder to account for the choice of the *terminus ante quem*, however, since Quantz provides no clue. The most likely possibility is that it was in 1716 that Quantz himself first encountered cadenzas; this was the year in which he arrived in Dresden, where Pisendel probably introduced him to some of the more brilliant violin concertos of Vivaldi[20] and other Italian composers, and where he probably also became familiar with Italian opera. Quantz does after all describe the cadenza as Italian in origin.

Whatever the sources of the dates which Quantz suggests, they deserve to be taken seriously; corroborative evidence is found in the writings of Tosi (*Opinioni*) and Marcello ('Il teatro alla moda'),[21] who both speak of the tradition as something already firmly established in Italian opera by the 1720s (but see Ch. 4 n. 7);[22] by the 1730s it was being used by keyboard composers in North Germany and in Austria. Those writers who speak of cadenzas in earlier music are in most cases describing composed cadential prolongations rather than genuine cadenzas.

Why did the cadenza arise at this particular stage in musical history? Ornamentation and prolongation of cadences goes back at least as far as medieval polyphony.[23] Could not a tradition of improvised cadenzas have established itself much earlier? The most likely answer lies in the emergence of the hierarchical key-relationships of major–minor tonality in the seventeenth century, a process associated particularly with the rise of the concerto, the first large-scale form to exploit these relationships. A higher level of structural significance than ever before was now acquired by the main cadences, and this in turn gave rise to a tendency on the part of both composer and performer to highlight them. Closely linked to this development was the emergence of ritornello form in the concerto and the aria; this form articulated the main key areas of a movement with more or less extended tuttis, characteristically preceded by a strong solo cadence. It was at such cadences in particular that the concentration of ornamentation developed which was to give rise to the tradition of the improvised cadenza.

---

[20] While it is argued in Ch. 3 below that many of the passages which Vivaldi labels 'cadenza' are actually capriccios, there are nevertheless examples of genuine cadenzas in the works of Vivaldi, Locatelli, etc.

[21] P. F. Tosi, *Opinioni de' cantori antichi e moderni, o sieno Osservazioni sopra il canto figurato* (Bologna, 1723), trans. J. E. Galliard (1742), ed. M. Pilkington, as *Observations on the Florid Song* (London, 1987). For Marcello, 'Il teatro alla moda', see *MQ* 34 (1948), 371 ff.

[22] A word of caution is necessary here. Neither Tosi nor Marcello give musical examples of cadenzas, in the absence of which it is hard to be sure exactly what they are describing.

[23] See C. W. Warren, 'Punctus Organi and Cantus Coronatus in the Music of Dufay', in A. W. Atlas (ed.), *Dufay Quincentenary Conference* (Brooklyn, 1976), 128 ff.

'. . . a concertante part'

Eine concertirende Stimme—to use Quantz's original expression—refers to an undoubled part.[24] An improvisation by definition cannot be doubled. In eighteenth-century Western music at least, in which there are strict conventions governing the harmonic and contrapuntal combinations which are acceptable, most improvisation is soloistic; simultaneous improvisation by more than one performer can succeed only if agreement on certain procedures has previously been reached. Different strands of a given musical text may be simultaneously ornamented, though care is needed if the ornamented lines are not to clash. Where there is no given text, as would be the case in a cadenza, simultaneous improvisation is much more difficult. There must be some form of communication between the performers, and there must always be one who takes the lead. In its simplest form, this need for communication is exemplified by the ending of a solo cadenza; the accompanying instruments need to know when the cadenza is about to conclude, so that they can prepare to re-enter together in time, and at the appropriate moment. Often, in order for this to work smoothly, it is necessary for the conductor or continuo player to take over the lead from the soloist during the cadential trill. In the duet cadenzas discussed by Quantz (see Chapter 2 below) the lead passes from one improvising soloist to the other in a most sophisticated manner, presupposing a high degree of skill and sensitivity on the part of both performers. More commonly cadenzas are improvised by a single soloist; if there are accompanying instruments, they normally pause until the cadential trill is reached.

In practice, and contrary to popular belief, the cadenza was by no means restricted to arias and concerto movements, to genres, that is, in which a solo performer is pitted against an orchestra; on the contrary, Quantz's reference to a concertante part applies equally to undoubled parts in chamber groupings. Thus the upper part in a duo, or the first violin in a string quartet, or a solo keyboard instrument in a sonata, may all be invited to supply cadenzas. Examples of some of these types will be encountered in the course of the present survey.

Cadenza or Cadential Prolongation?

It has been pointed out above that composers not infrequently wrote obbligato cadenzas, leaving the performer without the option of supplying his own. The most common instances of this, namely ensemble cadenzas and those found in concertos written for amateurs or students, have been mentioned. Yet there are factors other than purely practical ones at work here. The history of the cadenza was acted out against the backcloth of a changing relationship

---

[24] On this point see Quantz, *Versuch*, trans. Reilly, 2nd edn., p. xl.

between performer and composer. As is demonstrated in the course of the present survey, some developments in the cadenza were initiated by the performer and others by the composer, but the latter asserted himself more and more as the century progressed. Quantz's account of the origin of the cadenza describes a liberty taken by soloists on their own initiative; a century after the presumed date of this event Rossini was to write out in detail the embellishments he wanted from his singers, leaving them without freedom to improvise, and Beethoven was to write 'Non si fa una Cadenza ma s'attacca subito il seguente'[25] into the score of his 'Emperor' Concerto. The improvised cadenza was to be the last surviving bastion of the performer's rights to participate in the creation of a musical composition: and in the early nineteenth century it fell. Improvisation was still cultivated, both in the context of the performance of earlier music, and as an important element in the musical equipment of the virtuoso pianist, who would frequently improvise whole pieces at length; composers in the nineteenth century, however, seldom permitted any additions to be made to their scores.

When it is the composer rather than the performer who writes the cadenzas, a difficulty arises. How are obbligato cadenzas to be distinguished from other types of cadential prolongation? Composers in the eighteenth century, no less than at any other period in the history of Western music, would frequently extend and elaborate their cadences without reference to the tradition of inserted, improvised cadenzas which is the subject of this survey. One frequently encounters cadential prolongations which make use of some of the gestures of the eighteenth-century cadenza, and which may or may not be conscious references to this tradition.[26] While it may be true that pedal-points in toccatas and other organ works provided a repertory of figuration suitable for borrowing in the specific context of cadential improvisation over a dominant pedal at a later stage, as Knödt observes, it is misleading to assume with him that such passages are a form of cadenza.[27] The 'pedal-point' is an idiomatic feature of organ music, frequently found not only on the penultimate towards cadences, where it does at least resemble a cadenza, but also on the tonic at the beginning or end of an organ piece, where it cannot possibly be a cadenza.

What of such a passage as bars 152–69 of the finale of Mozart's F major Sonata, K. 533 (see Ex. 2)? This passage is described as having 'very much the character of' a cadenza in Paul and Eva Badura-Skoda's discussion of

---

[25] Or 'sequente', according to the 1st edn. (Leipzig, 1811).

[26] e.g. bars 141–51 from the Fugue in A minor by J. S. Bach, BWV 543; this passage is almost certainly not a conscious reference, given its early date and its continuity with the preceding music.

[27] 'Zur Entwicklungsgeschichte', p. 389. See the discussion below of the 'perfidia', Ch. 3. Interestingly, the French word for cadenza, 'point d'orgue', and the German word for pedal, 'Orgelpunkt', are etymologically equivalent.

Ex. 2.   *W. A. Mozart, Sonata in F, K. 533, finale*

Mozart's cadenza style,[28] although it contains neither a cadential fermata nor the label 'cadenza'. It has been seen that the use of the label 'cadenza' follows no consistent pattern during the period. The omission of an ambiguous label cannot in itself be sufficient to alter the nature of a particular passage. Yet it is obviously misleading to consider all cadential prolongations in the classical repertoire as a form of cadenza, unless some specific reference is made to the tradition of improvised cadenzas. For the purposes of the present survey it is necessary to define the cadenza clearly in order to be able to apply consistent criteria to the task of distinguishing between cadenzas and other types of cadential prolongation.

Definition of the Cadenza

While eighteenth-century definitions are of interest for the light which they can shed on contemporary understanding of the cadenza at particular times and places, they are inadequate to serve as the basis of a wide-ranging survey. Usages varied at different stages in the century and from one part of Europe to another. Some important aspects of the definition adopted in the present survey have already emerged during the discussion of various types of cadenza in the first section of this chapter: that the term 'cadenza' is restricted to passages occurring in a specifically cadential context, and that cadenzas are not invariably improvised, but may sometimes be prepared in advance by the performer or else be prescribed by the composer.

[28] E. and P. Badura-Skoda, trans. Leo Black, *Interpreting Mozart on the Keyboard* (London, 1962), 229.

Writers throughout the period insist that cadenzas must sound like improvisations even when they are not. The effect on the listener, whose experience of music is diachronic, must therefore be taken into account. If the listener is to believe that what he hears is an inserted improvisation, then it must somehow be set off from its surroundings. What is necessary if this articulation is to be achieved?

The earliest cadenzas were generally rhapsodic, unaccompanied, and single-line in texture. This in itself was usually sufficient to contrast them with their metrical, continuo-texture surroundings. The cadential fermata marked the point at which the metre was interrupted and the texture reduced. With the advent of regular metre and normal textures into ensemble cadenzas and polyphonic keyboard cadenzas, some other means of articulation became necessary; conventional methods of cadential preparation were developed which would lead to a sustained 6–4 or unison dominant, often via chromatic movement in the bass, and often using syncopations or an inverted pedal, or both, in the upper parts, and this came to be recognized as a signal that a cadenza was about to follow.

While it is not absolutely necessary that a fermata sign should appear in the score above the penultimate, the effect of a fermata is an essential part of the articulation, and a 'composed fermata' is necessary in the absence of a fermata sign. Nor is a dominant bass-note absolutely necessary at the beginning of a cadenza, as we have seen. For the listener to recognize the start of a cadenza occurring on an unconventional harmony, however, the articulation needs to be exceptionally clear in other respects.

As with any musical procedure which generates expectations of a particular type of continuation, it is possible for the composer to spring a surprise on the listener after a passage of conventional cadential preparation. That is to say, he might proceed directly with a simple, unprolonged cadence. One example of such a procedure is found in the finale of Mozart's F major Sonata, K. 332

Ex. 3.   *W. A. Mozart, Sonata in F, K. 332, finale*

(300 k), bars 230–2 (see Ex. 3). Such passages, in which the listener is led to expect a cadenza, but in vain, are known hereafter as 'false-start cadenzas'.[29] Bearing in mind that, in general, cadenzas approached by passages of this kind cannot be omitted, it should be pointed out that the effect of the unembellished, unprolonged cadence in the example mentioned is humorous. There is a certain incongruity in the almost banal cadence which follows the dramatic build-up, gently brushing aside the listener's expectations in order to proceed directly to the resolution.

Just as composers sometimes exploit the listener's expectations in order to achieve a surprise effect when it seems that a cadenza is about to begin, so also do they when it seems that a cadenza is about to end. It will be seen in Part II that numerous examples of passages here held to be cadenzas are clearly articulated at the opening, but much less clearly if at all at the ending, to the extent that it can be difficult to agree on the precise point at which the cadenzas end. On account of the diachronic perspective of the listener, however, it is maintained that the articulation of the opening is of more importance than the articulation of the ending. It is the beginning of a cadenza that is crucial if the passage is to register with the listener as an insertion. Irregularities of articulation at the end are of interest to the analyst and to the historian, but they do not significantly affect the character of the passage for the listener.

It follows from the above that cadenzas are articulated either by the contrast between their rhapsodic character and their metrical surroundings, or else through being introduced by a signal of some kind which an informed listener is able to recognize. There are, however, instances of cadential prolongation in which the metrical opening is not clearly articulated, but in which the conclusion is nevertheless rhapsodic. In view of the importance which is here attached to the clear articulation of the opening of the cadenza, these passages must be excluded from the category of cadenza: while it is evident from a glance at the score that such passages are improvisatory cadential prolongations, this only becomes evident to the listener half-way through. If there were a noticeable point at which metrical writing were to give way to rhapsodic writing, then that would be the point at which to locate the beginning of a cadenza. In cases where a rapid figuration or a trill simply continues while the sense of a regular beat is lost, it is impossible to isolate the moment when the change takes place (see Ex. 48, Chapter 10). For want of a better term such passages are known hereafter as 'deceptive cadenzas'.[30]

---

[29] Another example is found in the third movement of Haydn's Symphony No. 68. Here Haydn prepares a cadential 6–4 in the conventional way, the penultimate arriving in bar 108. Yet the expected prolongation does not come. The fortissimo of the preparation and penultimate is abruptly followed by a piano, then a pianissimo, as the 6–4 is repeated to a triplet figure. Then come two dominant chords, and the cadence is resolved with the return of the full orchestra in bar 111.

[30] A well-known example is found in the second movement of Beethoven's G major Piano Concerto. See Ch. 12.

A related hybrid case is that of the 'rallentando cadenza'. Here the gradual transition from metrical to rhapsodic writing occurs before rather than after the beginning of the cadential prolongation. If, as in Ex. 1*b*, it is impossible to identify a moment when an articulated insertion could be said to begin (since neither the arrival of the dominant in the bass nor the start of the rallentando is clearly articulated), then such a passage may also be excluded from the category of cadenza.

It may be helpful to illustrate some of the points made in the above discussion. Towards the end of the finale of Haydn's G major Piano Concerto, Hob. XVIII: 4, it is easy to recognize the point in bar 214 at which a cadential prolongation begins—a prolongation which continues until bar 258 (see Ex. 4). This effect is created by the use of conventional formulae of cadential preparation, leading to a tutti 6–4 with a composed fermata in bars 212–13 followed by a caesura and a solo entry in bar 214. In the absence of any clues in the notation of the passage—there is neither a fermata sign nor the word 'cadenza' to mark the beginning, the accompanying parts are given the exact number of bars' rest to count, and they actually participate in the cadenza from bar 241 onwards—it is only by reference to stylistic criteria that the passage can be identified as a cadenza at all. Such a cadenza may be termed a 'hidden cadenza', and numerous other examples are discussed in Part II.

In the finale of Mozart's F major Sonata, K. 533, there is no correspondingly clear articulation at the start of the cadential prolongation in bar 152 (see

Ex. 4.   *J. Haydn, Concerto in G, Hob. XVIII: 4, finale*

Ex. 4. – *Contd.*

Ex. 2). There is no cadential fermata indicated in the score, nor is there a 'composed fermata', nor is there a caesura between the arrival of the dominant in the bass and the start of the prolongation. The passage is continuous with the preceding music, the listener is unlikely to interpret it as an insertion, and so it cannot be included within the category of 'hidden cadenza': it is not a cadenza at all.[31] If, however, a comparison is made with the original version of this rondo (the Rondo in F, K. 494), then it becomes apparent that the passage is technically an insertion: bars 143–69 of the later version are not

[31] Taken out of context it looks exactly like one of Mozart's cadenzas, and performers may well be justified in playing it more freely in consequence. The Badura-Skodas may also be justified in treating it as an illustration of Mozart's cadenza style. Yet for our purposes it must be regarded as a cadential prolongation that makes deliberate reference to the tradition of the cadenza without itself exemplifying that tradition.

present in the original. Yet it is an insertion that merges seamlessly with its surroundings.

A cadenza may therefore be defined as an improvisation, or a passage intended to sound like one, inserted within a structural cadence, thereby causing it to be audibly prolonged.

2

On the Performance of Cadenzas

∽∾∾∽

WRITTEN evidence concerning the early history of the cadenza is not plentiful, as it was largely through the practice of spontaneous ornamentation by performers that the cadenza arose. From the 1750s onwards, however, a great deal of information becomes available, since it was at this time that the authors of treatises on performing practice began to devote considerable attention to the cadenza with a view to instructing students in the art of providing 'tasteful' examples. Texts concerning vocal cadenzas as well as those concerning instrumental cadenzas are relevant to our present purposes, and before proceeding to a more detailed examination of their recommendations, it may be useful to give a brief overview of the texts to be considered.

In 1757, Johann Friedrich Agricola issued a work entitled *Anleitung zur Singkunst*, which consisted of a translation, with extensive commentary, of Pier Francesco Tosi's *Opinioni de' cantori antichi e moderni, o sieno Osservazioni sopra il canto figurato* (Bologna, 1723). The original text had been in the form not of a didactic treatise, but rather of an essay on the current state of the art of singing. Thus, unlike most of the writers who are discussed in this chapter, Tosi did not offer systematic guidelines to the student, but rather a series of observations, mainly about the faults which, in his view, disfigured the art.

Agricola's commentary sheds light on some of the changes in attitude that had taken place during the intervening thirty-four years. Agricola recommends the chapter on cadenzas included in Quantz's *Versuch* (1752) to those wishing to investigate the matter further, and it is clear that much of what he has to say is borrowed from Quantz.[1] Johann Adam Hiller's *Anweisung zum musikalisch-zierlichen Gesang* (1780) represents a slightly later stage still, though he makes use of material taken from both Tosi and Agricola.

From the instrumentalist's point of view, Quantz was the first to devote attention to the subject of improvised cadenzas in a published treatise. The date of the original manuscript of Tartini's *Traité des agrémens de la musique* has not been conclusively established; it is thought by Petrobelli to be *c.*1740,[2] although the work was not published until 1771. Joseph Riepel, in his *Erläuterung der betrüglichen Tonordnung* (1765), includes a lengthy if somewhat rambling discussion of the cadenza, in the form of a dialogue between master and pupil. In part I of his *Versuch* (1753), C. P. E. Bach considers the

---

[1] e.g. he claims that the cadenza originated between 1710 and 1716. In discussing duet cadenzas he refers the reader to Quantz's *Versuch* for a more detailed treatment of the subject.

[2] *Giuseppe Tartini: Le fonti biografiche* (Venice, 1968), 113 f.

cadenza mainly from the point of view of the keyboard player who has to accompany the soloist, although a few remarks on the solo keyboard cadenzas in the *Probestücke* (H. 70–5) are included elsewhere. The earliest treatise in which a whole chapter is devoted to the matter of improvised cadenzas for solo keyboard is Daniel Gottlob Türk's *Klavierschule* (1789). Given the tendency of theory to lag behind practice, this seems an accurate reflection of the change in the role of keyboard instruments in ensembles which took place during the century: from providing continuo accompaniment to a leading position among the solo instruments for which concertos were written in the later classical period.

Specific Recommendations

Tosi evidently disapproved of the manner in which singers were wont to overload their cadences with tasteless ornaments. Interestingly, he claims that a similar fault had prevailed in the previous century, but that these excessive divisions had been 'banished without so much as attempting their correction'.[3] Among the faults that he finds with the cadential improvisations of the present generation is that they 'injure the time'[4]—in other words, they require the bass to pause. Owing in part to his view that the unaccompanied human voice soon becomes tiresome to the listener, he recommends a style of cadential elaboration which does not involve a pausing bass—the *cadenza fiorita*, in other words (see Glossary). In this view he is not followed by the other writers currently being discussed.

It seems unlikely that the cadential improvisations of the generation preceding his own were actually prolongations. Tosi had no first-hand experience of them, and both Hiller and Türk assume, from the witness of J. A. Herbst,[5] that cadential elaborations in the seventeenth century were of the type here described as *cadenze fiorite*. It is more likely that something akin to the rallentando cadenza was involved.

The most frequently quoted passage in Tosi's essay is the following:

Every air has (at least) three cadences that are all three final. Generally speaking, the study of the singers of the present times consists of terminating the cadence of the first part with an overflowing of passages and divisions at pleasure, and the orchestra waits; in that of the second the dose is increased, and the orchestra grows tired; but on the last cadence, the throat is set a-going, like a weather-cock in a whirlwind and the orchestra yawns.[6]

---

[3] P. F. Tosi, *Opinioni de' cantori antichi e moderni, o sieno Osservazioni sopra il canto figurato*, trans. J. E. Galliard (1742), ed. M. Pilkington, as *Observations on the Florid Song* (London, 1987), 53. Henceforth abbreviated as *Observations*.

[4] Ibid. 60.

[5] *Musica Moderna Prattica* (Frankfurt, 1653).

[6] Tosi, *Observations*, pp. 52 f.

A footnote by Tosi's English translator indicates that the three cadences described occur respectively at the ends of each of the first two parts (i.e. at the final solo cadences of each section) and at the end of the da capo. Elsewhere Tosi grants that a little extra liberty is permissible in the last of the cadences, but asserts that this liberty is intolerably abused.[7]

In the earlier part of the century, such a multiplicity of cadenzas occurring within a single piece was not uncommon, and while it may be more character-istic of the aria than of the concerto, examples do exist of concerto movements which invite both subsidiary and final cadenzas. None the less, perhaps because of the abuse to which such a liberal distribution of cadential fermatas could so easily lead, only the final one was to remain a normative feature in the classical period, and it became a focus of attention to a degree which would scarcely be possible if it were simply the last in a succession of cadenzas. Türk points out that most of the audience is more attentive during the cadenza than at any previous point.[8] For Riepel it was supposed to be a brief summary of the expression of the entire movement.[9] It has also been likened to a peroration,[10] following the eighteenth-century tradition of seeking parallels between rhetoric and music.

In fairness to the opera singers of the time it should be noted that excessively long and inappropriate cadenzas were not entirely caused by lack of taste on their part; the audiences were at least as much to blame. Writers are unanimous in recording that some of the worst excesses were extremely well received by the public, and it seems that if a singer wanted to please, he had to oblige by providing cadenzas of dazzling brilliance. Not for nothing was the cadenza likened by Mattheson to a farewell compliment.[11]

Some thirty years later a slightly different view found expression in the writings of both Quantz and Agricola. Neither objected in principle to the type of cadenza which required the bass to pause,[12] but both recommended that there should not be too many cadenzas in a single movement. Quantz suggests that there should be only one, and deplores the practice of some singers, who, by performing two cadenzas in the first part of a da capo aria (one subsidiary and one final), brought the total up to five.[13] Agricola, less

---

[7] Tosi, *Observations*, 59.

[8] *Klavierschule* (Leipzig and Halle, 1789), 313; trans. R. H. Haggh as *School of Clavier Playing* (Lincoln, Nebr., and London, 1982), 301; henceforth abbreviated as *School*.

[9] *Erläuterung der betrüglichen Tonordnung* (Augsburg, 1765), 81. This work is vol. iv of Riepel's *Anfangsgründe zur musikalischen Setzkunst* (1752–68). Henceforth abbreviated as *Erlaüterung*.

[10] F. Algarotti, trans. anon., *An Essay on the Opera* (London, 1767), 61.

[11] *Der Vollkommene Kapellmeister* (Hamburg, 1739), trans. and ed. E. C. Harriss (Ann Arbor, 1981), part II, ch. 3, par. 39.

[12] Few writers adopt Tosi's stand on this matter after the middle of the century, yet there is evidence that some are merely yielding to pressure of public demand. Riepel mentions a violinist who held out against the cadenza for a long time, but finally realized that he would have to incorporate cadenzas into his playing for fear that he might otherwise fail to satisfy his employer (*Erläuterung*, p. 81).   [13] *Versuch*, ch. XV, par. 5.

specific on this matter, merely observes that cadenzas should not occur too frequently, and that they should not be too long. It appears from another remark, however, that the number of cadenzas introduced into arias was lower than it had been in Tosi's day. In commenting on Tosi's preferred type of cadential embellishment—here termed *cadenza fiorita*—Agricola observes that this type is sometimes heard at the end of the first part of an aria, even when a genuine cadenza is to follow later.[14] The trend towards emphasizing the final cadenza was clearly under way.

A complaint made by almost every eighteenth-century writer who addressed himself to the subject of cadenzas concerns the inappropriateness of character of so many of the cadenzas that were performed: 'Some, after a tender and passionate air, make a lively merry cadence, and after a brisk air, end it with one that is doleful.'[15] The former was doubtless a more common fault. Performers must have been keen to show off their technical agility at every opportunity, whether it suited the character of the music or not. It is difficult to imagine many performers neglecting to do so when it might have been appropriate.

Quantz goes further when he recommends, as a means of ensuring that the cadenza maintain the appropriate mood, that it be based on a selection of the principal themes of the movement.[16] He mentions that this practice was not particularly well known, and it must be said that few of the examples studied from this period make use of Quantz's idea. Nevertheless it reappears in the writings of Agricola, Riepel, and Türk. Cadenzas that are thematically related to the parent movement are known hereafter as 'integrated cadenzas', while those that are not are termed 'interchangeable'. From the 1770s onwards integrated cadenzas were to become increasingly common.

Tosi does not specifically mention the 'single-breath rule', according to which a vocal cadenza might last no longer than it was possible to sustain a single breath, and yet it goes without saying that he would have expected this. Breathing during a cadenza meant breathing during a word, an abuse which he called 'an error against nature'.[17] Quantz and Agricola mention the rule specifically, although Quantz restricts its application to singers and wind players. String-players, he says, may make their cadenzas as long as they like, provided they are able to sustain interest.[18] Agricola is prepared to allow breaths in duet cadenzas, so long as they do not occur simultaneously. Riepel recommends the use of rests as a means of achieving greater length in a single-line cadenza.[19] The overall pattern to be observed is an increase in the length and scope thought desirable for a cadenza, and a gradual relaxation of the rules concerning brevity.

Tosi deplores the practice of using the same or similar cadenzas repeatedly, without variety, and he expects singers to be able to improvise afresh on each

---

[14] *Anleitung zur Singkunst* (Berlin, 1757), 202 f.
[15] Tosi, *Observations*, p. 60, note by Galliard. [16] *Versuch*, ch. xv, par. 8.
[17] *Observations*, p. 24. [18] *Versuch*, ch. xv, par. 17. [19] *Erläuterung*, p. 81.

performance. He holds in particular contempt singers who copy the 'graces' of others.[20] Essentially, then, he is attacking a style of ornamentation which lacks spontaneity. Given the small scale of the improvisations thought desirable by Tosi, it was not unreasonable to expect the singers to improvise them. As the cadenza grew in scope it became harder to do so. And if cadenzas were to be simultaneously improvised by more than one performer, a great deal of skill and technical knowledge was needed. While Quantz and others offered advice about how this might be done, they conceded that it would often be advisable in performance to use a cadenza that had been worked out in advance, either by the performers or by the composer. Nevertheless the need to achieve an effect of spontaneity is repeatedly emphasized; the listener should believe that he is listening to a genuine improvisation. The skill required for the invention of a good cadenza is like a polished wit; it cannot be taught or learned by rote, although it can be sharpened by observation of a skilful practitioner. Likewise the cadenza makes a good effect only if it is performed with the spontaneity of a witticism.[21]

Tosi's other remarks include a number of specific technical comments, including an interesting reference to the practice of performing the cadential trill not on the supertonic but on the mediant.[22] He deplores this practice, but it evidently persisted, for not only is it mentioned by other writers later in the century,[23] invariably in the context of music in the minor mode, but written examples exist of keyboard cadenzas in minor keys which cadence in this way (see Ex. 32).

For information on the content of early cadenzas it is necessary to look beyond Tosi's essay to the specifically didactic works written later in the century. Quantz was a pioneer in this field, and even though his book was written primarily from the point of view of a flautist, it is also addressed to string-players and singers.

Quantz considers it appropriate to introduce a cadenza not into any solo instrumental piece whatsoever, but only into 'pathetic and slow pieces, or . . . serious quick ones'. 'Serious quick' appears to mean common time, for he considers fast pieces in 2/4, 3/4, 3/8, 6/8, and 12/8 to be unsuitable.[24] Riepel is prepared to allow cadenzas in 3/8 or 3/4 movements, unless they are in minuet tempo.[25] In practice they are also found in movements in the shorter metres—Mozart's concerto finales offer examples of movements in 2/4 or 6/8 which contain cadenzas. The trend observable here is not so much a change in attitude towards the use of cadenzas, as an increase in the seriousness of music written in the shorter metres. Quantz's conception of a 2/4 Allegro was of a movement on a considerably lighter scale than the Finale of Mozart's F major Concerto, K. 459.

[20] *Observations*, p. 46.   [21] Quantz, *Versuch*, ch. XV, pars. 9, 18.
[22] *Observations*, pp. 54 f.
[23] Quantz, *Versuch*, ch. XV, par. 36; Bach, *Versuch*, ii. 262 f., *Essay*, p. 382.
[24] Quantz, *Versuch*, ch. XV, par. 4.   [25] *Erläuterung*, p. 90.

In Quantz's view, the cadenzas themselves should avoid regular metre. They should consist of detached ideas rather than sustained melodies.[26] No idea should be repeated more than twice, because variety both of metre and of material is needed in order to sustain interest and continue to surprise. If an idea is to be repeated at all, it should be at a different pitch. And yet, while contrasting ideas are needed for all but the shortest cadenzas, there should not be too many of them.[27]

Short cadenzas should not introduce any chromatic notes. Longer cadenzas may touch upon nearly related keys by a judicious use of accidentals, but may not move far from the tonic.[28] Dissonant and chromatic notes must be correctly resolved.[29]

In discussing the importance of maintaining the correct *Affekt* in a cadenza (matching that of the movement in which it occurs) Quantz suggests certain types of figuration that are suited to certain *Affekte*: leaps, trills, fast runs in an allegro, dissonances and small intervals in a slow, sad piece. He cautions against mixing these different types in a single cadenza.[30]

Hiller is more prepared than Quantz to allow a mixture of different types of expression within a single cadenza, thereby increasing variety and the possibilities for surprise.[31] He speaks more in terms of figuration, standard patterns based on the scale or the triad upon which the improvising soloist may draw, than of the motivic ideas which feature prominently in Quantz's discussion.[32] Perhaps this merely reflects the difference in outlook between a singer and an instrumentalist rather than a changed historical situation. The singer, prolonging a single vowel in the middle of a word, is perhaps more likely to conceive the cadenza as a single unbroken utterance than the flautist, who, with no words to consider, may be more likely to contrast motivic ideas.

Hiller also discusses the harmonic context of the cadenza in slightly different terms from most other writers. He speaks of three types. The first occurs when the 6–4 harmony over the bass dominant is prolonged, to be followed by a cadential trill on the supertonic over a 5–3 harmony on the same bass-note. The second occurs when instead of tonic harmony, dominant

Ex. 5.   *J. A. Hiller, example of a cadenza from* Anweisung

[26] Quantz, *Versuch*, ch. xv, par. 16.   [27] Ibid., ch. xv, pars. 10–12.
[28] Ibid., ch. xv, par. 14.   [29] Ibid., ch. xv, par. 13.   [30] Ibid., ch. xv, par. 15.
[31] *Anweisung zum musikalisch-zierlichen Gesang* (Leipzig, 1780), 117.   [32] Ibid. 113.

harmony is chosen, the tonic harmony appearing only incidentally. The third type involves drawing on more remote keys in the course of the cadenza.[33] With his first and third types, Hiller is clearly saying nothing new; but the suggestion that a cadenza might be based on dominant harmony appears to be original in didactic literature. In the example which he quotes of this type of cadenza (Ex. 5), the 6–4 harmony does in fact occur at the cadential fermata, but it moves on to dominant harmony immediately, and remains there throughout the cadenza. This is a fairly rare type.

Tartini's discussion is rather briefer than those of the above writers, but it contains many more written-out examples. His comments are principally applicable to the Italian violin concerto, a tradition very different from that to which Quantz belonged. It was a tradition in which virtuosity of a specifically violinistic nature was highly prized, and while the more cantabile style of the German wind concerto is also found in the Italian concerto, it is hardly surprising that a more technical style should have prevailed in the cadenzas. Tartini speaks in terms of 'tasteful artificial figures' (*modi artificiali di buon gusto*), and it is these which constitute the material of his cadenzas, rather than the thematic, cantabile ideas which appear in Quantz's examples.

Tartini begins with a slightly confused argument about the notes on which it is permissible for the solo part to pause in order to begin a cadenza.[34] His conclusion offers valuable evidence that performers were not expected to adhere literally to the form of notation used by the composer if they were going to perform a cadenza. Tartini suggests that the composer would indicate a cadenza by placing a fermata over the first of the two notes constituting a cadence, i.e. the supertonic, the note bearing the cadential trill over dominant harmony. Yet, he says, it is impossible for the soloist to pause on this note, because he must prepare for the trill on the supertonic by approaching it with 'tasteful artificial figures' from above or below. The emphasis on patterned figuration places Tartini closer to Hiller than to any of the other writers discussed so far. He argues that the only three possible notes are the three notes of the tonic triad, since the tonic is in the bass. Presumably he means that the tonic is the root of the triad, since it is the dominant which is in the bass.[35] The 6/4 convention may therefore legitimately be applied even where the score does not actually indicate this chord.

Tartini's advice on how to improvise the cadenza is more practical in orientation than Quantz's. He suggests a melodic outline to be filled in by means of *modi artificiali*. Starting from the note chosen for the fermata (which must, as he has argued, be drawn from the tonic triad), the soloist works

[33] Ibid. 112.

[34] *Traité des agrémens de la musique* (Paris, 1771), trans. and ed. E. Jacobi (Celle and New York, 1961), 118 f. Henceforth abbreviated as *Traité*.

[35] The idea that chords might be structured around roots rather than around bass-notes was a relatively recent development in musical theory, which may explain why Tartini's language is somewhat obscure at this point.

towards another of the notes of the triad, after which he wends his way to the supertonic for the cadential trill.[36] The musical examples illustrate the ways in which the figures were to be used, i.e. they were repeated on each degree of the scale or of the triad until the desired note was reached (see Ex. 6). Quantz's strictures on excessive repetition and on the use of regular patterns clearly do not apply here.

Ex. 6.   *G. Tartini, example of a cadenza from* Traité

The cadenzas quoted in Riepel's innumerable musical examples are closer in style to those of Quantz than they are to Tartini's, for they use thematic ideas as their material for the most part. The approach to the combination of different ideas is strikingly mathematical. Throughout this five-volume work, Riepel shows a great interest in the *ars combinatoria*,[37] the number of different possible arrangements and permutations of ideas or notes, and he takes delight in exploring the range of possible melodies based on a certain pattern. He quotes, in whole or in part, no fewer than sixteen possible cadenzas for a single aria, illustrating different ways of using the material of its opening phrase.

Riepel's discussion of the tonal construction of cadenzas illustrates this tendency even more clearly. It is demonstrated that the number of possible key-schemes using two or more out of the five most nearly related keys is 320.[38] A few possibilities are selected at random and illustrated.

This mathematical approach to the arrangement of material and tonalities in the cadenzas is Riepel's most original contribution to the discussion of improvised cadenzas. It is best interpreted as an aid to study, aimed at developing a facility for variety in improvisation rather than as a method to be adopted by professionals. There is no evidence that such a method was used otherwise. In other respects he represents a slightly more advanced stage than Quantz, particularly with regard to his views on the variety of expression,

---

[36] *Traité*, p. 121.
[37] For further discussion of this phenomenon in 18th-cent. music, see L. G. Ratner, 'Ars Combinatoria, Chance and Choice in Eighteenth-Century Music', in H. C. Robbins Landon and R. E. Chapman (eds.), *Studies in Eighteenth-Century Music: A Tribute to Karl Geiringer on his Seventieth Birthday* (London, 1970), 343 ff.
[38] Riepel, *Erläuterung*, p. 86.

mood, and dynamic permissible within a cadenza, on the possibility of repetition, either exact or varied, at the same or a different pitch, and on harmonic exploration—Neapolitan and diminished seventh effects are mentioned and illustrated.

The matter of signalling to the orchestra when they should make their re-entry after the conclusion of the cadenza is discussed by C. P. E. Bach in his *Versuch*, where he considers the cadenza from two angles. His comments on the performance of keyboard cadenzas in two or more parts are discussed in Chapter 6 below. Most of what he has to say on the subject, however, occurs in his discussion of the art of accompaniment.[39] Here he offers advice not to the soloist who is improvising the cadenza, but to the keyboard player who is accompanying. His observations, not surprisingly, apply exclusively to the beginning and the ending of the cadenza, as the keyboard player is silent in between these points.

The first requirement is that the accompanist should recognize when a cadenza is about to take place. In this matter the score cannot always be interpreted literally. In the first place, even if the composer has clearly indicated the place for a cadenza, the soloist might wish to omit it (see Ex. 7).

Ex. 7.   C. P. E. Bach, *example from* Versuch

Sometimes the performer feels disinclined to pause at the cadence, regardless of whether there is a fermata over the bass note; he usually indicates this to the orchestra by a movement of either the head or the body. When the accompanist notices this, instead of a sustained bass note he continues to play short notes as before, in order to preserve the ensemble and to indicate clearly to the other musicians the continuation in strict time.[40]

Conversely cadenzas might be inserted even when not indicated in the score (see Ex. 8).

In the case quoted below, in which the figuring makes no allowance for a pause over the bass at the cadence, the accompanist does not follow the written instructions, but plays above the G not 4–3 but 6/4–5/3, as soon as he notices that the soloist wishes to

---

[39] *Versuch*, ii. 259 ff., *Essay*, pp. 379 ff.

[40] *Versuch*, ii. 261, *Essay*, pp. 380 f. Dittersdorf, writing of a performance by the violinist Reinhard of six new violin concertos by Benda, had 'only one fault to find, which was that he shirked every cadenza, and passed on at once to the shake': *Lebensbeschreibung* (1801), trans. A. D. Coleridge as *Autobiography* (London, 1896), 50.

pause at the cadence, whether with or without embellishment. All similar cases should be dealt with in this way, however they are figured.[41]

Ex. 8.   *C. P. E. Bach, example from* Versuch

The keyboard player and the orchestral players needed always to be alert to the possibility that a soloist might wish to introduce a cadenza just before a tutti, whether or not there was any corresponding indication in their parts.[42]

Bach goes on to describe other situations in which the text would have to be modified in order to allow a cadenza to be improvised, even though a fermata is present. He explains that the right-hand harmony from the beginning of the bar in Ex. 9 should be sustained so as to produce a 6–4 over the final crotchet. It is at this point that the cadenza begins.[43]

Ex. 9.   *C. P. E. Bach, example from* Versuch

So the accompanist must be able to anticipate the intentions of the soloist regarding the inclusion or omission of cadenzas. It is up to the soloist to communicate his intentions 'by a movement of either the head or the body', but the accompanist must be prepared for either inclusion or omission, and if necessary he must amend his part accordingly.

Bach also discusses the manner of performing the 6–4 chord itself.[44] He recommends that the chord should be spread slowly and sustained in a slow tempo, but played quite short and then released in an allegro, in order to allow the soloist the opportunity to move quickly away from the 6–4 harmony should he so wish. Bach considers it inadvisable for the soloist to move away

[41] *Versuch*, ii. 265, *Essay*, p. 384.

[42] An illustration of the importance of this is found in the C minor Harpsichord Concerto, H. 474, by C. P. E. Bach. Here the bar in which the final tutti is marked in the orchestral parts actually corresponds to the penultimate at the beginning of an obbligato cadenza in the keyboard part. It is true that a fermata sign is placed over the rest which the orchestra is given to count before this entry, but it would still be easy to imagine a colossal error in performance if the orchestral players were not primed to listen out for a cadenza at this point.

[43] *Versuch*, ii. 263 f., *Essay*, pp. 382 f. Compare this passage with the similar recommendations of Tartini mentioned above.

[44] *Versuch*, ii. 262, *Essay*, pp. 381 f.

from the cadential harmony too quickly, but necessary that he be given the chance to do so. Ideally the soloist will pause for a little while on whichever note of the tonic triad he is playing, until the sound of the harpsichord has had a chance to die away, and the listeners have registered in their minds the harmony which is to be prolonged. Only then will the cadenza begin. This recommendation provides evidence that conventional notation might be disregarded in one further respect, namely that the bass need not be sustained, even when a sustained bass-note is present in the orchestral parts. Indeed, in some instances in which Bach writes a sustained orchestral bass-note in his concerto scores, the cadenzas which he wrote later would jar unpleasantly with the bass dominant if it were in fact to be sustained.[45]

The signal that the cadenza is about to finish is a trill on the second degree of the scale (or sometimes the third degree in a minor key). Care is needed on the part of the accompanist, who must play a dominant chord underneath this trill, but must do so neither too soon nor too late.[46] It may be, particularly if the soloist uses a chain of trills in his cadenza, that a trill of this kind will occur in the middle of the cadenza, and the accompanist must not mistake such a trill for the cadential trill. If he does, then the soloist will either be obliged to cut his cadenza short, or else he will ignore the accompanist and continue, creating dissonance with the unresolved dominant harmony underneath. Particular care is needed when the trill occurs on the third degree of the scale, and here, Bach says, the soloist must be prepared to sustain the trill for a long time if he wishes to conclude in this way—the accompanist will want to wait in order to make sure that it really is the cadential trill. On the other hand he owes it to the soloist not to wait so long that the trill begins to lose its brilliance. Some soloists, Bach informs us, take a perverse pleasure in deceiving the accompanist into thinking that they are ready to conclude, and then as soon as he has sounded his dominant chord they launch off into quite unrelated harmonies in order to make him look a fool. One wonders whether Frederick the Great treated Bach in this way! In such cases, Bach declares, the accompanist need feel no shame; his own conduct was entirely professional.

Türk's recommendations continue along the lines established by Quantz and Agricola, to whom he refers in his text. He defends the cadenza in principle, claiming that good composers make use of it, and even that learned philosophers argue in its favour,[47] although he deplores its frequent abuse by performers. He stresses the importance of matching the character of the movement, indeed of providing a concise summary of its expression in the cadenza; in advocating the use of material from the movement in order to achieve this, he observes that cadenzas produced by this method (integrated

---

[45] e.g. cadenzas 15 and 60 from H. 264 (see ch. 6), both written for the first movement of H. 414, would clash with the sustained A which Bach gives to the bass instruments during the cadenza, since both approach the final flourish via an arpeggiated diminished triad on a bottom G sharp.

[46] *Versuch*, ii. 262 f., *Essay*, p. 382.   [47] *Klavierschule*, p. 309, *School*, p. 298.

cadenzas) can only be performed in the context of one particular parent movement.[48] By this time interchangeable cadenzas were becoming less common. While reiterating Quantz's opposition to regular metre in the cadenza, he does allow that certain passages in the cadenza might retain the metre of the parent movement, but he warns against too much regularity. He suggests that such passages should be mixed with apparently unconnected ideas in the manner of a dream, so as to achieve the desired effects of surprise and spontaneity. He is prepared to allow more variety of expression in the cadenza than Quantz.[49]

As for the harmonic range, he concedes that performers will probably wish to explore harmonies other than those of the cadential chords, but advises that the tonal range of the cadenza should not exceed that of the parent movement.[50] While he thinks that cadenzas should ideally be improvised, he advises preparation as the safer method.[51] Like C. P. E. Bach he points out that cadenzas may be introduced in places where the composer has not indicated them, but he says that this happens only seldom, and he seems to be thinking more in terms of solo sonatas than of concertos.[52]

In many respects then, there are certain advances over the recommendations of Quantz and Agricola, partly no doubt because Türk was writing over thirty years later, but partly too because of the increased scope offered by the keyboard as solo instrument. Yet Türk's examples do not exploit the possibilities of idiomatic keyboard style even to the extent that Mozart's had done ten years earlier. He does distinguish between simple and multiple cadenzas, i.e. those written with only a single voice and those with two or three obbligato voice parts.[53] Although he makes use of idiomatic keyboard figures in simple cadenzas, he never uses idiomatic keyboard textures with a variable number of parts.[54] In this respect his cadenzas resemble those of C. P. E. Bach. There are frequent references to Bach in the treatise, and it appears that Türk was addressing himself primarily to clavichordists in whose repertoire the works of Bach would have featured prominently.

It is unusual for small-scale keyboard cadenzas to be other than simple or two-part; the use of idiomatic keyboard textures with a variable number of parts was not surprisingly a somewhat later development, facilitated by the

---

[48] *Klavierschule*, p. 310, *School*, p. 299.
[49] *Klavierschule*, p. 312, *School*, pp. 301, 498.
[50] *Klavierschule*, p. 311, *School*, p. 300.
[51] *Klavierschule*, p. 313, *School*, p. 301.
[52] *Klavierschule*, p. 310, *School*, p. 497.
[53] *Klavierschule*, p. 310, *School*, p. 298.
[54] There is arguably a single exception to this rule. In spite of Türk's claim that cadenzas are either simple or multiple, there is one example, the most shocking of those which illustrate how not to write cadenzas (*Klavierschule*, pp. 316 ff., *School*, pp. 304 f.: no. 4), in which a variable number of parts is used. Türk does not mention this when listing its many faults, so he evidently was not opposed to the idea that cadenzas might be written using such textures.

growth in scale which the cadenza underwent in the later part of the eighteenth century.[55]

Duet Cadenzas

On account of the importance of cadenzas in two or more real parts for the growth of the keyboard cadenza, it is necessary to examine also the recommendations made by the didactic authors, principally Quantz, on this subject.

The added interest provided by an extra voice is considerable. It not only introduces a harmonic dimension to the cadenza, but also the possibility of imitation. In both respects the result is likely to be a move towards a more structured improvisation, one which is further removed from the ideal of spontaneity which Quantz emphasizes so much. This is not only because so many duet cadenzas were prepared in advance; especially, perhaps, when duet cadenzas were improvised there was a need for an agreed structure of some kind.

The simplest type of two-part writing consists in chains of thirds or sixths. While it was scarcely desirable that an entire cadenza should proceed in this way, it was highly likely that at some point the parts would move in parallel. Quantz explains that it was necessary for one player to anticipate each move, so that the other player might know whether to ascend or to descend.[56]

Imitations, particularly those involving suspensions, constitute the raw material of a good duet cadenza as conceived by Quantz. Considerable skill was required to improvise such a cadenza well. The leader not only had to invent ideas which lent themselves to imitation by the other player, but also to prepare a suspension during the answer, and if possible to vary the intervals to some extent.[57] Effectively it was necessary to know a variety of patterns of two-part suspensions and resolutions, to embellish these in different ways, to be able to move from one pattern to another, and to communicate such a move to the partner through the choice of imitative figure.

Perhaps the most crucial piece of communication between the players concerned the timing of the approach to the cadential trill. Quantz indicates that the cue was the tritone between the leading-note and the fourth scale degree. If, while one player was sustaining the fourth scale degree, the other contrived to arrive on the leading-note, this was to be interpreted as a signal for the two parts to converge in a standard cadential figure.[58]

On account of the greater scope offered by the combination of two parts, greater length is permissible in a duet cadenza than in a solo, and the taking of

---

[55] Isolated examples do exist, however, of small-scale polyphonic keyboard cadenzas, e.g. C. P. E. Bach, Sonata, H. 208, second movement, closing bars, and G. Sammartini, Concerto Op. 9 No. 3, second movement, final solo cadence.

[56] Quantz, *Versuch*, ch. xv, par. 24.

[57] Ibid., ch. xv, par. 26.   [58] Ibid., ch. xv, par. 29.

breaths is allowed. The variety and the flexibility of metre which Quantz emphasizes in his treatment of the solo cadenza is also desirable here, although it is harder to achieve. The best method is to vary the imitative figures which serve to embellish the basic patterns of two-part suspensions and resolutions, and Quantz provides several illustrations of how this may be done.

C. P. E. Bach approaches the multiple cadenza from a somewhat different angle in part I of his *Versuch*,[59] which appeared only one year after Quantz's treatise. He addresses himself briefly to the keyboard player who is performing a solo obbligato cadenza in two or more real parts, such as those found in the middle movements of the fourth and sixth of the *Probestücke*. His comments are discussed more fully in connection with the particular cadenzas to which they apply (see Chapter 6). Again his main concern is that the effect of improvisation be achieved in spite of the use of imitation.

The comments made by the didactic writers provide a useful summary of the growth of the cadenza and the changes which it underwent as it was adapted to the nature of the different instruments on which cadenzas were performed. It will be seen in Part II that examples exist of keyboard cadenzas in all the categories described above, ranging from the single-breath, rhapsodic style, through the patterned violinistic style described by Tartini, to harmonically varied and thematically complex cadenzas in two or more real parts, such as Türk describes.

It must be borne in mind that the recommendations made by the didactic authors describe not so much the type of cadenza that was actually heard, but rather the ideal cadenza as they conceived it. Indeed, some of the most revealing comments they have to offer, from the point of view of the historian anxious to know what eighteenth-century cadenzas were really like, come in their occasional asides about the abuses that were common, and the faults into which all too many performers tended to fall. It may be useful to cast a brief glance at some further documentary evidence, in which actual performances are described, in case the prescriptive writings to which this chapter has been devoted give too one-sided a picture.

Anecdotal evidence is available in plenty to testify that performers often improvised for far too long, and ranged too widely in their harmonic explorations. One of the best-known tales is that related of the violinist Dubourg, who improvised a cadenza during a concert in Dublin which Handel was conducting.

One night, while HANDEL was in Dublin, Dubourg having a solo part in a song, and a close to make, *ad libitum*, he wandered about in different keys a great while, and seemed indeed a little bewildered, and uncertain of his original key . . . but, at length, coming to the shake, which was to terminate this long close, HANDEL, to the great delight of the audience, and augmentation of applause, cried out loud enough to be

---

[59] C. P. E. Bach, *Versuch*, i. 131 f., *Essay*, pp. 164 f.

heard in the most remote parts of the theatre: 'You are welcome home, Mr. Dubourg!'[60]

By the early years of the nineteenth century abuses were even greater, as may be seen from the following account concerning the violinist Boucher related in Spohr's autobiography:[61]

As his concluding subject he played a rondo of his own composition which had at the end an impromptu cadence. At the rehearsal he had begged the gentlemen dilettanti to fall in right vigorously with their final tutti immediately after the shake of his cadence, and added that he would give them the signal by stamping with his foot. In the evening, when this concluding piece began, it was already very late, and the dilettanti were growing impatient to get home to supper. But when the cadence in which *Boucher* as usual exhibited all his artistic *tours de force* seemed never likely to end, some of the gentlemen put their instruments into their cases and slipped out. This was so infectious, that in a few minutes the whole orchestra had disappeared. *Boucher*, who in the enthusiasm of his play had observed nothing of this, lifted his foot already at the commencement of his concluding shake, in order to draw the attention of the orchestra beforehand to the agreed signal. When he had now concluded the shake he was fully satisfied of what would follow, namely the most vigorous entry of the orchestra and the burst of applause it was to bring down from the enraptured audience. His astonishment may therefore be imagined when all that fell upon his ear was the loud stamp of his own foot. Horrified he stared aghast around him, and beheld all the music desks abandoned. But the public, who had already prepared themselves to see this moment arrive, burst out into an uproarious laughter, in which *Boucher*, with the best stomach he could, was obliged to join.

Perhaps the historian needs to be on his guard against taking the didactic treatises too much at face value.

[60] C. Burney, 'Sketch of the Life of Handel', *An Account of the Musical Performances in Westminster Abbey . . . in Commemoration of Handel* (London, 1785), 27 n. Henceforth abbreviated as 'Sketch'.
[61] L. Spohr, *Lebenserinnerungen*, ed. F. Göthel, 2 vols. (Tutzing, 1968), ii. 65 f.; trans. anon. *Louis Spohr's Autobiography*, 2 vols. (London, 1865), ii. 71 f.

3

When is a Cadenza not a Cadenza?

IT is useful at this stage to consider some of those types of improvisation or improvisatory writing which are related to the cadenza, but which for one reason or another stand outside the particular tradition of improvisation under examination here.

The Embellished Fermata

It is possible to distinguish a number of different types of embellished fermata, according to the context in which they occur. Indeed the cadenza itself ought strictly to be included under this heading, since it is after all a particular type of fermata embellishment. For present purposes, however, it is convenient to group a number of types together under this heading, while dealing separately not only with the cadenza, but also with the *Eingang*, a form of embellished fermata which occurs with great frequency in the classical concerto.

(*a*) The first type is the *halbe Kadenz* described by Quantz.[1] This is essentially a decorated Phrygian cadence. Unlike the cadenza itself, the *halbe Kadenz* serves not as a confirmation of a tonality, but as a linking passage, a question mark pointing ahead to an important new event that will provide an answer. As Quantz points out, it was used a great deal in music of a slightly earlier generation, especially in compositions in the church style, but was rather rarer in his own day.

Not surprisingly for a figure that had been somewhat overused in earlier music, it tended to appear in highly conventional forms. Quantz recognizes only one form, namely that in which a 7–6 suspension over the sixth degree in a minor key cadences onto a dominant chord (Ex. 10*a*). The decoration had to be introduced on the suspended seventh, outlining and embellishing the arpeggio of the seventh chord, before resolving on to the sixth above the bass. If there were a second participating soloist, he would sustain the third above the bass during this embellishment, which he would then imitate a fifth below or a fourth above, arriving on the sharpened leading note as the other parts cadenced onto the dominant (Ex. 10*b*).

(*b*) Quantz also describes a second type of embellished fermata,[2] namely

---

[1] *Versuch*, ch. xv, pars. 32–34.   [2] *Versuch*, ch. xv, par. 35.

Ex. 10. *J. J. Quantz*, Versuch: (a) *example of a plain* halbe Kadenz, (b) *example of an embellished* halbe Kadenz

that which sometimes occurs at the first vocal entry in an aria. Here the embellishment is normally restricted to tonic harmony, in which it starts and finishes. The normal type, quoted by Quantz, is that in which the voice part falls a fifth, as shown in Ex. 11a. Quantz describes how it tended to begin with a *messa di voce*, the tone swelling and diminishing, and then to outline the notes of the triad either above or below; it had to return to the original pitch, however, after which it would descend to the tonic via a trill on the third scale degree (Ex. 11b). Quantz is quite specific about the way this trill must be executed: it must be approached from above and must not be provided with a termination. As Quantz explains, it was rare for such an embellished fermata to occur in an instrumental movement, although it was not unknown in the slow movements of concertos. It is an embellishment directly related to those improvisatory opening entries sometimes given to the solo instrument in Mozart's concertos just before the main theme is restated (e.g. the first movements of K. 219 and K. 450).[3]

(c) It is necessary to turn to C. P. E. Bach for a discussion of less specific types of embellished fermata.[4] As an expressive ornament, he writes, a fermata awakens 'unusual attentiveness',[5] and provides an opportunity for a

Ex. 11. *J. J. Quantz*, Versuch, *examples of initial vocal entries*: (a) *unembellished* (b) *embellished*

[3] Arguably it is also related indirectly to the improvisatory flourishes at the start of the 'Emperor' Concerto.
[4] *Versuch*, i. 112 ff.; *Essay*, pp. 143 ff.   [5] *Versuch*, i. 112 f.; *Essay*, p. 143.

heightening of the *Affekt*. It normally occurs at a cadence of some kind, though not necessarily one that is of particular structural importance. Bach recommends the use of a fermata sign to mark both the point where the embellishment is to begin and the point where it is to end,[6] although in practice it is usually only the ending which is marked. Sometimes an embellished fermata involves a progression from one chord to another, as is the case with the *halbe Kadenz*; at other times the embellishment takes place within a single harmony, as is the case with the initial vocal entries described above. What distinguishes the types of embellished fermata under consideration here from those discussed earlier is that they are neither tied to a particular harmonic context nor fulfil an important structural function; the example quoted in Ex. 12, taken from Bach's *Versuch*, is an expressive ornament rather than a form of structural articulation.

Ex. 12.　*C. P. E. Bach, example of an embellished fermata from* Versuch

The Eingang

It is necessary to look ahead to Hiller's *Anweisung* to find a reference to this further category of embellished fermata. The term *Eingang* is not Hiller's but Mozart's; Hiller speaks of an *Übergang*, and he does so not in a separate section, but in the same paragraph in which other types of embellished fermata are discussed.[7] It is in fact closely related to the type of fermata embellishment that may occur at an imperfect cadence, with the addition of a linking passage that leads into the next section, often the return of a rondo theme. It follows that *Eingänge* tend to occur at moments of some structural significance, more perhaps than is the case with other embellished fermatas, since they offer a means of highlighting a new event. *Eingänge* may occur not only before the return of a rondo theme, but also before a recapitulation,

---

[6] *Versuch*, i. 113; *Essay*, p. 143.
[7] J. A. Hiller, *Anweisung zum musikalisch-zierlichen Gesang* (Leipzig, 1780), 122 f.

before a second subject, or before a new section in a different tempo or metre. They differ functionally from cadenzas in that they point ahead to what follows, like a pair of opening quotation marks, whereas cadenzas serve essentially as full stops to conclude the paragraph that has gone before. In general, *Eingänge* tend to occur on dominant or dominant seventh harmonies, and to remain within a single harmony. It has been observed, however, that there are cadenzas of which this could be said, and *Eingänge* of which it could not;[8] the two types clearly belong to different traditions of improvisation but, as will be seen in other instances too, different traditions sometimes converge. It is important that the distinction between two such traditions should be made on the basis of function rather than character, especially where the latter is such a variable quality.

Functional distinctions, however, are not without their difficulties. It is often only the addition of a linking passage into the following section which distinguishes an *Eingang* from an embellished fermata on a dominant harmony. The presence or absence of a caesura can have important implications for the function of an embellishment of this kind.

In several of Mozart's concerto finales the cadenza is followed not by a rousing tutti, as might be expected, but by a further statement of the rondo theme from the soloist; the cadenza concludes not with a cadential trill, but with a linking passage. In such cases the cadenza clearly fulfils a dual function, combining the roles of cadenza and *Eingang*. Passages of this kind are known hereafter as 'rondo cadenzas'.[9] Since the function of a cadenza is of greater structural significance than that of an *Eingang*, however, the primary function of a rondo cadenza is always cadential articulation, and the local articulation of a thematic statement is a secondary function. In this way the retention of the term 'cadenza', which Mozart himself used in preference to *Eingang* as a label for such passages, can be justified.

The cadenza-related forms of improvisation considered above were categories recognized and discussed by eighteenth-century didactic writers. Two further phenomena remain to be considered, namely the perfidia and the capriccio; although not discussed in contemporary writings, they nevertheless played an important part in the development of the Italian violin concerto in the early eighteenth century, and have been considered by some to stand in a close relation to the cadenza.

The Perfidia

The label 'perfidia' is attached to three brief passages by Giuseppe Torelli, lasting respectively 29, 28, and 13 bars. Each is scored for two violins and

---

[8] Knödt, 'Zur Entwicklungsgeschichte', p. 377.
[9] Paul Mies takes the view that rondo cadenzas should be classed as *Eingänge*; see *Die Krise der Konzertkadenz bei Beethoven* (Bonn, 1970), 54 f.

bass. Franz Giegling quotes the incipits in his thematic catalogue, which appears as an appendix to *Torelli*,[10] where they are assigned the numbers 65–7.

In each of the perfidias the bass simply sustains a pedal-note, while the upper parts busy themselves with brilliant triadic figurations and scales. Not unreasonably, Giegling assumes that they must form parts of some larger work or works. The openings of the first two (Ex. 13) seem to support this assumption, since neither the single adagio chord with which TV65 begins nor the opening two bars in TV66 make much musical sense except as references to some larger context. Giegling suggests that the perfidias could have functioned as introductions to a sonata da chiesa, or as middle movements flanked by brief adagios.[11]

He goes on to suggest that Torelli's music, as well as other contemporary Italian violin music, contains many further examples of perfidias, by which he means passages occurring within larger works and resembling these three passages in character. (All subsequent references to the perfidia, unless otherwise stated, relate to the type which resembles TV65–7 in character, and not to these three passages themselves.) It seems that Giegling has in mind such passages as Ex. 14, taken from Corelli's solo Violin Sonata, Op. 5 No. 3. He claims that this sort of passage 'anticipates the later solo cadenza of the great instrumental concertos of the eighteenth century'.[12]

Care is needed when the relationship between the perfidia and the cadenza is discussed. Heinrich Knödt suggests that the perfidia made a somewhat indirect contribution to the growth of the cadenza.[13] On the one hand it served to emphasize the structural importance of cadences, thereby helping to pave the way for a tradition of improvisation at these important structural moments; and on the other hand it served as a testing-ground for composers and performers to develop the type of idiomatic figurations which were later to form the substance of the cadenza, in which the same problem of sustaining interest in an unchanging harmonic context would obtain.

It is certainly true that the use of perfidias in the music of Corelli, Torelli, and Vivaldi played a part in the process whereby cadences came to be articulated with all manner of virtuoso prolongations, both composed and improvised. It must be emphasized, however, that a direct line cannot be drawn between the perfidia and the classical cadenza, since the true successor of the perfidia was the type of composed cadential prolongation which, like the perfidia, was not articulated at the beginning: we have seen an example of

[10] F. Giegling, *Giuseppe Torelli: Ein Beitrag zur Entwicklungsgeschichte des italienischen Konzerts* (Kassel and Basle, 1949).   [11] Ibid. 27.   [12] Ibid. 64 f.

[13] 'Zur Entwicklungsgeschichte', p. 389. Knödt does not actually use the word 'perfidia', but his discussion of 'cadenza-like passages' in Italian violin music of the late baroque period clearly refers to the same phenomenon. He uses the Corelli passage quoted here in Ex. 14 to illustrate his point. The frequent use of the term 'perfidia' for such passages in more recent writings probably derives from Giegling: in the 18th cent. it was used inconsistently (see Giegling, *Torelli*, p. 27).

Ex. 13.   *G. Torelli, openings of perfidias, TV 65 and TV 66*

Ex. 14.   *A. Corelli, Sonata, Op. 5 No. 3, second movement*

this in Mozart's F major Sonata, K. 533. Moreover, Knödt's assertion that the perfidia provided a vocabulary of figurative formulae for the cadenzas of the future is questionable. It is probably Vivaldi that he has in mind here; yet most of Vivaldi's so-called cadenzas are not in fact cadenzas at all, according to the usage adopted in the present survey, but capriccios (see below). The perfidia undoubtedly used many of the idiomatic figurations of violinistic virtuosity that were to reappear in the capriccio; but Vivaldi's genuine cadenzas were very different, and much more vocal in idiom. The importance of correctly defining terms and distinguishing between them cannot be overstressed—in this instance it significantly affects the conclusions to be reached.

The Capriccio

The label 'capriccio' is attached to each of a series of extended, unaccompanied, and extremely brilliant passages for solo violin found in Pietro Antonio Locatelli's 'L'arte del violino', Op. 3 (Amsterdam, 1733). This publication contains twelve solo violin concertos, each with three movements in a fast-slow-fast relationship; each of the twenty-four outer movements is supplied with a capriccio towards the end. Most of the capriccios are optional, in the sense that the movement may be terminated immediately before them, should the performer so wish. This is because they follow what appears to be the concluding ritornello in the tonic. In every such case another brief tutti in the tonic is supplied after the capriccio as an alternative conclusion. (See the figure below).

P. A. Locatelli, Violin Concerto, Op. 3 No. 8, finale, conclusion (solo violin part only)

Four capriccios, however, are preceded by a dominant harmony, in some cases a dominant seventh; clearly the movement cannot be terminated here and some continuation is needed. These four capriccios could be described as examples of cadential prolongation since they articulate a move from dominant harmony to the tonic. The other twenty do not articulate a cadence—they end precisely where they began, on a tonic 5–3. All twenty-four capriccios are clearly articulated, unlike the perfidias discussed above. There would appear to be a strong case, then, for including the 'cadential' capriccios within the category of cadenza, stronger in fact than the case for including any of the other types of improvisatory insertion discussed in this chapter.

It is worth noting that Locatelli actually uses the word 'cadenza' over a blank bar at the end of eighteen of the capriccios. At this point he presumably expected a cadential improvisation that would lead into the concluding tutti. So a distinction is made between capriccios and cadenzas: the cadenzas being the improvised embellishments of the cadences occurring at the end of the capriccios. From the written-out examples of cadenzas that appear in some of Locatelli's other publications,[14] it is possible to observe how he conceived the differences between the two phenomena.

[14] The last movement of the Violin Sonata Op. 6 No. 12 consists entirely of a capriccio, ending with a written-out cadenza (quoted in P. Whitmore, 'Towards an Understanding of the Capriccio', *JRMA* 113/1 (1988), 49). This cadenza is longer than most; more characteristic examples occur in the first movements of Op. 6 Nos. 7 and 11.

Locatelli's distinction between these two terms seems to reflect not so much a radical difference between the cadenza and the capriccio as a difference between the traditions to which each belongs. It has been shown that four of Locatelli's capriccios are in fact cadential prolongations, albeit on a vast scale, and it is also the case that the cadenzas written in the later eighteenth and early nineteenth centuries were frequently similar in length, difficulty, and self-sufficiency to Locatelli's capriccios. Yet to group the four 'cadential' capriccios together with Locatelli's 'cadenzas' would obscure the enormous differences between th m, as well as the obvious place occupied by the former within the tradition of the capriccio, in which a cadential context was by no means essential.

Vivaldi was the first composer to include capriccios in his concertos. They were frequently preceded by the instruction 'Qui si ferma a piacimento' (Here one may pause/stop at will). In some cases Vivaldi's capriccios were ad libitum in the sense that the performer was invited to supply his own.[15] In other cases, though, Vivaldi wrote the capriccio out. Unfortunately he labelled these written-out passages not 'capriccio' but 'cadenza'. Yet they closely resemble Locatelli's 'capriccios' and, like them, some occur within a cadential context, while others follow the 5–3 chord that marks the completion of a cadence and a possible ending to the movement. For present purposes, then, the blanket label 'cadenza' is misleading.

Occasionally, Vivaldi's capriccios conclude with rhapsodic passages articulating the final cadence and clearly set off from their metrical surroundings.[16] These passages stand in the same relation to the whole capriccio as do the final ad libitum cadenzas of Locatelli's capriccios to the capriccios themselves. In other words, the same distinction which Locatelli draws between capriccios and cadenzas obtains in Vivaldi's music, the fact that Vivaldi makes no such terminological distinction notwithstanding. Vivaldi was writing before either term had acquired the definite meaning it was to hold for Locatelli.[17]

The same problem arises here as was encountered in our discussion of Locatelli's capriccios, namely that those capriccios which occur in a cadential context actually fall within the terms of the definition of the cadenza here adopted. A similar solution is recommended in both cases, namely that these passages be held to belong to the tradition of the capriccio and not to that of the cadenza, even though they might appear to belong to the latter category when viewed outside their historical context.

In Tartini's work the traditions of capriccio and cadenza were to converge

---

[15] See e.g. the concerto published as Op. 7 No. 11, RV 208a, discussed in Ch. 5.

[16] One example occurs in the B flat Concerto, RV 583, finale—the conclusion of the capriccio is quoted in Whitmore, 'Capriccio', p. 51. Another is found in the finale of the C major Concerto, RV 581.

[17] Once again we see the importance of applying consistent definitions, and evaluating critically the terminology used in the 18th cent. A compilation of the many different uses of the word 'cadenza' would be of more philological than historical interest, and it would be hard to produce a coherent account of such material.

still further. While he retains both words and distinguishes between them in the same way that Locatelli had done, his capriccios differ in two important respects from Locatelli's: they are usually thematically constructed and introduced within a cadential context.[18] Like Vivaldi's, they are sometimes ad libitum, although sources vary on this point. Tartini's written-out capriccios often terminate in cadenzas, sometimes in ad libitum cadenzas. In addition to his use of the capriccio, Tartini frequently invites ad libitum cadenzas in his concertos, unlike either Vivaldi or Locatelli, and he obligingly includes a discussion of the cadenza in his *Traité* (see Chapter 2), from which it is evident that his understanding of the cadenza was of something quite unlike the metrical, thematically constructed capriccios, with their double and triple stops, which appear in certain of his concertos.[19] In theory, then, the distinction is maintained, but in practice it can be very difficult to decide to

Ex. 15.   *G. Tartini, Capriccio from Concerto, D. 103, finale*

[18] Only one of Locatelli's capriccios (that of the first movement of Op. 3 No. 9) makes extensive use of thematic material from the parent movement. Others borrow certain patterns of figuration on a more or less casual basis. Only four occur within a cadential context.

[19] Evident, that is, from the examples he uses and from his discussion of how to shape a cadenza. Nevertheless he makes a revealing comment, that 'nowadays every singer or instrumentalist feels entitled to lengthen [the cadenza], and with such different expressions that it is unreasonable to speak of a "cadenza" but rather should one say "capriccio", since the capriccio can be as long as one likes and be made up of different pieces and sentiments, with varied bar time' (*Traité*, pp. 117 f.).

which category a certain passage belongs. The 'capriccio' in the finale of D. 103[20] is given in Ex. 15. By Tartini's own standards it is hard to see how it could be labelled as other than a cadenza.

Tartini was the last major exponent of the capriccio, in the sense understood here. Isolated examples do occur in concertos written later than *c*.1740, but these seem to be consciously modelled on Locatelli's celebrated Op. 3, and no longer to form part of a living tradition. The word itself came to be used to describe an independent display piece, and in this sense Locatelli's capriccios have been seen as the ancestors of the 'Caprices' of Paganini. In the concertos of Tartini the phenomenon of the capriccio became associated increasingly with a cadential context, while the cadenza grew in proportions and scope until the two became indistinguishable. It is here maintained, however, that in the earlier part of the eighteenth century the traditions of capriccio and cadenza were quite distinct, and that to group the capriccios of Vivaldi or Locatelli together with their cadenzas is to overlook the immense differences between them, and is bound to give rise to unhistorical judgements about the state of the cadenza in the early eighteenth-century Italian violin concerto.

[20] F-Pn MS 9795/15, autograph.

4

Growth and Decline

THE evolution of the keyboard cadenza followed a pattern not unlike that of the keyboard concerto. Whether or not J. S. Bach's transcription for keyboard instruments of concertos originally written for melody instruments is held to mark the origin of the new genre, the fact remains that the earliest keyboard concertos are written like transcriptions. That is to say, they make little use of the tremendous resources which a keyboard instrument can offer in a concerto: it can compete on equal terms with the orchestra, it can accompany, enter into dialogue, or stand entirely alone, unlike a melody instrument. Once the keyboard concerto had developed to the stage where it made full use of these resources, it was able to become a leading genre. In a similar way, the keyboard cadenza, once it had matured beyond the idiom of transcription, possessed far greater potential for expansion and development than did the melody-instrument cadenzas which had helped to form it.

The only example of a solo keyboard cadenza known by the writer to have been transcribed directly from a pre-existent cadenza is that of J. S. Bach's E major Violin Concerto, which was retained in the harpsichord arrangement (see Chapter 5). Since Bach added a harmonization not present in the original, he altered its character considerably. Most concerto transcriptions, if they contain cadenzas at all, contain newly composed ones added by the transcriber.[1] Many of the cadenzas by C. P. E. Bach contained in H. 264 (see Chapter 6) are of the type which uses a single part over a stationary bass, i.e. they are written in the idiom of a transcription. Occasionally the bass-note may be changed to allow a brief harmonic digression, but it remains accompanimental and does not join with the right hand in the substance of the cadenza.

An important stimulus to the development of the keyboard cadenza was provided by the ensemble cadenza. This type, found in many vocal duets, arias with an instrumental obbligato, and concertos for more than one solo instrument, had been discussed by Quantz, Agricola, Riepel, and others (see Chapter 2), and it developed with particular speed during the vogue for the 'symphonie concertante' in Paris from the 1770s onwards (see Chapter 10). It is obvious that the presence of more than one contrapuntal strand increases the scope of the cadenza considerably. Indeed, there is a danger that the

---

[1] e.g. the cadenzas which occur in L. Frischmuth's 'VI concerti del Signor Giuseppe Tartini accommodati per il cembalo', Op. 4, are absent from the original violin concertos.

advent of harmonic and contrapuntal interest might rob the cadenza of its improvisatory character altogether. Quantz, in his discussion of the duet cadenza, reiterates his opposition to regular metre in cadenzas, partly on account of his concern that the character of improvisation should be preserved, but it is easy to see the difficulties involved in following this recommendation. The need to co-ordinate the different strands of a polyphonic texture had after all been a significant factor influencing the initial development of systems of mensuration some centuries previously. Most of the ensemble cadenzas from the Parisian symphonie concertante repertory do in fact observe regular metre (i.e. they are cadenzas in tempo) for much if not all of their duration.

For a keyboard player, though, it is not at all difficult to co-ordinate a number of contrapuntal strands in a non-metrical improvisation. Keyboard instruments are ideally suited to improvisation, since they combine the possibility of a full polyphonic texture with total control by a single performer. Harmonic, textural, registral, and metrical variety are all possible without any difficulties in co-ordination; even if a cadenza were to be prepared in advance it ought not to be difficult to achieve the effect of an improvisation in performance.

It has been seen that Türk recognizes a category of keyboard cadenza using a fixed number of parts and termed here a multiple cadenza. This type may have originated in the transcription of ensemble cadenzas, although in view of the scarcity of surviving examples this must remain a hypothesis.[2] Once the composers or improvisers of keyboard cadenzas no longer felt bound by the need to observe a strict number of parts throughout, then the stage of the fully idiomatic keyboard cadenza was reached, and the potential for growth was virtually unlimited.

As the cadenza grew, it became difficult to sustain interest simply with neutral, rhapsodic, or figurative passage-work. Increasingly composers of cadenzas tended to draw upon the thematic material of the parent movement, and to write what are here termed 'integrated cadenzas'. (It will be remembered that Quantz had recommended this procedure, but in his case merely as an expedient to guarantee consistency of *Affekt*.) Most of Mozart's and most of Beethoven's piano concerto cadenzas are of this kind. Yet only a small number of C. P. E. Bach's cadenzas are integrated, largely those written for the later concertos. A general trend towards greater integration may be observed throughout the history of the classical cadenza. The earlier examples of integrated cadenzas frequently drew upon the motivic or thematic idea heard immediately before the cadential fermata, especially where this fermata was preceded by a tutti passage. Later and more extended examples tended to quote the principal theme of the movement, or perhaps a number of different

---

[2] Examples do exist of transcribed cadenzas in which a keyboard instrument takes one or more of the parts (see Ch. 10), but in all cases known to the writer another instrument is also present. These are consequently ensemble cadenzas.

themes; passage-work was another possibility, either in the form of literal quotation, or in the form of a new extension of a pattern of figuration. All these types are illustrated in Part II.

As mentioned earlier, Türk pointed out in his *Klavierschule* that interchangeability was lost when cadenzas became thematically integrated with the parent movement. A certain type of cadenza was dependent on interchangeability, namely the type published in sets for the use of amateurs who might be unable to improvise or compose their own. As long as cadenzas were provided in each of the most commonly occurring keys, ideally with alternatives for fast and for slow movements, the amateur performer was able to use these collections in order to supply ad libitum cadenzas for almost any occasion.[3] The seeds of future developments lay in the practice of increasing integration, however; and it was not only performers, but also composers who used various techniques to integrate the cadenza more and more closely into their compositions until it made no sense to leave any room for an ad libitum insertion.

It may be useful to take another look at the growth of the cadenza from the point of view of the composer, whose changing methods of making provision for the introduction of cadenzas are themselves of considerable interest.

Cadential Context

'. . . a little passage over a moving bass'

In this way Quantz describes the kind of cadential embellishment which preceded the birth of the cadenza (see Chapter 1); the 'moving bass' was supplied by the composer, the 'little passage' improvised by the soloist. Quantz seems to attribute the origin of the cadenza mainly to the performer's initiative, and in this he is probably correct: where ornamentation was concerned, composers at this stage in history were not usually consulted. Yet they did have a part to play in the early development of the cadenza; by increasing the virtuosity of solo parts as the main cadences were approached, especially final cadences, they contributed to the climactic effect of the cadences which in turn seemed to call forth extra virtuosity from the performer.

One particularly interesting compositional procedure connected with the increasing emphasis placed upon cadences is found in some seventeenth-

---

[3] An interesting example of the use of interchangeable cadenzas is mentioned in Dittersdorf's *Autobiography*, where he relates the story of his childhood triumph when performing at sight six new concertos by Benda. He had prepared for this by practising cadenzas in various keys, which he was then able to incorporate into his performance of the concertos wherever a cadential fermata appeared in the score. His teacher was so impressed with the compositional talent shown in the cadenzas that he arranged for Dittersdorf to begin lessons in composition (Dittersdorf, *Lebensbeschreibung*, pp. 54, 76, *Autobiography*, pp. 52, 76).

century Italian cantatas. It was common in these works for the composer to supply a melismatic vocal passage after a cadence, either perfect or imperfect, under which in many cases the final words of text would be repeated. It has been claimed that this procedure was later to be expanded and give rise to the coda.[4] Extension and repetition of cadences was indeed to become a common feature of eighteenth-century music, and the simple practice described here contains in embryo many of the techniques of achieving length that were to be used in later tonal music. What is of particular interest to the student of the cadenza is the repetition of the last few words under a melisma.

In order for it to be possible for a singer to improvise a cadenza in an aria, it was usually necessary for a textual repetition of this kind to occur. While theory and practice clearly did not always concur in such matters, there was a strong consensus that singers ought not to breathe in the middle of a word (see Chapter 2). A cadenza was normally delivered on a single vowel, and to breathe in the middle of a cadenza would have involved interrupting a word, hence the rule limiting the length of a cadenza to a single breath. Yet if the cadenza was to contain any substance at all, it was necessary for the singer to take a breath at or shortly before the beginning, so as to have enough breath to sustain it. It was convenient, therefore, for the singer to repeat a word or phrase immediately before the cadenza, in order to arrive on a suitable vowel with enough breath remaining to deliver an effective peroration.

While cadential fermatas are conspicuously absent from Handel's arias, as indeed they are from most Italian operatic arias until the early 1730s, this cannot be taken to mean that no cadenzas were introduced in performance.[5] Composers frequently took care to write the main cadences in such a way as to facilitate the introduction of a cadenza: firstly, the scoring is often reduced, so that the accompanying instruments might not obscure such vocal embellishments as it should please the soloists to add; secondly the cadences themselves are often written in considerably longer note-values than those preceding them, so that an effect of remarkable blandness would result if no embellishments were made; and thirdly the feature described above is often found, that is to say the last few words of text are repeated in a final phrase beginning shortly before the cadence, and this phrase is commonly introduced by a rest over which there might appear a fermata. Examples of such cadences are given in Ex. 16. Many composers would mark such cadential phrases 'adagio'.[6] It is significant, too, that the style of the cadences continued unchanged after it

---

[4] Knödt, 'Zur Entwicklungsgeschichte', p. 378, where these ideas are attributed to Hugo Goldschmidt.

[5] See Ch. 5 for an example of a cadenza written for a Handel aria during Handel's lifetime (Ex. 25).

[6] An 'adagio' marking does not necessarily indicate that improvisation is expected, since similar 'adagio' cadences are commonly found in Handel's choral and orchestral music. It should be seen as a feature which facilitated the introduction of cadenzas where this was appropriate. In other instances its function was to lend an added seriousness to the cadence, to give to it the character of peroration without recourse to embellishment.

Ex. 16. *Examples of vocal cadences in which the last few words are repeated after a rest:* (a) G.
F. *Handel*, Messiah, *'But Who May Abide'*, (b) A. *Scarlatti*, Griselda, *'Quella tiranna'*

became customary to include cadential fermatas above them, a change which appears to have taken place quite suddenly in the early 1730s.[7] It is possible, of course, indeed it is likely, that many of the embellishments introduced at cadences before it became customary to include fermata signs were simply *cadenze fiorite*. The practice of improvising cadential prolongations must, however, have become established during the 1720s and 1730s, for notational developments of this kind usually postdate changes in the actual practice of performers.

Further evidence that vocal cadenzas were introduced despite the absence of cadential fermatas in the scores is provided by the following remark in Burney's *History*, in connection with the aria 'Brilla nell'alma' from *Alessandro* (1726): '[Handel] has given the Faustina an opportunity of displaying her taste and fancy in a cadence, *ad libitum*, at the end of each part of this song; a compliment but seldom paid to vocal performers at this period of time.'[8] There are in fact no cadential fermatas in this aria, but the cadences are of the type described above. Although Burney was writing about a performance which took place in the year of his birth, his testimony should be respected, as his *History* was evidently researched with great diligence and drew on many conversations with witnesses of the occasions described. Interestingly, this passage suggests not only that the practice of introducing cadenzas predates that of introducing cadential fermatas, but that Handel rarely tolerated it. There can have been few singers who were able to improvise cadenzas to his satisfaction.

That composers tended to write their cadences with a view to facilitating cadential embellishment on the part of the singers is attested by none other than Tosi. 'Composers leave generally in every final cadence some note sufficient to make a discreet embellishment.'[9] Which note does Tosi mean? As we have seen, Tartini argues that the place for a cadential embellishment was on a note of the tonic triad occurring over a dominant penultimate immediately before a cadential trill, although he suggests that composers did not always introduce the appropriate note here, and that it frequently fell to the performer to adapt the score accordingly. In fact composers of arias do 'leave

---

[7] Compare e.g. the autograph of Porpora's *Siface* (Acts i–ii, GB-Lbl Add. MS 14116, written in 1726), in which there are no cadential fermatas, with that of the same composer's *Mitridate* (Acts ii–iii, GB-Lbl Add. MS 14115, written c.1733), in which there are a great many; or compare Hasse's *Artaserse* (GB-Lbl Add. MS 32582, this copy written c.1730) in which there are no cadential fermatas, and the same composer's *Alessandro nell'Indie* (GB-Lbl Add. MS 30838, this copy written c.1736), in which there are several. Although D. J. Grout's edn. of A. Scarlatti's *Griselda* (Cambridge, Mass., and London, 1975) includes several general pause bars over which appears a fermata and the word 'Cadenza', it is evident from Scarlatti's autograph of the work (GB-Lbl Add. MS 14168, written in 1721) that the word 'Cadenza' is an editorial addition. Presumably the fermata indicated that the general pause bar might be lengthened at will, and the cadenzas, if any, would have been performed at the cadences, which usually follow a bar or two later.

[8] C. Burney, *A General History of Music*, 4 vols. (London, 1776–89), iv. 312; ed. F. Mercer in 2 vols. (London, 1935), ii. 740 f.   [9] Tosi, *Observations*, p. 60.

generally' some such note as Tartini describes in every final cadence, although a certain type of cadence, the 'bass-cadence', one in which the voice part descends a fifth from the dominant to the tonic, is an exception. Quantz expresses an amusing opinion in connection with this matter, namely that composers more than twenty years previously had actively sought to prevent singers from improvising cadenzas by writing 'bass-cadences'.[10] Tosi mentions that these cadences were the 'most prevailing' in his day, although he sees no other merit in them 'but of being the easiest of all, as well for the Composer as for the Singer'.[11] He does not suggest that composers used them in order to prevent singers from improvising cadenzas, but it is certainly true that they do not lend themselves so readily as the other types to cadential elaboration.

Phrasing

It has been seen that vocal cadenzas frequently form part of a phrase that begins just before the penultimate, to a repetition of the last few words of text. At the arrival of the penultimate the voice-part reaches a vowel suitable for prolongation, and the singer continues in the same breath while delivering the cadenza itself. For an instrumentalist, the problems of arriving at a suitable vowel and of avoiding breaths during words do not arise, and this means that a somewhat greater flexibility obtains in the matter of phrasing.

   In an instrumental cadenza the same pattern may be followed as described above, or there may be breaks in phrasing in the soloist's line immediately before the penultimate, or immediately after it. That is to say, the phrase may begin before, at, or after the penultimate. There is a certain chronological sequence here. The older type of cadential embellishment (*cadenza fiorita*) was unlikely to introduce breaks in phrasing at any stage during the embellishment: a cadence is, after all, a part of the phrase which it completes. The prolongation of cadential embellishments which constituted the birth of the cadenza, however, marked the beginning of a process in which the continuity of the cadenza with the preceding music is shifted to a higher level of structure: as the cadenza grew, it naturally tended to fall into separate phrases itself. The first stage in this process may be observed in the vocal cadenzas described, where a new phrase begins just before the penultimate; the cadenza remains a part of this phrase, but it has grown in proportional length from being a mere 'finishing touch' to the point where it constitutes the greater part of the phrase. The next stage is represented by those instrumental cadenzas in which the surface continuity of phrasing is broken immediately before the penultimate. Here the cadenza consists of an entire new phrase in itself, although at a higher level of structure it still functions as the completion of the passage which precedes it. It should be pointed out that in such cases the

---

[10] *Versuch*, ch. xv, par. 3.   [11] *Observations*, p. 52.

surface continuity with the preceding music is provided by the accompanying instruments. In other words there is tutti reinforcement of the cadential approach, and this itself marks a step forward in the evolution of the cadenza (see below).

The passage in the *Versuch* in which C. P. E. Bach considers whether the continuo player should sustain or release the penultimate (see Chapter 3) implies that the soloist himself would normally participate in the penultimate, and that if the accompanist were to release the chord, he would do so before the soloist moved on to other notes. This in turn implies the type of phrasing in which there is no caesura after the penultimate. Broadly speaking, caesuras after the penultimate are more likely to be found in long cadenzas than in short ones. If the cadenza corresponds in length to a single breath (i.e. a single phrase), there is unlikely to be a caesura after the penultimate; if it consists of more than one phrase, however, in other words if there is a caesura within the cadenza, then it is more likely that there will also be a caesura after the penultimate.

It is not only in respect of the length of the cadenza that the presence of a caesura at this point increases the range of possibilities open to the soloist. It releases him, for example, from the need to begin within the harmony of the penultimate. There are ad libitum cadenzas by Beethoven in which the first chord is a chord other than a 6–4 (see Chapter 12). This type of phrasing increases the clarity with which the opening of the cadenza is articulated, and consequently allows it to make considerably greater dramatic impact. The clearest and most dramatic articulation of all is achieved when the soloist is silent during the preparation and the penultimate, beginning his cadenza only after the penultimate, this chord and the preparation having been entrusted to the tutti.

Placing

Closely linked to the changes which took place in connection with phrasing at the start of the cadenza are those which affected the placing of the cadenza within the structure of a ritornello movement. It has been observed that the number of cadenzas per movement dwindled to one at a fairly early stage, it being felt almost universally that the best effect was to be achieved by holding the cadenza in reserve until the final solo cadence. As the dramatic possibilities offered by the cadenza were increasingly exploited, it was felt that a greater effect might be achieved by approaching the cadential fermata via a tutti. The effect of this development on the phrasing of the cadenza has been mentioned, but the larger structural implications are no less significant.

The cadenza had previously been introduced at those points where a solo section cadenced into a tutti. Such cadenzas are known hereafter as 'pre-tutti' (see Ex. 17). The first examples of tutti preparation took the form of simple reinforcement of the last few moments before the cadenza (Ex. 18). Symmetry

Ex. 17.   *Example of a pre-tutti cadenza: G. A. Benda, Concerto in F minor, second movement*

Ex. 18.   *Example of simple tutti reinforcement of cadence: C. P. E. Bach, Concerto in D, H. 433, second movement*

increasingly demanded, however, that the cadence marking the end of the exposition solo be recalled at the end of the recapitulation solo, with the result that a type of cadential preparation arose in which the solo cadenced into a brief tutti passage, perhaps lasting only one or two bars, and perhaps via an interrupted cadence, as in Ex. 19. In such an 'extended cadence' it is clear that the final ritornello does not begin until after the cadenza.[12] The logic of this development, however, and the demands of symmetry in larger scale concertos with longer trills at the final solo cadences, pointed towards what is hereafter termed an 'inserted cadenza', i.e. one which is inserted into the final ritornello. In Ex. 20 the ritornello clearly begins at the point marked 'X', but is interrupted by a cadential fermata (marked 'Y'), only to resume after the cadential trill at the point marked 'Z'. In practice it can often be hard to decide to which category a particular example belongs, since borderline cases are commonly found. More important than precise classification is an awareness of the gradual evolution of the inserted cadenza through various methods of extension of the cadence and tutti reinforcement of the approach.

---

[12] It was equally possible for such an extension of the cadence to occur without tutti reinforcement, in which case the effect was similar to that of a pre-tutti cadenza.

Ex. 19. *Examples of extended cadences, with and without interruption:* (a) *J. Haydn, Concerto in D, Hob. XVIII: 11, second movement,* (b) *J. B. Vanhal, Concerto in C, second movement*

The growth of the classical style took the form of increasingly dramatic articulation of the crucial events in a tonally constructed movement; the history of the cadenza offers an illustration of this process, for the effect of separating the cadenza from the final solo cadence by sandwiching it between tutti passages was to heighten its dramatic effect. The cadence which it served to prolong was no longer simply the ending of a phrase or section, but an artificially inserted cadence interrupting the final section of the movement. The approach bars no longer formed part of a musical phrase like any other, but existed simply for the sake of cadential preparation. The conventions of cadential preparation which arose at the same time served to underline the dramatic effect of the arrival of the cadential fermata still further. Such dramatization of the approach was scarcely possible with a pre-tutti cadenza.

The structural significance of an inserted cadenza cannot be merely local. A cadence normally marks the ending of a phrase or section, derives its meaning from its position at the end of the phrase or section, and serves to release some or all of the tension built up in the course of the phrase or section. In the case of the inserted cadenza it is exactly the other way round. The approach derives its meaning from the cadence which it serves to prepare, and it builds up

Ex. 20.   *Example of an inserted cadenza: W. A. Mozart, Concerto in G, K. 107 No. 2, first movement*

tension specifically for the sake of dramatizing the cadence. Taken out of context, such a passage makes no musical sense. It can only be understood at a higher level within the context of the entire movement, deriving its meaning from its position towards the end of the movement, and resolving the tensions of the entire movement.[13]

It will be readily understood that one feature of the earlier cadenza is lost in the process of dramatization—it can no longer be omitted on the spur of the moment. When the cadence serves no other function than to provide a context for a cadenza, as is the case with the inserted type, then omission of the cadenza would render it meaningless.[14] The dramatic build-up would be

---

[13] It is arguable that it is the cadenza rather than the final solo cadence which marks what Heinrich Schenker would call the descent onto $\hat{1}$ in the *Urlinie* of an aria or concerto movement containing an inserted cadenza in the final ritornello.

[14] But see the discussion of false-start cadenzas in Ch. 1; here the effect is humorous.

followed by a moment of supreme anticlimax as a simple cadence in long notes ushered in the final tutti. There is normally a periodic accent on the penultimate and another on the downbeat of the tutti entry, an effect which can only make sense if the accents are separated by a substantial utterance. Should a performer or an arranger wish to omit such a cadenza, it would be necessary to omit the preceding tutti passage as well, and to proceed directly from the final solo cadence to the tutti following the cadenza.[15] A cut of this kind must obviously be planned in advance.[16]

It is not suggested that each type of cadenza placing discussed was superseded by the following one; on the contrary it frequently happens that different types of cadenza placing occur in different movements of the same work, or even within a single movement. The evolution of the three types took place in the chronological sequence described, but earlier stages in the process were retained and used in conjunction with later ones. Pre-tutti placing, for example, remained common in slow movements, while the more dramatic extended and inserted types are more commonly found in first movements.

It will be realized that the above account of the changes in placing and style of approach undergone by the cadenza assumes a context in an aria or concerto, that is to say a work in which a soloist is pitted against a larger ensemble within a ritornello framework. It was principally in such surroundings that the evolution of the cadenza took place, for it was there that the resources for maximum exploitation of the dramatic potential of the cadenza existed. Nevertheless, examples of instrumental cadenzas in other music existed at all stages during the growth of the classical cadenza, from C. P. E. Bach's solo keyboard sonatas to Beethoven's Sonata for Cello and Piano, Op. 5 No. 1. In many cases, however, the cadenzas which occur in other music borrow the gestures of the larger, more dramatic concerto and aria. It was in the latter that the principal developments in the history of the cadenza took place.

Decline and Metamorphosis

One factor which led to the decline of the cadenza was the rise of the so-called virtuoso concerto, a type used increasingly by travelling virtuosi such as Steibelt, Field, and Hummel. Conceived primarily as display pieces, these

---

[15] A curious exceptional case occurs in Cramer's edn. of Mozart's C major Concerto, K. 467 (London, 1827). Here the cadential fermata in the first movement is omitted, but the preparation is retained, the 6–4 and the following dominant chord are indicated as staccato crotchet chords each followed by a crotchet rest, and the ritornello begins in the following bar. The effect is that of a 'false-start cadenza', though this was surely not what Mozart intended!

[16] The most usual way of indicating such a cut was to use the instruction 'Vide', placing the syllable 'Vi-' at the beginning and the syllable '-de' at the end of the cut. Haydn used this method for indicating his revisions to the score of *Il ritorno di Tobia* for the 1784 performance, in which many of the cadenzas were omitted and the ritornellos shortened correspondingly. See Ch. 9.

concertos usually had somewhat perfunctory tuttis, the focus of attention being the spectacular virtuosity of the solo sections. Apart from first and second subjects, the bulk of the material would consist of sheer bravura. Trills at the ends of solo sections might be extended for anything up to twenty-two bars (see Chapter 13). In such a concerto, where virtuosity was distributed fairly evenly throughout the movement, it made little sense to articulate dramatically a moment of particular virtuosity towards the end; the cadenza had either to be conceived on an enormous scale, or it had to be omitted altogether. Instances of both may be found, but the logic of this development pointed away from the use of cadenzas altogether. Hummel, himself a composer of this type of concerto, remarked in the 1820s that the cadenza was fast becoming a thing of the past.

The pause denoting that an extemporaneous embellishment was to be introduced, appeared formerly in concertos &c. generally towards the conclusion of the piece, and under favour of it, the player endeavoured to display his chief powers of execution; but as the Concerto has now received another form and as the difficulties are distributed throughout the composition itself, they are at present but seldom introduced. When such a pause is met with in Sonatas or variations of the present day, the Composer generally supplies the player with the required embellishment.[17]

The rise of the inserted cadenza and the use of a caesura after the penultimate allowed the cadenza to increase in scale; thematic integration tied it more closely to its parent movement. In the finales of his London violin concertos, Giovanni Battista Viotti went one step further by incorporating orchestral accompaniment into the cadenzas, seeking in this way to emulate the scale and the drama of the keyboard cadenza, while at the same time integrating the cadenza more closely than ever before with the parent movement. Clear articulation of the ending of the cadenza, normally achieved by the entry of the tutti, was thereby lost, although the articulation of the opening retained the conventional gestures. For present purposes, these cadenzas are considered to end at the soloist's final cadence, where the tutti bursts in to conclude the movement. Increasingly, however, in the works of Viotti and Beethoven, the articulation of the ending is blurred. The logic inherent in this process of growth and integration pointed towards blurring the articulation not only at the end of the cadenza, but also at the opening.

This is precisely what happened in the course of the nineteenth century. Schumann's Piano Concerto contains a passage labelled 'cadenza' towards the end of the first movement, and this passage undoubtedly has a certain amount in common with the classical cadenza. Its length, its position, its developmental treatment of thematic material, its climactic, dramatic, bravura character, all suggest kinship with the ad libitum cadenzas of Beethoven, for

---

[17] J. N. Hummel, *Ausführliche theoretisch-practische Anweisung zum Piano-Forte-Spiel* (Vienna, 1828); Eng. trans., *A Complete Theoretical and Practical Course of Instructions on the Art of Playing the Piano Forte* (London, 1828), i. 66 n.

example. Yet it is so closely integrated that the character of insertion is lost. The underlying harmonic progression is a movement from an augmented sixth chord on F via E major, the dominant of A minor, back to the tonic key for the coda, in which the piano participates. The corresponding passage in Rachmaninov's First Piano Concerto progresses from a 6–5 on E to a dominant minor ninth on F sharp, and this in a movement written in F sharp minor! (See Ex. 21.) These passages are integrated not only thematically, but also harmonically. They retain the dramatic function of the mature classical cadenza, but they do not retain its defining characteristic, namely the clear articulation of a structural cadence.

Ex. 21.   *Harmonic schemes of first-movement cadenzas in* (a) *Schumann's Piano Concerto and* (b) *Rachmaninov's First Piano Concerto*

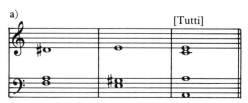

The 'cadenza' in the first movement of Mendelssohn's Violin Concerto is still further removed from the tradition of the classical cadenza. Although it proceeds from a dominant seventh harmony to the tonic and the opening is clearly articulated, it seems to make more sense, in view of its position immediately before the recapitulation, to link it functionally with the embellished pauses and the traditional bursts of virtuosity frequently found at this point in the classical repertoire. Its function is not so much to articulate the end of a musical paragraph (the function of a cadenza) as the beginning of a new one. Nevertheless, in terms of its thematic content and its dramatic and expressive character, it may be linked with the romantic cadenza.

Brahms, however, uses genuine cadenzas in two of his concertos; in the first movement of the Violin Concerto he invites the soloist to supply an ad libitum cadenza, in order to articulate a cadence between a 6–4 on the dominant and a solo restatement of the main theme (i.e. a 'rondo cadenza'), while in the finale of the D minor Piano Concerto he provides a written-out cadenza, articulating the progression from a 6–4 on the dominant to an orchestral entry. The second movement of this concerto also contains a passage labelled 'cadenza'.

The passage in question is an unmeasured prolongation of dominant harmony leading to the final solo cadence of the movement. The passage is strongly reminiscent of the corresponding one in the slow movement of Beethoven's G major Concerto, and could be classified as a deceptive cadenza for present purposes.

It must be stressed that once the cadential function of the cadenza is lost, once it becomes primarily a dramatic feature that may occur in a variety of harmonic contexts, the cadenza has evolved into something substantially different from the object of the present study, and from what Quantz and C. P. E. Bach meant by this term. Through all its many and varied manifestations, the 'classical' cadenza was rooted in its harmonic function. In so far as romantic composers continued to write cadenzas, then, they reinterpreted their classical models, preserving some outward resemblance, but profoundly altering the structural significance. From now on the classical cadenza would only be used by composers as a deliberately historical gesture, as in Brahms's Violin Concerto.

The subsequent history of the cadenza followed two quite distinct paths. There are many instances of cadenzas written by performers from the nineteenth and twentieth centuries for use in classical concertos, especially for those of Mozart and Beethoven. Until the Second World War it was customary for performers to provide cadenzas in their own style, rather than that of the concertos, as indeed the composers would have expected. Yet the resulting incompatibility of style proved unacceptable to the taste of the more historically conscious post-war years, and a trend arose towards imitating the style of the composer of the concerto.[18] Eva and Paul Badura-Skoda were pioneers in this new approach, and in their book *Interpreting Mozart on the Keyboard* they offer guidelines to the pianist on how to imitate Mozart's cadenza style.

The other strand in the subsequent history of the cadenza is of course the development of the romantic cadenza and its twentieth-century offshoots. No attempt is made in the present survey to follow either of these paths; the final stages in the history of the classical cadenza as seen in the music of Beethoven and his contemporaries provide a convenient point at which to conclude.

---

[18] For an instance of unusually restrained 19th-cent. cadenzas, written with rare sensitivity to the style of the concerto, see Riemann's edn. of W. F. Bach's Concerto in F major, F. 44 (Leipzig, 1894).

PART II

5

Late Baroque Cadenzas

As a preliminary to the more particular study of the history of the classical cadenza, to which the remainder of this book is devoted, it is useful to consider a few early manifestations of the phenomenon. Its origins have been shown to lie in the early eighteenth century, pre-eminently in the soloistic genres of aria and concerto. At around the same time the first keyboard concertos were written, Handel and J. S. Bach being pioneers in the genre. In this chapter an attempt is made to situate these two leading composers within the history of the cadenza, and also to survey briefly the evidence regarding the style of cadenzas in the late baroque period more generally.

Handel's Organ Concertos

It was Handel's custom to improvise an organ concerto during the intervals in performances of his oratorios.[1] More than any other concertos of the period, Handel's organ concertos are filled with 'ad libitum' markings, which reflect the improvisatory origin of these works. Does this mean, then, that cadential improvisations over a pausing bass are likely to have occurred during Handel's performances?

The 'ad libitum' markings refer to improvisation of several different kinds. Some movements in the Op. 7 set, usually slow movements, are left to be improvised entirely. Also in the Op. 7 set there are a number of instances in which the soloist is required to improvise part or the whole of a solo episode of unspecified length (the finale of Op. 7 No. 6 in B flat is the most extreme example: here none of the solo episodes is given in full—only the beginnings and the endings of each are supplied). The Op. 4 set does not offer any instances of either of these types of improvisation, but both sets give the soloist ample opportunity for improvised ornamentation—this too is sometimes indicated by an 'ad libitum' instruction.

The cadenza is a form of inserted improvisation and, of the three types of 'ad libitum' passage discussed above, it resembles most closely the improvisation of a solo episode between tuttis. According to Burney, Handel

after his blindness . . . played several of his *old* organ-concertos, which must have been previously impressed on his memory by practice. At last, however, he rather

---

[1] For the later French practice of improvising organ concertos at the Concert Spirituel, see Ch. 10.

chose to trust to his inventive powers, than those of reminiscence: for, giving the band only the skeleton, or ritornels of each movement, he played all the solo parts extempore, while the other instruments left him, *ad libitum*; waiting for the signal of a shake, before they played such fragments of symphony as they found in their books.[2]

This being the case it is not surprising that the manuscripts from which the Op. 7 concertos were posthumously compiled contain so many 'ad libitum' markings. It is not only in these works that Handel's text leaves gaps for inserted improvisations, however, for in the aria 'Vo' far guerra' from *Rinaldo*, published by Walsh in 1711, there are several points at which a harpsichord improvisation is indicated simply by a blank bar in which is written the word 'Cembalo'. No doubt a part of the huge success of Handel's first London opera derived from these inserted harpsichord improvisations, which, if William Babell's reconstructions are at all accurate,[3] must have been quite spectacular. The organ concertos published as Op. 4, even though the printed text does not invite inserted improvisation, probably arose in the same way—the solos are left unaccompanied, and appear to be written-out improvisations.

It has been suggested that two passages from the Op. 4 set invite the introduction of a cadenza.[4] The first occurs in the second movement of the second concerto in bar 114 (Ex. 22), and the second occurs in the first movement of the fourth concerto at bar 101 (Ex. 23). Both passages come immediately before the final solo cadence, which is of course the normal place

Ex. 22.   *G. F. Handel, Organ Concerto, Op. 4 No 2, second movement*

Ex. 23.   *G. F. Handel, Organ Concerto, Op. 4 No. 4, first movement*

[2] Burney, 'Sketch', p. 30.   [3] HG xlviii. 230 ff.
[4] Knödt, 'Zur Entwicklungsgeschichte', pp. 400 ff. and *HHA* IV: 2. 46, 80.

for the introduction of a cadenza in the later eighteenth-century concerto. Unlike some printed editions,[5] Handel's autograph score[6] contains no fermata at either point, but only an 'ad libitum' marking added above the system during the final solo episode, and lacking any precise alignment over a particular point in the music.[7] This being the case, is it possible to agree that the introduction of a short cadenza at these two points would be appropriate?

It seems unlikely that Handel would have envisaged a clearly articulated cadential fermata interrupting the metric flow at these points. An alternative interpretation of these 'ad libitum' markings has been put forward:

In some cases, Handel did add the words 'ad libitum' over the final solo episode of the organ part, but his practice at such times was to replace totally the written episode with an improvised one. Handel always improvised final solo episodes when he repeated a concerto that had already been heard in previous seasons; and this practice was common in the concertos of the 1740s where one often finds blank measures in the sources together with an indication to complete the movement by improvisation.[8]

Extended improvisation could and did take place in any solo episode in an organ concerto, and it could be varied in content and length entirely according to the whim of the improvising performer; needing no orchestral accompaniment, the organist was not restricted by the need to co-ordinate his improvisation with the accompanying harmonies, as a singer or a soloist playing a melody instrument would have been. In the aria or the concerto for melody instrument improvised ornamentation could certainly take place during accompanied solos, but inserted improvisations, of the kind which might be varied in length and content according to the whim of the performer, could be introduced only over a pausing bass. In the improvised organ concerto there was no need to interrupt the metre and to pause on one particular bass-note in order to simulate an improvisation within an improvisation. It would of course have been possible to do so, but there is no evidence that Handel ever did. Quite the contrary, in fact, for to judge by the 'written-out improvisations' of the organ concertos, his aim was to improvise solo episodes which 'sounded composed', and not to produce fantasia-like passage-work which 'sounded improvised' as C. P. E. Bach's (written-out) fantasias do. The custom of inserting a cadenza at the final solo cadence in the concerto was still largely a thing of the future, and it was to be used in concertos of which the final solo had been composed, and in most cases supplied with an orchestral accompaniment. The 'ad libitum' markings in the autographs of these two Handel concertos, then, are best interpreted as an indication for the soloist that the entire episode might be recast, that it could be lengthened, shortened,

[5] e.g. Six Concertos, Op. 4 (London, 1738).

[6] GB-Lbl King's MS 317 (dated 1735).

[7] In Op. 4 No. 2 it is towards the end, and in Op. 4 No. 4 it is near the beginning of the episode.

[8] William D. Gudger in his edn. of Handel's 'Six Concertos for the Harpsichord or Organ', *Recent Researches in the Music of the Baroque Era*, 39 (Madison, 1981), p. xi.

or rewritten at will. They also served as a warning for the orchestral players. There is evidence in the autograph of Op. 4 No. 4 that Handel recomposed the final solo cadence here, making it slightly shorter, and it may have been for this reason that he decided to alert the orchestral players to the possibility of longer or shorter versions being performed; it would be disastrous for the orchestral entry to occur in the wrong place.

Once the later practice of introducing cadenzas at final solo cadences became established, however, soloists began to introduce them in their performances of Handel's concertos as well. Some evidently did so quite arbitrarily: W. T. Best's edition of Op. 4 No. 1, 'as performed at the Handel Festivals, Crystal Palace, in 1871 and 1883' (London, 1883) contains a fifty-six bar cadenza rudely thrust into the organ part a bar before the tutti entry.

In conclusion, then, there is no evidence that such cadential prolongations as Handel may have included in his concerto improvisations were set off clearly from their surroundings by the interruption of regular metre, or by any other means. It would be anachronistic to introduce such improvised cadential prolongations into modern performances of Handel's concertos.

The Keyboard Concertos of J. S. Bach

While Handel introduced the genre of the organ concerto to England, and was to exert a profound influence on the development of the keyboard concerto in that country during the remainder of the eighteenth century, it was J. S. Bach who established the keyboard concerto in Germany. He began by making transcriptions for organ solo of concertos for melody instruments by Vivaldi and others. Through this exercise he gained familiarity with the Italian concerto style, which was to shape not only the original concertos he later composed, but also his style in many other genres. Bach's concertos for harpsichord and orchestra are mostly arrangements of his concertos for melody instruments. In some cases the originals have been lost, but it is thought unlikely that any of the harpsichord concertos was actually conceived as such.[9] Bach's sons and other pupils, however, started to compose concertos specifically for the harpsichord, following the lead which he had given.

Bach's three-movement fast–slow–fast scheme, his use of the ritornello layout, the style of the thematic material in outer movements with its motoric rhythms, its firmly diatonic, triadic, and scalic character, the aria-like quality of the slow movements, all this came from Vivaldi. So too did Bach's tendency to concentrate virtuosity around the final solo sections in outer movements. There are examples of capriccios and of perfidias, sometimes terminating in

---

[9] It is thought, however, that the Concerto for Two Harpsichords and Strings, BWV 1061, may have been written originally for two harpsichords without accompaniment. See *Grove*, i. 816.

genuine cadenzas, exactly as was found to be the case in certain Vivaldi concertos.

As an example, let us consider the first movement of Bach's organ arrangement, BWV 594, of Vivaldi's D major Violin Concerto, RV 208. The final solo of this movement exists in variant versions, both in its original scoring and in the transcription.[10] Vivaldi's autograph[11] is marked 'Qui si ferma a piacimento' in the bar immediately preceding the entry of the final ritornello, a bar of dominant harmony. A manuscript copy of the Violin Concerto at present located in Schwerin[12] expands this single bar into thirty-seven bars. Bach's autograph of the organ transcription gives the thirty-seven bar version found in the Schwerin source, but a copy in Kellner's hand[13] simply breaks off after the first crotchet of the first bar[14] and resumes with the final ritornello. The thirty-seven bar expansion is not articulated with particular clarity, and might therefore be classed as a perfidia (although it lacks the sustained bass-note characteristic of the perfidias discussed by Giegling). Were a cadential prolongation to be improvised by a performer playing from the Kellner source of the Bach transcription or from the autograph of the original concerto, it is likely that it would be set off rather more clearly from its surroundings, in other words that it might be recognizable as a cadenza.[15]

This same work includes the first known example of a capriccio (in the Locatellian sense) for an instrument other than the violin. Once again there are variant versions of the passage among the sources of the Vivaldi original. The autograph score contains the instruction 'Qui si ferma a piacimento' at the end of the finale, followed by a further seven bars of tutti.[16] The Schwerin source contains a lengthy written-out capriccio between the tuttis in place of Vivaldi's instruction.[17] The printed edition of the concerto, RV 208a, however, comes to an end at the point where the autograph instruction had appeared, and there is no trace of the instruction, the capriccio, or of the

---

[10] See P. Ryom, 'La Comparaison entre les versions différentes d'un concerto d'Antonio Vivaldi transcrit par J. S. Bach', *DAM* (1966–7), 91 ff., and *NBA* IV: 8, *Kritischer Bericht*, pp. 43 ff.

[11] I-Tn, Renzo Giordano Collection, vol. v, no. 29, fols. 167ʳ–181ʳ.

[12] D-SWl Mus. 5565. See Ryom, 'La Comparaison', pp. 101 ff. and *NBA* IV: 8, *Kritischer Bericht*, pp. 47 f., 100 ff. A critical edn. has recently been published of yet another version of the cadenza/capriccio passages from the outer movements of this work. The title of the publication is *Antonio Vivaldi: Cadenze per il concerto RV 208/F1, 138 'Grosso Mogul' per violino, archi e b.c.*, ed. M. Grattoni (Udine, 1986), and the source is a manuscript at Cividale del Friuli. See M. Grattoni, 'Una scoperta vivaldiana a Cividale del Friuli', *Informazioni e studi vivaldiani*, 4 (1983), 3 ff. The Cividale versions are very similar but not quite identical to the Schwerin versions.

[13] See *NBA* IV: 8, *Kritischer Bericht*, pp. 44 f., for details of this source.

[14] See *NBA* IV: 8, *Kritischer Bericht*, p. 54.

[15] A parallel may be drawn here with Mozart's insertion of 27 extra bars into his Rondo in F, K. 494, discussed in Ch. 1 above. In view of the 'seamless' character of the expansion, it cannot be regarded as a cadenza.

[16] Ryom, 'La Comparaison', p. 97; *NBA* IV: 8, *Kritischer Bericht*, p. 47.

[17] Ryom, 'La Comparaison', p. 102; *NBA* IV: 8, *Kritischer Bericht*, pp. 101 ff.

subsequent tutti. Bach's transcription includes the capriccio from the Schwerin source (bars 180–282), although Kellner omits the last sixty-five bars.[18] So this work provides examples of Bach's use of both the perfidia and the capriccio, each transcribed directly from a Vivaldi source.

The capriccio in the finale of BWV 594 may be seen as a significant precedent for the long harpsichord solo in the first movement of the Fifth Brandenburg Concerto. This passage is best understood as a thematically based, cadential capriccio, like those found in many of Tartini's concertos. It is articulated principally by the sudden disappearance of all the other instruments. Although frequently called a 'cadenza' by commentators, it is sixty-five bars long, it is metrical, it modulates freely, treats material from the movement extensively, and makes considerable use of sequential patterns. It is probably the earliest thematically based capriccio, yet this should come as no surprise; it was characteristic of Bach in his adaptation of the Vivaldian concerto form to thicken the texture with innumerable motivic references, especially in solo sections. This capriccio is much better integrated in every respect than the transcribed capriccio in BWV 594. It is true that Bach does not use the label 'capriccio' in either case, but simply 'Solo', yet 'capriccio' seems a better label than 'cadenza' which is not Bach's either. While admittedly this passage, like the capriccios of Tartini, falls strictly within the terms of the definition of the cadenza that is used here, it makes little historical sense to interpret the passage as an unprecedented and unrepeated anticipation of the classical concerto cadenza; surely there is a stronger case for linking it with the capriccio tradition and pointing to Vivaldi as the model.

The earlier nineteen-bar version of the passage[19] is unthematic and fantasia-like in style (it closely resembles the last third of the longer version), but is still better understood as a capriccio than as a cadenza.

Another original composition by Bach in which his methods of embellishing and prolonging structural cadences may be observed is the D minor Harpsichord Concerto, BWV 1052.[20] The earlier version of this work[21] contains in the solo part just before the final tutti entry in the finale a dominant seventh chord, under which the marking 'ad libitum' appears. It seems likely that some form of improvised cadential prolongation, probably a deceptive cadenza, was required here.[22] In the later version a fully written-out cadential prolongation is supplied, but without a caesura of any kind to mark where it begins; hence the extra music cannot be regarded as a cadenza. When the cadence itself is reached there is a fermata on a dominant seventh harmony (bar 272), followed immediately by an adagio cadence. This is a common

---

[18] See *NBA* IV: 8, *Kritischer Bericht*, p. 58.

[19] *NBA* VII: 2, *Kritischer Bericht*, pp. 120 ff.

[20] This work is thought to be an arrangement of a lost violin concerto; for a reconstruction of the supposed original, see *NBA* VII: 7.

[21] BWV 1052a. An edn. is found in BG xvii. 275 ff.

[22] The words 'Cadenza al arbitrio', which appear a few bars earlier in the Bach-Gesellschaft edn., are absent from the sources (see *NBA* VII: 7. 29 and the corresponding *Kritischer Bericht*, p. 57).

method of articulating structural cadences in baroque music, as we have seen, and while it may sometimes be intended as an invitation for an improvisation, it is more often intended simply as an expressive gesture. Since this cadence is notated polyphonically, in four real parts, unlike the utterly bland cadences which serve to indicate that the soloist is free to embellish, it makes more sense to interpret this passage as an expressive cadence, requiring no further embellishment. In this revision Bach integrates the cadential prolongation seamlessly into the parent movement. The spirit of the revision is a move away from soloistic freedom towards compositional control and integration.

Ex. 24.   *J. S. Bach, E major Violin Concerto, BWV 1042, first-movement cadenza* (a) *with harmonization borrowed from Bach's harpsichord arrangement, BWV 1054, and* (b) *with simpler harmonization*

An example of a subsidiary cadenza composed by Bach is found in the first movement of the E major Violin Concerto, BWV 1042 (see Ex. 24). Here the violin arrives on the ninth (E) of a dominant minor ninth harmony at the end of a section in G sharp minor. The accompanying instruments drop out, and the violin continues for two bars at a slower tempo marked 'adagio'. The change of tempo and the disappearance of the accompaniment is sufficient to give this passage the character of a rhapsodic insertion; although written in strict time it sounds free. Interestingly there is no cadential trill, nor is there any accompaniment indicated by Bach at the resolution of the cadence, when the violin arrives on the temporary tonic, G sharp. A harmonization is, however, provided by Bach in his arrangement of this work as a Harpsichord Concerto in D major, BWV 1054. In some editions of the violin concerto it is suggested that the continuo player might supply this harmonization, suitably transposed, at the equivalent point (as in Ex. 24a).[23] Musically this may seem to be more satisfactory than an unharmonized version, given the structural importance of the cadence, but it makes the passage sound composed rather than improvised. On the other hand, as we have seen, Bach was not so anxious as Quantz to preserve the illusion of improvisation in his cadential embellishments, and it would be quite mistaken to apply Quantz's comments about cadenzas uncritically to those which occur in Bach's concertos. It might be added that there seems to be a difference between earlier and later forms of cadential embellishment in Bach's concertos; it is the later versions which sound composed, the earlier ones being more improvisatory in effect. A case could thus be argued for leaving the cadenza in the E major Violin Concerto with only a straightforward dominant to tonic harmonization, as in Ex. 24b, and interpreting the harpsichord version given in BWV 1054 as a later reworking of the passage intended to integrate the cadenza more closely into the composition, and arguably causing it to lose the character of a cadenza.

This movement is one of those written in a large da capo form, that is to say the da capo involves a repetition of more than just the opening ritornello, which is quite commonly restated at the end of a concerto movement. Whereas a more typical concerto movement would be based on a pattern comparable to an expanded first section of a da capo aria, this movement is closer to the form of a complete da capo aria, with its middle section exploring related minor tonalities.[24] The cadenza occurs at the end of the middle section, immediately before the da capo. Perhaps it is on account of the unusual closeness to aria form that Bach introduces a cadenza at this point —the cadence marking the end of the middle section in an aria was frequently embellished by a cadenza. The resemblance to aria form also helps to explain the abruptness of the key-change from this cadence in G sharp minor to the repeat of the opening E major material. Schering tentatively suggests that the cadenza be extended so as to provide a smoother transition to E major, in other words that an improvisation combining the functions of cadenza and *Eingang* be introduced.[25] Such a procedure would be entirely inappropriate; it would obscure Bach's deliberate reference to da capo aria form with its clear sectional articulation. The desire expressed by Schering for a smoother return to the home key reflects an attitude that did not become prevalent until later in the eighteenth century; even in sonata movements it was not uncommon in the pre-classical period for an abrupt switch to occur from a cadence in a related minor key (usually the relative minor) at the end of the middle section to a recapitulation in the tonic major.

Another instance of a genuine cadenza composed by Bach occurs in the

[23] e.g. BG xxi/1, p. 28; A. Schering (ed.), Eulenburg miniature score (London and Zurich, 1929), 15.

[24] The finale of the Fifth Brandenburg Concerto is another such da capo movement.

[25] Eulenburg miniature score, p. vii.

finale of the Triple Concerto, BWV 1044. The movement is derived from a keyboard fugue in A minor, BWV 894, to which ritornellos have been added, and numerous revisions made. One such revision occurs in bar 208 of the concerto finale, which corresponds to the penultimate bar of the fugue; at this point a cadential prolongation is inserted, which, on account of the clear articulation achieved by a fermata and a change in texture at this point, is clearly recognizable to the listener as an insertion.

The existence of alternative versions of the final solo cadences in the D minor Concerto, the Fifth Brandenburg Concerto, as well as numerous Vivaldi concertos with particularly brilliant concluding solo sections, suggests not so much an ad libitum tradition of cadential improvisation as a penchant for recomposition at this sensitive point in the structure of a concerto movement. Bach's practice seems to have moved from a more improvisatory style of cadential prolongation, occasionally involving genuine cadenzas, towards a more integrated style in which the accompanying instruments participate, and in which maximum continuity is maintained. So Bach's personal development in cadential treatment seems almost to reflect the entire history of the eighteenth-century cadenza in microcosm.

Some of the distinctions offered here between cadenzas and non-cadenzas in the music of J. S. Bach may seem somewhat tenuous. It is readily admitted that Bach is unlikely to have thought in such terms himself, any more than Vivaldi did. If the distinctions offered here are of any significance at all, they are so only in the light of subsequent developments in the concerto. Bach's sons and pupils were to expand the specifically cadential improvisatory prolongations into something entirely *sui generis*, in a way that J. S. Bach's cadenzas were not. But the question has to be asked whether J. S. Bach made use of the cadenza himself, and the answer offered here is that he did, though only as one of a number of possible ways of prolonging the cadences, and one which he frequently avoided when revising his concertos.

Inevitably, most of what we know about the content of eighteenth-century cadenzas is based on extant written-out examples. Their testimony is invaluable, but at the same time they cannot be assumed to be entirely accurate records of actual improvisation. One has to ask why they were written down at all, and by whom—questions which are often difficult to answer, and which may suggest didactic or commercial interests rather than concern for scrupulous accuracy. Such evidence needs to be complemented by that of contemporary writings, including those considered in Chapter 2. This documentary evidence also has its limitations, both because of the subjective outlooks of the writers, and because of the inadequacy of words alone to describe music. Yet indirect evidence of this kind is all that there is, and in the first half of the eighteenth century it is particularly slender. All we have from this early period are a few glimpses of what improvised cadenzas were like.

In the discussion of the origins of the cadenza provided in Part I, the question of precisely where it originated was deliberately avoided—and with good reason, for the scarcity of the evidence makes the question virtually unanswerable. Probably the cadenza had its origins in many different parts of Europe at around the same time. What may be said with some confidence, however, is that in whichever part of Europe we see cadenzas appearing, they sprang from the soil of Italian opera. By the 1720s and 1730s Italian opera, or an Italianate style derived from it, was well established in all of Europe except France. In this sense, then, the cadenza may be regarded as 'vocal' and 'Italian' in origin, because even the early instrumental examples from Northern Europe borrow the gestures of the Italian aria. So before moving on to a more detailed examination of extant keyboard cadenzas, it may be useful to consider some early vocal examples.

Some Early Examples of Vocal Cadenzas

One of the few great singers from this period about whose improvisations a certain amount is known is the castrato Farinelli. Particularly well known is the following account by Burney of a triumph which took place in Rome in the early 1720s. (Admittedly it was reported only much later to Burney, who had not been born at the time.)

. . . there was a struggle every night between [Farinelli] and a famous player on the trumpet, in a song accompanied by that instrument: this, at first, seemed amicable and merely sportive, till the audience began to interest themselves in the contest, and to take different sides: after severally swelling out a note, in which each manifested the power of his lungs, and tried to rival the other in brilliancy and force, they had both a swell and a shake together, by thirds, which was continued so long, while the audience eagerly waited the event, that both seemed to be exhausted; and, in fact, the trumpeter, wholly spent gave it up, thinking, however, his antagonist as much tired as himself, and that it would be a drawn battle; when Farinelli with a smile on his countenance, shewing he had only been sporting with him all this time, broke out all at once in the same breath, with fresh vigour, and not only swelled and shook the note, but ran the most rapid and difficult divisions, and was at last silenced only by the acclamations of the audience.[26]

In the absence of the musical sources of the aria in question it is impossible to be certain whether this improvisation was genuinely a cadential embellishment.[27] It seems perhaps more likely that it was an embellished fermata on a single harmony intended to be followed by a silence; otherwise the problems of co-ordination between the players themselves and with the

[26] C. Burney, *Dr. Burney's Musical Tours in Europe*, ed. P. Scholes, 2 vols. (London, etc., 1959), i. 153. Henceforth abbreviated as *Musical Tours*.
[27] Haböck believes the opera to have been Porpora's *Eomene*, although he mentions the possibility that it may have been Riccardo Broschi's *L'isola d'Alcinea*. Both works appear to be lost. See F. Haböck, *Die Gesangskunst der Kastraten* (Vienna, 1923), p. xvi.

orchestra, which evidently did not make its re-entry at the close of the
improvisation, would surely have been insuperable. Clearly the two soloists
had not worked out their improvisation in advance, as it was normally
necessary to do, and the element of competition between them would hardly
have been conducive to the kind of rapport required for a harmonically active
duet cadenza of the type described by Quantz.

A few genuine cadenzas are contained in a manuscript of arias sent by
Farinelli to the Empress Maria Theresa, and dated March 1753. Both the aria
'Quell' usignolo' from Giacomelli's *Merope* and Riccardo Broschi's 'Son qual
nave', composed for use in Hasse's *Artaserse*, are presented here in heavily
ornamented versions with extraordinarily brilliant cadenzas.

The first of these is one of the four arias that Farinelli apparently sang to
King Philip V of Spain every night for ten years.[28] Thus it is not surprising
that it should have developed into a particularly remarkable showpiece. The
first part contains two long cadenzas, one at the subsidiary cadence into the
dominant and one at the final cadence, in addition to two long embellished
fermatas, while the middle section contains one long final cadenza. If Farinelli
performed both cadenzas in the first part both times it was sung, then this aria
would be an example of the type complained of by Quantz, in which as many
as five cadenzas are heard in a single aria. The setting of 'Son qual nave' is
more restrained, including only a single cadenza[29] which is considerably
shorter than those written for 'Quell' usignolo'.

Although Farinelli first sang both these arias as early as 1734, the

Ex. 25.   (a) *Two cadenzas for an aria from Handel's* Poro; *(b) the cadence at which the above
cadenzas were inserted*

---

[28] Burney, *Musical Tours*, i. 154 f. Burney does not identify the fourth aria, but Haböck has shown
that it must have been this one. Haböck, *Gesangskunst*, pp. xlii, xliv.
[29] The cadenza is quoted in Burney, *Musical Tours*, i. 127, editor's footnote.

ornamented versions given in the Viennese manuscript are somewhat later in origin. The arias have been extensively rewritten as well as ornamented.[30] It seems that all the arias contained in the 1753 manuscript have been adapted so as to represent the style of the singer rather than that of the original composers. Thus the manuscript offers an indication of the kind of cadenza performed by an exceptionally brilliant singer in private to a Spanish king around 1750, and cannot be taken to be representative of operatic style in the 1730s and 1740s.

What may, however, be rather more representative are the cadenzas quoted in Ex. 25a. They are intended to be introduced as first and second time cadential embellishments at the final solo cadence of the first part of a da capo aria, namely 'Vil trofeo d'un alma imbelle' from Handel's *Poro* (1731). They are found in a manuscript score from the first half of the eighteenth century, and are written into the blank Violin 2 and Viola staves immediately above the voice part. We have seen that Handel does not write cadential fermatas into his scores. In fact the cadence where these cadenzas belong is shown in Ex. 25b—they are intended to be inserted at the point marked with an asterisk.[31]

Most early keyboard cadenzas tended to be similar in style to those written for voice or melody instruments, that is to say they corresponded to the length of a single breath and were restricted to a single part over a stationary bass, even though there were no technical limitations requiring keyboard cadenzas to conform to this model. It is in this sense that the priority of vocal cadenzas over instrumental is best understood. The beginnings of the emancipation of the keyboard cadenza from vocal style can be detected in the work of C. P. E. Bach.

[30] Haböck quotes both the ornamented and the original versions.
[31] I am indebted for this information to Dr H. D. Johnstone, who kindly brought these cadenzas to my attention.

6

C. P. E. Bach and the Cadenza

CARL Philipp Emanuel Bach was one of the earliest keyboard composers to make extensive use of the keyboard cadenza. It is not only his concertos which include cadential fermatas, but also, interestingly, many of the solo keyboard sonatas, ranging from the earliest examples written during the 1730s right up until the last decade of his life. These merit a brief consideration here.

Solo Sonatas

Almost all the cadential fermatas which occur in the sonatas are found over the penultimate bar of the middle (slow) movement.[1] In relatively few of the sonatas is a cadenza written out; normally the final cadence, over which the fermata appears, is unembellished, written in longer notes than those which immediately precede it, and it is approached via some expressive chromaticism (Ex. 26). Bach makes frequent use of dynamic markings at this point; indeed he tends to exploit extreme contrasts of dynamics here, producing a much higher concentration of dynamic markings than is normally found in other parts of the movement. The slow movements are naturally the most affective in Bach's sonatas, and these cadenzas should be seen as opportunities to provide an expressive, affective climax rather than a display of technical virtuosity. The affective use of dynamics itself suggests this climactic effect. In view of the small scale of many of the movements

Ex. 26. *C. P. E. Bach, Sonata, H. 25, second movement*

---

[1] In the concertos too there is a higher incidence of cadential fermatas in the slow movements than elsewhere.

which contain cadential fermatas, it would be inappropriate for the cadenzas to be long—the single-breath rule offers a good indication of the most appropriate length. The majority of written-out cadenzas found in Bach's sonatas consist of a single part over a stationary bass, remaining within the given 6–4 harmony until the dominant seventh chord which accompanies the cadential trill.[2]

Somewhat exceptional are the cases of the three written-out cadenzas in the *Probestücke*, H. 70–5, written as musical illustrations for the first part of the *Versuch*. Here the slow movement of the second sonata contains a single-part cadenza, that of the fourth sonata a two-part cadenza, and that of the sixth a three-part cadenza. The multiple cadenzas are written respectively in two and in three real parts throughout; the sustained notes which one part holds while another performs an imitation are written as void notes, in order to express the rhythmic freedom desired in performance.

The tonality of the two-part cadenza in the fourth sonata is unusual: it prolongs a cadence in F sharp minor at the end of a movement in D major, the move to F sharp minor occurring only in the bar before the cadential fermata. F sharp minor is in fact the key of the following movement, so that the cadenza is best seen not as an affective climax to the second movement, but rather as a link between the second and third movements. The tonality of the *Probestücke* is somewhat unconventional in any case, since none of the 'sonatas' ends in the key in which it began, all six consisting of three movements in three different keys. (Hence the slightly cryptic title *18 Probestücke in 6 Sonaten*.) The slow movement of the fourth 'sonata', however, is the only individual movement which appears to end in a different key from that in which it began.

The two-part cadenza is unusually long—more than a quarter of the length of the whole movement. This may best be explained by reference to its linking function, since it makes little sense if the cadenza is considered a part of the second movement. The three-part cadenza, more conventionally, is much shorter.

Bach comments on the correct style of performance for the two- and three-part cadenzas in the following passage from the *Versuch*:

In two-part or three-part cadenzas there is always a slight pause between entries, before the next part comes in; in the *Probestücke* I have indicated these pauses occurring at the ends of each entry by using void notes, without recourse to the more usual ties, and with no other purpose in mind. These void notes are to be sustained until they are resolved by others in the same part. It should be noted that when another part crosses over the sustained one, then it will be necessary to release the key briefly; nevertheless it should be depressed again as soon as the moving part has moved away. Should both hands be involved in this procedure, then the key should be retaken at once by the original hand before it is released by the hand that has just restruck it. In this way the note continues to sound without having to be struck afresh. The pauses on

---

[2] See H. 36/ii for an example.

the white notes are required so that the effect of two or three persons in spontaneous conversation may be achieved; one must imagine that each pays careful attention to the other, to see whether he has finished what he has to say or not. Otherwise the cadenzas would lose their natural character, and it would seem as if, instead of a cadenza, one were presented with a strictly metrical composition using tied notes. At the same time these pauses must be forgone whenever the resolution of the harmony preceding the void note requires that the note written above it should be struck simultaneously with the void note.[3]

Evidently, then, in spite of the presence of imitation and harmonic change, an effect of improvisation is desired. This is achieved not only by the free rhythm which Bach describes, but also by the dovetailing of imitative entries, in the manner of an improvised duet cadenza. In the two-part cadenza, the first occasion on which two notes are struck simultaneously occurs during the approach to the cadential trill; in the three-part cadenza simultaneous attack occurs more frequently, but dovetailed entries are still common.

Many of the slow movements which do not contain a cadential fermata nevertheless terminate in cadences very similar in style to those of slow movements which do. Türk, as we have seen, pointed out that cadenzas might be introduced even when the composer did not indicate them, and he seemed to have Bach's solo sonatas in mind. This being the case it would be unwise to base too many conclusions on the distribution of cadential fermatas throughout Bach's sonatas. It seems to have varied according to the market for which he was writing. None of the *Six sonates pour le clavecin à l'usage des dames*, H. 204–7 and 184–5 (Wq. 54, 1770), contains a cadential fermata, but all except one of the slow movements from the Württemberg Sonatas, H. 30–4 and 36 (Wq. 49, 1744), do.[4] Suffice it to say that the appearance of a cadential fermata in the slow movement of a Bach sonata is by no means so unusual as it is in the sonatas of later composers. Not surprisingly, though, cadential fermatas occur with rather greater frequency in Bach's concertos.

The position of the Cadenza in C. P. E. Bach's Keyboard Concertos

Like the solo sonatas, Bach's fifty-two keyboard concertos were written throughout his creative life, the first dating from 1733 when he was a student at the University of Leipzig, and the last dating from 1788, the year of his death. One is written for two solo harpsichords and orchestra, one for solo harpsichord, solo fortepiano, and orchestra, and the rest for solo harpsichord and orchestra.[5] Thirty-eight of the concertos were written during the Berlin

---

[3] *Versuch*, i. 131 f., *Essay*, p. 165.

[4] The exception is the slow movement of H. 33.

[5] In two instances (H. 444 and 446) the organ is mentioned as an alternative solo instrument, while at least six concertos (H. 430, 434, 437, 444, 465, 467) also exist in arrangements for flute, oboe, or cello with orchestra.

period (1738–68), only eleven falling into the Hamburg period—Bach's last twenty years.

Setting aside for a moment the freedom of performers to introduce cadenzas at will, specifically mentioned by Bach in the *Versuch*, it can be shown that Bach directly authorized the use of cadenzas in all but two of the concertos.[6] In most cases he did this by introducing a cadential fermata at the final solo cadence. In some instances, however, even though no fermata is present in the source of a concerto, Bach himself provided a cadenza for it in an important manuscript collection of original cadenzas made towards the end of his life, H. 264. For example there are no cadential fermatas at all in the score of the E minor Concerto, H. 428, but H. 264 contains four alternative cadenzas for the slow movement.

Putting together the information conveyed by the scores and the manuscript cadenzas, it becomes clear that cadenzas were envisaged by Bach in the great majority of slow movements, in about half of the first movements, but only in a handful of finales. In two finales it is at a subsidiary cadence immediately before the recapitulation that the cadential fermata occurs.[7] Some finales require fermata embellishments at this point rather than cadenzas. So a pattern of cadenza usage emerges that is shared by many of Bach's North German contemporaries—a conservative approach to finales with little opportunity to introduce cadenzas, a preponderance of slow-movement cadenzas, reflecting the prevailing 'rhetorical' understanding of affective slow music, and a prophetic use of first-movement cadenzas, which, to judge from the examples in H. 264, could sometimes be fairly substantial.

Bach generally favours the pre-tutti type of cadenza placing.[8] More often than not the orchestra is silent during the cadential approach. In those instances in which the orchestra does participate, however, its contribution is not always limited to doubling the bass of the solo or providing a chordal accompaniment. Bach frequently uses the tutti in order to dramatize the approach in a way that anticipates the development of the inserted cadenza, without, in most cases, going so far as to make a clear separation between the final solo cadence and the cadenza.

In nineteen instances there is effectively a snatch of tutti immediately before the arrival of the cadential chord, for the solo part simply doubles the

[6] The exceptions are H. 479 and H. 472. An arrangement of H. 479 for two pianos alone by H. Schwartz (Leipzig, 1914) contains editorial cadenzas added to the first and last movements. An explanatory note in the preface makes clear that these are not indicated in Bach's original, and that they may be omitted at will, or others substituted. According to the flexible principles outlined in the *Versuch*, such arbitrary addition of cadenzas might seem to have Bach's blessing, except that by the end of his life he was inclined to prepare his cadenzas more dramatically. It is perhaps more likely that by 1788, when H. 479 was composed, he would have indicated a cadenza had he envisaged one at all.

[7] H. 411 and H. 429.

[8] Indeed in those few instances where the approach consists of a structural tutti, it is hard to sustain Bach's view that the cadenza might be omitted on the spur of the moment, given the anticlimax which this would produce after a passage of dramatic preparation.

Ex. 27.   *C. P. E. Bach, Concerto, H. 430, first movement*

orchestra at this point. Thirteen of these passages are marked *ff*,[9] an exceptionally loud dynamic in the eighteenth century. In most cases the snatch of tutti seems more like a dramatic interruption than a structural event. In some instances, though, there occurs what is best described as a false start to a structural tutti which turns out to be nothing of the kind; in Ex. 27 bar 205 seems like the beginning of such a tutti, but the soloist soon takes over and leads into the cadenza without any accompaniment.[10]

There are other instances of tutti reinforcement of the cadential approach in which, after what appears to be the final solo cadence, the tutti enters on an

Ex. 28.   *C. P. E. Bach, Concerto, H. 441, first movement*

[9] Compare Bach's use of dynamics at cadential fermatas in sonata slow movements, discussed above.
[10] Another instance of this procedure, again on a rather small scale, occurs in H. 416/ii.

unexpected harmony—submediant, flat submediant, #6–3 on the submediant, 4–2 on the flattened seventh, etc. Such a tutti may be as short as a single bar (Ex. 28) and is never longer than three bars, so it can hardly be considered a structural tutti in its own right, but it is undeniably a significant modification of the pre-tutti type of cadenza placing; it finds echoes in the interrupted cadences at the corresponding points in Mozart's G major Concerto, K. 453, and in Beethoven's Violin Concerto. In some cases the approach to the cadenza consists of a dialogue in which fragments of the thematic material are passed between solo and tutti, usually concluding with a loud, perhaps *ff*, contribution from the tutti to articulate the arrival of the penultimate.[11]

There are two instances of fully fledged inserted cadential fermatas, each preceded by a final solo cadence and a few bars of tutti, namely the first movements of H. 419 and H. 476. The latter contains a hidden cadenza in tempo. Interestingly, in the Brussels source at least,[12] H. 419 also contains a cadenza in tempo at this point.[13] Neither passage is labelled as a cadenza, and in both cases the orchestra is given the requisite number of bars' rest to count.[14]

In conclusion it may be observed that while Bach seldom has recourse to the clear separation of final solo cadence from cadenza that is characteristic of the inserted cadenza, he frequently employs techniques of articulation which render the pre-tutti and extended cadenza placing more than usually dramatic.

The Penultimate

In most cases the tutti, if it participates in the penultimate at all, plays simply the dominant note. In the solo part, however, there is seldom a simple octave or unison at this point. The most frequently encountered notation is of a plain or compound fourth, with just a single note in each hand. Full 6–4 chords, as well as sixths (compound or simple), and a few simple octaves are also found, normally as a consequence of the part-writing immediately before the penultimate—the sources are generally notated in such a way that the cadenza could be omitted without doing violence to the melodic line.

[11] e.g. H. 471/i.

[12] Included in B-Bc 5887.

[13] The Berlin source, however—D-B Mus ms Bach St 499—gives only the cadential fermata.

[14] It is likely that the Berlin source of H. 419 represents the performing material used at the time of composition of the work (1745), and that the Brussels source, copied by Michel and therefore dating from Bach's Hamburg period, is much later in date. Although in the Hamburg version Bach appears to have chosen to provide a particular cadenza for this work, it does not necessarily follow that he would have objected to its replacement by another. Probably the Hamburg revision was carried out with a particular occasion in mind, rather than as a definitive improvement.

In view of the flexibility with which the notation of this bar in a concerto could be interpreted, it is quite striking that the uppermost right-hand pitch found under the cadential fermata in the scores is identical to the opening pitch of the corresponding cadenza in H. 264 in as many as thirty-four instances. This is a fairly high figure, because although there are fifty-five cadenzas assigned to particular concerto movements in H. 264, a number of these begin with a rest in the right-hand part, and a number are assigned to movements with no cadential fermata marked in the scores.[15]

By far the most important musical source for an examination of the content of Bach's cadenzas is the manuscript collection H. 264. This will accordingly be treated in some detail. Only one other source need be considered here—the set of six concertos published in Hamburg in 1772, which usefully complements the manuscript collection.

A Manuscript of Original Cadenzas by C. P. E. Bach

The manuscript collection H. 264 is interesting for a number of reasons; it constitutes the most significant corpus of keyboard cadenzas written for use in the concertos of a single composer before those of Mozart, and is the largest collection of keyboard cadenzas from this relatively early stage in the development of the phenomenon. Moreover, as examples of the work of C. P. E. Bach, an astounding improviser by all accounts, and a key figure in the development not only of the keyboard cadenza and concerto but of all forms of instrumental music in the eighteenth century, they well repay study.

Formerly a part of J. J. H. Westphal's collection of C. P. E. Bach's manuscripts, the Brussels source of H. 264, B-Bc 5871, contains seventy-five 'cadenzas' copied by Michel, Bach's principal and most reliable Hamburg copyist. It is described in Alfred Wotquenne's 1905 thematic catalogue[16] as follows: '80[*sic*] keyboard cadenzas, which he prepared for his keyboard concertos and sonatas, together with an indication of the concerto to which they belong. Ms.' Wotquenne's description is in fact taken verbatim from that given by Westphal in his much earlier thematic catalogue.[17] The reference to sonatas is therefore worth taking seriously as a possible clue to the use

---

[15] The cadential chords in H. 264 frequently appear with a fuller sonority than those found in the corresponding concerto sources, and occasionally with a less full sonority, but the identity of the uppermost right-hand pitch is the significant factor which allows the cadenzas to be conveniently inserted.

[16] A. Wotquenne, *Thematisches Verzeichnis der Werke von Carl Philipp Emanuel Bach (1714–1788)* (Leipzig, 1905; repr. 1964).

[17] J. J. H. Westphal, 'Catalogue thématique des œuvres de Ch.-Ph. Emm. Bach', Ms. B-Br, Fonds Fétis 5218 II (4140). Wotquenne repeats Westphal's counting error in his own catalogue, and all but the most recent literature has perpetuated it. Since the back page is left blank, there can be no question of five cadenzas having been lost.

intended for those cadenzas in the collection which are simply labelled with a tempo indication: Westphal must have corresponded with Bach about the contents of this manuscript.

The manuscript cannot have been written any earlier than 1778, since it begins with a cadenza for the first movement of H. 478, quoting the main theme of that movement, and H. 478 was composed in 1778. A manuscript entitled 'Cadenzen zu verschiedenen Concerts' is mentioned by Bach's widow, Johanna Maria, in a list of her husband's works contained in a letter to Sarah Levy dated 5 September 1789.[18] The following year the *Nachlassverzeichnis* was published, listing on page 53 'Cadenzen' among the works offered for sale by Bach's widow in Hamburg. It is possible that these are references to the manuscript in question, but they could also refer to a manuscript now lost, but formerly in the possession of the Königliches Akademisches Institut für Kirchenmusik in Berlin. This manuscript is discussed briefly by Knödt,[19] who describes it as follows: 'In the library of the Königliches Akademisches Institut für Kirchenmusik in Berlin there are 73 cadenzas for concertos by C. P. E. Bach. The headings assign the cadenzas to particular concertos, but are evidently incorrect[20]—probably oversights on the part of the copyist.' Although the manuscript mentioned by Knödt is lost, there is a copy in the Staatsbibliothek Preussischer Kulturbesitz in Berlin which was made early this century and acquired by the then Königliche Bibliothek in Berlin in 1909 from Gustav Beckmann.[21] It contains only seventy-four cadenzas, the last of the Brussels cadenzas being absent; otherwise the contents of the two manuscripts are virtually identical, except that nos. 60 and 61 appear in reverse order in the Berlin source.

Westphal is known to have been an avid collector of Bachiana,[22] and the majority of the manuscripts in his possession were prepared for him under Bach's supervision. It seems likely, then, that B-Bc 5871 was also prepared and dispatched to Westphal in Schwerin during Bach's lifetime, i.e. before 1788, and that the manuscript forming part of Bach's estate is the one which found its way to Berlin; while the possibility that Westphal may have acquired his manuscript from Bach's widow cannot be ruled out, this would leave no obvious explanation for the existence of a second manuscript. It may, therefore, be dated with some confidence to the period 1778–88.

[18] Quoted in C. H. Bitter, *Carl Philipp Emanuel Bach und Wilhelm Friedemann Bach und deren Brüder*, 2 vols. (Berlin, 1868; repr. 1973), ii. 309.
[19] 'Zur Entwicklungsgeschichte', p. 408 n.
[20] The labels are in fact correct according to the numbering used in *Nachlassverzeichnis*, i.e. *Verzeichnis des musikalischen Nachlasses des verstorbenen Capellmeisters Carl Philipp Emanuel Bach* (Hamburg, 1790). Also available in facsimile, ed. R. W. Wade, as *The Catalog of Carl Philipp Emanuel Bach's Estate: A Facsimile of the Edition by Schniebes, Hamburg, 1790* (New York and London, 1981). Presumably Knödt was unfamiliar with this numbering.
[21] D-B Mus ms Bach P 800.
[22] R. W. Wade, *The Keyboard Concertos of Carl Philipp Emanuel Bach: Sources and Style* (Ann Arbor, 1981), 45.

The contents of the Manuscript

Each of the 'cadenzas' bears a label. Fifty-seven of them are assigned to particular concerto movements (see Table 1), although two of these fifty-seven are labelled 'fermata', and are not cadenzas—a fact which was evidently recognized by Bach, since the label 'cadenza' is avoided.[23] The assignations to particular movements use the numbering of the concertos found in the *Nachlassverzeichnis*. Rachel Wade[24] argues that this numbering, although published posthumously, actually corresponds closely to Bach's own numbering, so it does not follow that the assignations were themselves posthumous.[25]

Table 1. *The cadenzas by C. P. E. Bach contained in H. 264*

Cadenza no.	Concerto movement / other annotation
1	H. 478/i
2	H. 429/i
3	H. 429/iii
4	H. 428/ii
5	H. 423/ii
6	H. 428/ii
7	Adagio
8	Adagio
9	H. 444/i
10	H. 444/ii
11	H. 444/iii—Fermate
12	H. 433/ii
13	H. 444/i
14	H. 428/ii
15	H. 414/i
16	H. 414/ii
17	H. 428/ii
18	H. 430 (432)/i
19	H. 430 (432)/ii
20	Einfall allo. assai
21	H. 420/i
22	H. 420/ii
23	H. 434 (436)/ii
24	H. 429/i
25	H. 444/i
26	H. 417/ii
27	H. 417/i
28	H. 429/iii
29	H. 444/ii
30	H. 444/iii—Fermate

[23] Bach deals with cadenzas and fermatas in separate sections of the *Versuch* (see Chs. 2 and 3 above).

[24] Wade, *The Keyboard Concertos*, p. 6.

[25] If there were any discrepancies between the *Nachlassverzeichnis* numbering of the concertos and Bach's own, as there are for certain other works (Wade, *The Keyboard Concertos*, p. 6), it might be possible to establish that the labels were posthumous. In fact, however, Bach's numbering of the concertos matches that of the *Nachlassverzeichnis* in every case.

C. P. E. Bach and the Cadenza

Table 1. – *Contd.*

Cadenza no.	Concerto movement / other annotation
31	H. 437 (439)/ii
32	H. 440/i
33	H. 416/ii
34	H. 407/ii
35	H. 447/i
36	H. 447/ii
37	H. 447/iii
38	H. 424/i
39	H. 424/ii
40	H. 418/ii
41	Adagio
42	Adagio
43	Adagio
44	Adagio
45	H. 441/i
46	H. 427/ii
47	H. 427/iii
48	H. 429/i
49	H. 429/iii
50	H. 442/ii
51	Cadenz
52	Fermate
53	H. 469/ii
54	H. 408/ii
55	Adagio oder vielmehr Andante
56	Allegro
57	Allegro
58	Adagio
59	H. 469/i
60	H. 414/i
61	H. 408/ii
62	H. 414/ii
63	H. 433/ii
64	H. 442/ii
65	H. 440/ii
66	Adagio
67	H. 417/ii
68	H. 417/i or iii
69	Allegro
70	H. 413/ii
71	H. 444/i
72	Cadenz zu einem Andante von 3/4 Tact aus dem C dur
73	Cadenz zu einem Andante aus dem C dur
74	H. 409/ii
75	Fermate zum Arioso der Sonatine no. 1 (H. 449/i)

Note: Two different Helm numbers are given when a concerto also exists in an arrangement as a cello concerto. Bach's labels seem to suggest that the cadenzas here are intended for the cello arrangements, but they could equally well be performed on the harpsichord.

Of the remaining eighteen 'cadenzas', one is a fermata for use in the First Sonatina, H. 449, and another is a fermata for an unnamed work in G major.[26] There are nine cadenzas assigned unspecifically to Adagio movements,[27] three to Allegros, and two to Andantes, of which the first is said to be in 3/4 (the cadenza is itself barred in 3/4 time); one is simply labelled 'Cadenz' —nothing further.

The one remaining 'cadenza' is actually nothing of the sort; it is labelled 'Einfall—All° assai'. According to Wade[28] the label 'Einfall' is also found above brief excerpts of a sketch-like character contained in a manuscript

Ex. 29.   *C. P. E. Bach,* (a) *'Einfall' from H. 264, and* (b) *Concerto, H. 434, first movement, closing bars*

<hr />

[26] This unnamed work cannot be the finale of H. 444, the location for the remaining fermatas in the collection, because in this instance, although the tonality would be compatible, the harmony occurring on the beat before the fermata, a ♯6–3 on E, would not.
[27] This figure includes cadenza 55, marked 'Adagio oder vielmehr Andante'.
[28] *The Keyboard Concertos,* pp. 65 f.

known as 'Miscellanea Musica', B-Bc 5895, again in Michel's hand—a collection of jottings, including teaching notes, contrapuntal exercises, and snatches of late compositions.[29] The passage in question in H. 264 seems to be a jotting for the last few bars of the first movement of H. 434, or perhaps for the end of its opening ritornello, which, as so often, is similar. Although the tempo indication for the first movement of H. 434 is not 'allegro assai' but 'allegretto', the bass at the places mentioned resembles the bass of the 'Einfall' to a degree that seems more than coincidental (see Ex. 29). Possibly the 'Einfall' represents a sketched realization of what the soloist might have played during the closing bars of the movement. If so, this would provide an interesting piece of evidence for the debate over precisely how keyboard soloists did fill in the tutti sections in concertos—and one which would conflict with the widely held view that they played either a background continuo role or possibly some form of keyboard reduction of the tuttis.[30] It is more likely, though, that we are faced simply with a sketch for H. 434, possibly a sketch for the conclusion of the final solo, although the finished version of that solo does not in fact resemble the presumed sketch. This raises the question why it should have been included in this manuscript at all.

A striking feature of the manuscript, evident in Table 1, is the haphazard sequence of cadenzas. They follow no logical sequence either of key or of chronology.[31] Even though it sometimes happens that cadenzas for a particular concerto are grouped together (see those for H. 447, for example), it is more common to find the various cadenzas for a single concerto or movement scattered indiscriminately (see those for H. 444 or H. 428). One can only assume that Michel was working his way through a pile of Bach's manuscripts, simply copying the cadenzas (and fermatas) in the order in which he found them. Thus it is not hard to imagine that the 'Einfall' may have been included simply because it appeared to belong to a concerto. One can picture Michel just as uncertain what to make of it as the present-day scholar is. According to this hypothesis, he then gave it the benefit of the doubt and included it in his collection of 'cadenzas'. It seems almost certain that it was included in error, for it seems not to belong here at all.

This hypothesis assumes that Bach's autographs of the cadenzas in question were scattered throughout his concerto manuscripts, and that he did not assemble them himself—if this is correct, then the Berlin manuscript of cadenzas cannot have been an autograph. While these assumptions cannot be proven, it seems unlikely that Bach himself would have assembled the

---

[29] Beethoven also used 'Einfall' to label certain of his sketches. See R. W. Wade, 'Beethoven's Eroica Sketchbook', *Fontes Artis Musicae*, 24 (1977), 288.

[30] See H. Heussner, 'Zur Musizierpraxis der Klavierkonzerte im 18. Jahrhundert', *M-Jb* (1967), 165 ff.

[31] It is the chronology of the concertos that is meant here, since that of the cadenzas is unknown.

cadenzas in such a haphazard sequence, or that he would have included
sketches which appear out of place in the collection.

About a third of the fifty-five cadenzas assigned to particular movements
have some motivic or thematic connection with the movement for which they
were intended. In most cases they simply use the motive heard immediately
prior to the cadential fermata. In only four cases is this motive of thematic
significance in the movement as a whole (Ex. 28, taken from H. 441, is one
such case). The technique of using the most recently heard idea underlines the
spontaneity of these cadenzas. It would be natural for an unprepared improvisation to set out in this way. Where a thematic fragment is used that is not
found in the approach bars, the reference is usually no more than a suggestion.
Ex. 30 shows the way in which the opening of H. 430 is suggested in the
first-movement cadenza written for it.

Ex. 30. *C. P. E. Bach, (a) cadenza 18 from H. 264, and (b) Concerto, H. 430, first
movement, opening*

a)

b) **Allegro assai**

Thematic connections, then, between these cadenzas and their associated
concerto movements, while not entirely absent, are not especially prominent.
Bach has little to say in the *Versuch* about the content of cadenzas, since he is
mainly concerned with their accompaniment rather than their performance.
Yet the style of the cadenzas in H. 264 suggests that he may have shared
Quantz's views on the use of motivic material from the parent movement: that
it was to be recommended as an expedient to guarantee consistency of *Affekt*,
rather than as an intrinsically desirable procedure.

The exception that stands out conspicuously is the first cadenza in the
collection, namely that written for the first movement of H. 478 (1778). This
cadenza begins with a quotation of the opening bars of the concerto over a
dominant pedal (see Ex. 31); the phrase is prolonged by repetition of figure 'x'
in different harmonic and melodic guises, and this leads into a rhapsodic,
fantasia-like chromatic passage in demisemiquaver arpeggios. The continuation is not thematic, but the clear reference at the opening, as well as the
length and scale of this cadenza, place it in quite a different category from any

Ex. 31.   *C. P. E. Bach, beginning of cadenza 1, H. 264*

etc.

of the others contained in H. 264. It may have been influenced by other cadenzas which Bach had heard by 1778, perhaps coming from the concertos of South German composers.

More than two-thirds of the cadenzas use a single-part texture over a stationary bass. If the harmonies are occasionally filled in for the left hand at the penultimate or at the cadence, this does not alter the essentially single-part character of the cadenzas. Idiomatic keyboard textures are rarely used. Bach does sometimes use idiomatic keyboard figurations, however, as in no. 24, but even here he avoids the free-voiced polyphonic texture so characteristic of his fantasias.

Twelve cadenzas are written in two or three real parts (i.e. they are multiple cadenzas), sometimes in simple homophony, with many parallel thirds and sixths, and sometimes in imitative two-part counterpoint. The use of two-part imitative cadenzas is natural enough in the case of the two cadenzas supplied for the concerto for two harpsichords, H. 408. It is perhaps more surprising in the cadenzas for solo harpsichord concertos—H. 414, 424, and 442. A cadenza for an unspecified Adagio in A minor is also of this type. Two- or three-part non-imitative cadenzas frequently allude to some passage in the concerto movement, especially the cadential preparation (e.g. H. 417, second movement, cadenza 26).[32]

Not all of the 'cadenzas' contained in H. 264 are of the kind which begins on the penultimate. Cadenza 1, as mentioned earlier, is exceptionally advanced and the opening as here presented is presumably intended to follow a caesura after the penultimate (Ex. 31). Cadenza 9, another advanced cadenza, also begins after the penultimate, but here at least the penultimate is notated in the manuscript. In several cases the right hand begins only after a caesura, but the left hand enters with the penultimate and sustains it.

Changing harmonies, while they frequently occur in those cadenzas written in two or three parts, are not entirely absent from the more typical examples in H. 264. About a fifth of those using the characteristic texture of a single line over a stationary bass contain at least one change of harmony, usually a semitonal descent and reascent in the bass towards the end, with a diminished triad or diminished seventh above the sharpened fourth degree. It is this, perhaps, more than anything else which demonstrates the need for the orchestra to be silent during the cadenza, rather than to sustain the 6–4 or the plain dominant throughout. The average length is one and a half lines of music, perhaps twice the length of a normal breath capacity.

The majority of cadenzas in H. 264 end with a trill on the supertonic, although many, particularly those in minor keys, cadence as in Ex. 32, with a

---

[32] No. 46 is a rather curious three-part five-bar passage assigned to the slow movement of H. 427. It is barred throughout, with no rhapsodic writing, and it begins not on a 6–4 but on an upbeat diminished 7th harmony. It seems unlikely to be a cadenza, given its marked dissimilarity to all the others in the manuscript. Probably it is an alternative reading of the last few bars of the final solo included in error by Michel—and this time labelled in error as well.

Ex. 32.   *C. P. E. Bach, cadenza 33 from H. 264*

trill on the mediant.[33] It is rare, but not unknown, to find a metrical conclusion to a cadenza, and in other instances a brief metrical continuation for the soloist may be supplied in the score of the concerto, but this is also a rare occurrence.

The question of authorship

The case for the authenticity of the cadenzas contained in H. 264 seems strong. Michel worked frequently with Bach during his Hamburg years, and was notably conscientious.[34] Some of the cadenzas found in H. 264 are also found in other sources.[35] Pippa Drummond[36] argues on stylistic grounds that the cadenzas are probably authentic, since they resemble the style of the written-out cadenzas in the set of six concertos, H. 471–6, published in Hamburg in 1772.

It was in fact quite characteristic of Bach to prepare written-out versions of material normally improvised. His 'Sonaten mit veränderten Reprisen', H. 136–40 and 126 (Wq. 50), is a well-known example, but there are other instances of his concern to guide the 'Liebhaber' in this difficult matter. According to the advertisement, the set of six concertos, H. 471–6, contained 'adequate ornamentation', as well as written-out cadenzas, and they were easier to play than many of his earlier concertos, specifically out of considera-

---

[33] See Ch. 2.

[34] Wade, *The Keyboard Concertos*, p. 26.

[35] B-Bc 5887, H. 409 contains cadenza 74. D-B Mus ms Bach St. 523, H. 407 contains cadenza 34. D-B Am Bib 100, H. 408 contains cadenza 54. GB-Lbl k. 7 i. 10, H. 429, contains cadenzas 2, 3, 24, 28, 48, and 49. In some cases slight variations exist between one version and another.

[36] *The German Concerto: Five Eighteenth-Century Studies* (Oxford, 1980), 317 ff.

tion for the amateur.[37] Another manuscript, H. 164,[38] contains 'Veränderungen und Auszierungen über einige Sonaten für Scholaren von C. P. E. Bach'. The manuscript consists largely of blank bars with only those passages notated which depart from the printed text of the sonatas in question. Other sources exist in which these very embellishments are written into the text, so it is clear that written-out 'improvisations' are not only frequently encountered in Bach sources, but also that they were circulated to some extent.

Internal evidence provides a few more pointers towards Bach's authorship. Not only is the numbering used in the assignations to particular concerto movements identical to Bach's own, but the cadenzas themselves are clearly the work of someone familiar with the concertos, few of which were published at the time. There are numerous motivic references, of course, but the frequent identity of pitch between the uppermost opening right-hand note in the cadenzas and that found under the cadential fermata in the autograph scores is also striking. There thus seems every reason to believe the claim made on the cover that these are indeed 'Cadenzen von C. P. E. Bach'.

The Six Hamburg Concertos, H. 471–6 (Wq. 43)

At the request of many amateurs of music six easy harpsichord concertos by Capellmeister C. P. E. Bach are to be published. Without losing any of their appropriate brilliance these concertos will differ from the other concertos of this composer in so far as they are more adapted to the nature of the harpsichord, are easier both in the solo part and the accompaniment, are adequately ornamented in the slow movements and are provided with written-out cadenzas.[39]

The works referred to in the advertisement quoted above were Bach's six harpsichord concertos, H. 471–6, written in Hamburg. Here is not the place to discuss their many formal innovations—the linking of movements, cyclical elements, and the extraordinary four-movement design of H. 474 in which the outer movements actually constitute a single movement interrupted by the insertion of an Adagio and a Minuet. Our present concern is with the cadenzas, which, as indicated in the advertisement, are written into the score. Since they were conceived at the time of composition of the concertos, and since Bach clearly intended them to be used, they should be regarded as obbligato cadenzas. There is a single cadenza in each concerto with the

[37] See below.
[38] Autograph D-Bds Mus ms Bach P 1135; copy in Michel's hand B-Bc 5885; facsimile, *The Collected Works for Solo Keyboard by Carl Philipp Emanuel Bach (1714–1788)*, 6 vols., ed. D. Berg (New York and London, 1985), v. 233 ff.
[39] The advertisement appeared in *Hamburgischer Unpartheiischer Correspondent*, 69, Apr. 1771; trans. in L. Crickmore, 'C. P. E. Bach's Harpsichord Concertos', *Music and Letters*, 39 (1958), 237.

exception of H. 472;[40] in H. 471, 473, 475, and 476 the cadenza occurs in the first movement, whereas in H. 474 it occurs in the finale.[41] All except H. 474 make use of orchestral participation in the approach, and a *ff* dynamic is found in the tutti each time.

In H. 471 the cadenza is approached via a brief dialogue between solo and tutti. The cadenza itself is mainly cast in the familiar texture of a single part over a stationary bass, but there is a brief passage of two-part writing in the

Ex. 33.   (a) *C. P. E. Bach, Concerto, H. 473, first movement* (b) *C. P. E. Bach, Concerto, H. 475, first movement*

[40] H. 472 contains a composed cadential prolongation for the soloist leading into the final solo cadence in the first movement, but the start of the passage is not clearly articulated.

[41] And yet the finale, as demonstrated by Crickmore ('Concertos', p. 235), functions as the conclusion of the first movement after the interruption caused by the insertion of the second and third movements.

treble register early on, and the bass moves down to a subdominant and back towards the end.

H. 473 and 475 both lead into the cadenza via an interrupted cadence and a brief tutti (see Ex. 33). In the cadenza to H. 473 the orchestra is given twelve bars' rest to count, concluding with a fermata. This is a curious indication; the cadenza itself is unbarred, and it contains a fair amount of rhapsodic writing such that it is virtually impossible to identify twelve distinct bars. In practice it gives the orchestra a rough guide to the length of the cadenza and alerts them as to approximately when to expect the cadential trill; yet listen out they must, and the indication of a specific number of bars of silence is potentially

Ex. 34.   *C. P. E. Bach, Concerto, H. 476, first movement*

Preparation, Opening, and Conclusion of Cadenza

misleading.[42] The cadenza is not thematically related to the concerto, it uses a free-voiced keyboard idiom, with changing harmonies, and a mixture of measured and rhapsodic writing.

In H. 475, however, the orchestra, more conventionally, is simply given a single bar's rest with a fermata at the point where the cadenza occurs. The cadenza is short, unbarred, affective rather than brilliant, single-part, and non-thematic; it would not appear out of place in H. 264.

The C major Concerto, H. 476, contains a hidden inserted cadenza in tempo; the orchestra counts seventeen bars of rest during the passage. The cadenza is written in an idiomatic keyboard texture ranging from two to four parts, mostly with a melody in the right hand and accompaniment in the left. It is only loosely related thematically to the movement: four bars are devoted to figure 'x' which is a contraction of the related figure 'y' heard in the opening tutti and elsewhere. A dominant pedal is maintained for the first four bars, after which the cadenza proceeds as if it were an ordinary solo episode; apart from its preparation, its opening on a 6–4, and its improvisatory conclusion, the passage is scarcely distinguishable from a normal solo episode (see Ex. 34). The clear opening articulation is unmistakable, however, and in terms of the movement's overall structure the four bars of preparation and the seventeen bars of cadenza are undeniably an insertion: there is no equivalent passage at the cadence into the middle ritornello.

Mention has been made of the daring movement sequence of the fourth concerto in the set, in which an Adagio and a Minuet are inserted within a single split movement; it should be added that there are reminiscences of the two inserted movements during the obbligato cadenza in the 'Finale'. So Beethoven's Ninth Symphony is anticipated in this device by a cadenza written over fifty years earlier! The passage is a hidden cadenza, with no label; nevertheless its clearly dramatized preparation, its opening on a 6–4 after a composed fermata on the dominant (Ex. 35), and its improvisatory style with changing metres and a rhapsodic conclusion, leading to the customary cadential trill, leave the listener in no doubt that he is listening to a cadenza. The 2/4 'poco adagio' theme is quoted at the opening of the cadenza, in C

Ex. 35.   *C. P. E. Bach, Concerto, H. 474, 'Finale'*

poco allegro

---

[42] For a similarly misleading indication of the duration of the orchestra's silence in H. 474, see Ch. 2 n. 42.

minor now, marked 'poco allegro', and in augmentation to suit the prevailing common time. Then come four bars of 3/4 in which the opening of the Minuet is quoted, again in C minor. A pause over an abrupt silence is followed by a return to the 'allegro assai' of the 'Finale' (i.e. the continuation of the first movement) and a vigorous dotted figure is quoted from the tutti material of that movement. It leads by extension to more gentle non-thematic arpeggios in triplets, ushering in the dominant pedal, at which point a rhapsodic single-part passage, which in H. 264 might have constituted an entire cadenza in its own right, leads to the customary cadential trill.

As it happens, then, the five cadenzas contained in this publication cover the whole range of types found in the substantial corpus of Bach's written-out cadenzas: short, extended, measured, unmeasured, thematic, non-thematic, harmonically static, harmonically active. It is easy to point out the 'prophetic' passages—the short preparatory tuttis, the climactic juxtaposition of earlier unrelated themes in H. 474, and the obbligato character of the cadenzas. It would be a mistake, however, to see these six works as a turning point in Bach's concerto production. They simply illustrate his never-ending delight in experimentation, and his eagerness to meet the challenge of producing novel works tailored to the requirements and taste of an amateur public, who lacked the necessary expertise to provide their own cadenzas. There are no obbligato cadenzas in the three concertos Bach was still to compose—in H. 479, in fact, there are no cadential fermatas at all. It may be that he was influenced by concertos from Southern Germany and Austria when composing H. 471–6. It has been observed earlier that at least one of the cadenzas in H. 264 seems to betray the influence of Southern composers. And yet Bach's inventive mind hardly needed the stimulus of other types of music in order to conceive novel compositional procedures. Even a consideration of such a small area of output as keyboard cadenzas reveals him to have been an exceptionally imaginative and original composer.

7

Other Composers in Germany and Austria

෴

Berlin

C. P. E. BACH was one of many distinguished composers and performers to be attracted to the Prussian capital as a result of the musical interests of King Frederick the Great. Whereas Frederick's father, King Frederick William I, had shown little interest in promoting the arts, the Crown Prince had employed a small band of musicians at Ruppin and later at Rheinsberg even before his accession to the throne in 1740. After his father's death, Frederick was able to augment his musical establishment considerably.

There were those who expected the arts to flourish under the new king, a great admirer of French culture, an enthusiastic musician, and a keen advocate of the philosophy of the Enlightenment. As far as music was concerned these hopes were only partially fulfilled. Frederick was a competent, though not outstanding musician; his enthusiasm for music-making and opera were matched by his obstinacy in demanding only the kind of music which he happened to like. His taste, while moderately advanced at the time of his accession to the throne, was largely unchanged, and thus highly conservative, at the time of his death in 1786. Burney wrote in 1772 in connection with the musical life of Berlin that 'with respect to the *general* and *national* style of composition and performance, it seems at present, to be formed so much upon *one model*, that it precludes all invention and genius'.[1]

Frederick did not particularly like the music of his court harpsichordist, C. P. E. Bach, and he preferred the much blander but more accessible style of his Kapellmeister Carl Heinrich Graun. The King's other musical idol was Johann Joachim Quantz. Flute concertos by Quantz, written for Frederick to play, formed the core of the repertoire performed at the evening concerts in Sanssouci, the royal palace in Potsdam. It is likely that most of the thirty-eight concertos that C. P. E. Bach wrote in Berlin were performed not at court, but at concerts in the city.

Owing to the presence of so many distinguished performers and composers in the court musical establishment, it was possible for music in the city to flourish as never before, and the many independent concert series which sprang into existence as a result were not constrained by the narrow tastes of the King. So the young genre of the keyboard concerto, first cultivated in

---

[1] Burney, *Musical Tours*, ii. 206.

Germany by J. S. Bach, and now beginning to spread further afield through the work of his sons and pupils, was able to grow freely. Hans Uldall, in his seminal study of the Berlin keyboard concerto, takes the view that it was principally in town circles that the genre developed, since the King, a flautist, appears not to have been particularly interested in this genre himself.[2]

Nevertheless the physical isolation of Berlin, and the concentration of composers who were relatively cut off from musical developments elsewhere as a result of the conservative tastes of the King, produced a somewhat insular type of keyboard concerto, according to Uldall. A predominantly serious tone was its main distinguishing feature. Polyphony reminiscent of J. S. Bach is encountered not infrequently, ritornello structure is consistently maintained, while dance movements, binary movements, variation sets, and rondos are scrupulously avoided. With regard to thematic character, there is some variety. The more conservative composers such as Schaffrath and Schale wrote themes which suggest Bachian or Vivaldian inspiration; the more progressive composers such as C. H. Graun and G. A. Benda, on the other hand, showed a degree of *galant* inspiration, a more vocal style of melody, and a liking for contrasting ideas that suggests the influence of Tartini. One feature mentioned by Uldall, which appears almost obsessively in the more *galant* of the Berlin concertos, is the juxtaposition of duplet and triplet rhythms in a primarily melodic texture. The keyboard writing tends to be more old-fashioned than that found further south; instead of Alberti basses it is more common to find repeated chords as accompaniment, and the melodic style, when it is not reminiscent of Bach and Vivaldi, is likely to be more stylized than cantabile. Three movements, fast–slow–fast, are the rule. It is rare for the finales to contain cadential fermatas, but first movements frequently do; it is in slow movements, however, that by far the greatest number is found. Most are pre-tutti, although some occur after extensions of the final solo cadence; examples of the inserted cadenza are extremely rare.[3] In all these respects it can be seen that the concertos of C. P. E. Bach reflected the prevailing Berlin style.

North Germany outside Berlin

Although the concertos of the Berlin composers do invite cadenzas, and some extant written-out examples for this repertoire do exist, it cannot be denied that Berlin was somewhat conservative in its cadenza treatment. The same

---

[2] H. Uldall, *Das Klavierkonzert der Berliner Schule* (Leipzig, 1928), 12.

[3] Uldall seems to be working with a much broader definition of the cadenza, perhaps including extended pedal passages of the perfidia type and various forms of embellished fermata, when he makes the otherwise inexplicable claim that 'solo cadenzas are found mostly at the end of the final solo in all three movements, but they also occur at the close of other solos', *Klavierkonzert*, p. 23.

was true of Northern Germany generally. J. S. Bach's eldest son, Wilhelm Friedemann, made rather more sparing use of cadenzas in his handful of keyboard concertos than did his better known younger brother. Nor did he follow a consistent pattern in this matter. In one case he introduces a cadential fermata at a cadence in the mediant at the end of the development section,[4] and in another the fermata appears over a submediant chord before a final solo cadence![5] All Friedemann's final cadenzas are of the pre-tutti type: he makes no use of the more dramatic forms of placing.[6]

Other pupils of J. S. Bach working in North Germany tended also to be conservative in their use of the cadenza. Johann Ludwig Krebs (1713–80) included in his B minor Concerto for Harpsichord, Oboe, and Strings a capriccio-like passage possibly modelled on the capriccio from Bach's Fifth Brandenburg Concerto.[7] As Uldall observed, his work remained firmly within the musical language of his teacher.[8]

Johann Gottfried Müthel (1728–88), another Bach pupil and a good representative of the North German *empfindsamer Stil*, made sparing use of the cadenza, principally in slow movements. From an extant written-out example, probably intended for use in a work for organ solo,[9] it appears that his own cadenza style made use of extended sequences and elaborate suspensions, not very commonly encountered in the repertory at any stage. Perhaps this particular example, intended as it was for the organ, was exceptional even in Müthel's work.

Johann Friedrich Reichardt (1752–1814) was a slightly later Prussian composer, and one much associated with the *Sturm und Drang* movement. He is better remembered for his songs and dramatic works than for his instrumental music, and Eugene Helm has said that 'his concertos are not as progressive as those of C. P. E. Bach'.[10] None the less they do represent an advance over those of C. P. E. Bach in their consistent placing of cadential fermatas in the dramatic position after the final solo cadences of first movements.[11] The concertos are actually fairly youthful works, all having

---

[4] F. 41/i. This is the only cadential fermata in the whole concerto, and it occurs during a tutti!

[5] F. 43/ii.

[6] The F minor concerto variously attributed to C.P.E., J.C., and W. F. Bach, and published in R. Maunder (ed.), *The Collected Works of Johann Christian Bach: 1735–1782*, xxxii. *Keyboard Concertos I: Six Early Concertos* (New York and London, 1985), is actually by J. C. Bach. See Jane R. Stevens, 'Concerto no. 6 in F minor: By Johann Christian Bach?', *RMA Research Chronicle*, 21 (1988), 53 ff. In this concerto each of the first two movements contains a cadential fermata separated from the final solo cadence by a brief snatch of tutti.

[7] First movement, bars 150–85. The capriccios included in A. C. Kunzen's set of eight keyboard concertos (B-Bc 6127) are probably modelled directly on Vivaldi or Locatelli. They were written in the 1760s.

[8] *Klavierkonzert*, p. 94.

[9] Variations on *Jesu, meine Freude*. See *Orgelwerke*, ii (Innsbruck, 1985), 10.

[10] *Grove*, xv. 706.

[11] With the exception of some of the six concertos published as Op. 1, 'à l'usage du beau sexe', which are naturally somewhat lighter in idiom than the other concertos.

been written while the composer was in his twenties, so clearly they do not represent his most advanced work.

Dresden

The Dresden court composer Christlieb Siegmund Binder is described by Günter Hausswald as one of the 'middlemen between baroque and classical style, between North and South [who] . . . represents the Italian period of Hasse in Dresden, but . . . also established links with the German baroque art of Frederick's Berlin'.[12] Much the same could be said of the musical establishment at Dresden in the mid-eighteenth century generally. A Catholic court in Protestant Saxony (the Elector of Saxony who succeeded in 1694 had become a Catholic in order to strengthen his claim to the throne of Poland), situated closer to Prague than to Berlin, it not surprisingly combines elements of the cultures of North and South. The figure of Hasse, who set Metastasio's libretti for the magnificent court opera in Dresden, dominated the musical establishment there until his dismissal in 1763, and he, together with a corpus of imported singers, including his wife Faustina Bordoni, contributed greatly to the Italianate style of Dresden's musical life. In the field of instrumental music the Vivaldi pupil Georg Johann Pisendel, leader of the orchestra from 1712 to 1755, introduced his teacher's style to the court, and helped to disseminate Vivaldi's music in Germany. Yet Berlin was not so far away, and Leipzig was even closer. Names such as Quantz, Heinichen, and Naumann are found among the members of the court's musical establishment, and these belong to a rather different, North German tradition. The keyboard concertos written and performed at the court in Dresden tended to be by Saxon or Prussian composers, and the roots of their style are to be found more in the North than in the South.

The court at Dresden in the years preceding the Seven Years War (1756–63) has been described as musically the most brilliant in Europe.[13] Many changes occurred in Dresden's musical life in 1763. The war had wreaked havoc on the city, which had been devastated by the Prussian bombardment of 1760. Two electors died in 1763, the year of Saxony's final defeat, and many of the court musicians (including Hasse and his wife) were dismissed as a consequence of the many economies which had become necessary. The death of the Elector Friedrich Christian in December 1763 was followed by a five-year period of administration by Prince Xaver, the brother of the deceased elector, before the latter's son Friedrich August III, the last elector and first king of Saxony, began to reign in person.

---

[12] *MGG* i. 1857.
[13] A. Yorke-Long, *Music at Court: Four Eighteenth-Century Studies* (London, 1954), 77.

Friedrich August III is of some significance for the present study, since he was a keen keyboard player. Burney says of him:

He is of a reserved disposition. Naumann, his *maestro di capella*, and Gasman, had informed me, that his highness was so good a musician as to accompany readily, and in a masterly manner, on the harpsichord, at sight; but was so shy of playing before company, that even the Electress, his consort, had hardly ever heard him.[14]

While the Elector was by no means so timid as Burney suggests, it is true that he never performed in public. The Elector's private music collection[15] contains arrangements for two harpsichords of a wide range of late eighteenth-century music, including, for example, symphonies and quartets by Haydn and Mozart. The reason for this is that the Elector liked to play duets with his court harpsichordists Peter August or Christlieb Siegmund Binder.[16] Most of the library's manuscript sources of keyboard concertos from this period, even if they do exist in orchestral parts, exist also in arrangements for two harpsichords. Thus the three keyboard concertos by Peter August[17] exist also, together with three other concertos by August, in arrangements for two harpsichords alone.[18] The method of arrangement is essentially the same as that used today when practical editions of piano concertos are published as arrangements for two pianos—the second player performs a keyboard reduction of the orchestral parts while the first player performs the solo part. Presumably, since the orchestral scores are autographs, the concertos were written to be performed with orchestra before an audience, probably by August himself, and yet it is clear that they were also performed privately by the Elector with one of his harpsichordists. Two of the six concertos by August require cadenzas, which are written out in full in the arrangements and elsewhere, though not in the autographs themselves. It seems most probable that these cadenzas were written specially for the Elector. They thus constitute an early example of 'private', 'domestic' cadenzas, written not for the purpose of impressing an audience with a brilliant display of technique, but rather for private, personal satisfaction. In this they anticipate some of the cadenzas published later in the century, either in independent collections[19] or else included in printed editions of specific concertos that were destined for amateur consumption.[20] It may be for this reason that the cadenzas by August place more emphasis on thematic reference to the concerto movement than on display. Such allusions to material from the

---

[14] Burney, *Musical Tours*, ii. 141.

[15] Now housed in D-Dlb.

[16] I am indebted for this information to Dr Ortrun Landmann of the Sächsische Landes-bibliothek in Dresden.

[17] D-Dlb Mus 3065-O-8, 1–3.

[18] D-Dlb Mus 3065-O-7, 1–6.

[19] e.g. T. Giordani, *Cadences* (see Ch. 10).

[20] e.g. G. J. Vogler, *Sei concerti facili*, Op. 2.

movement were relatively unusual in the 1760s when these works appear to have been written.

Christlieb Siegmund Binder (1723–89) was a much more prolific composer of concertos.[21] The great majority require cadenzas in both of the first two movements but not in the finale. Relatively few are written out, and most of these are found in the concertos for two harpsichords and orchestra. It is apparent from the written-out cadenzas for single harpsichord, however, that what Binder expected to be performed at these points was quite simple. They tend to be written as a single part over a stationary bass, and to rise and fall in pitch by means of small non-thematic figures repeated over and over again. The shape of the cadenzas seems to be determined largely by these somewhat aimless patterns of rising and falling pitch. Fleischer not unreasonably expresses disappointment at the quality of these cadenzas.[22] Yet he also draws attention to the much higher level of inspiration found in the double cadenzas. Here, the shape seems to be determined more by considerations of drama than by gratuitous changes in figuration and melodic direction, at least in the cadenza written for the first of the three double concertos.

Younger Sons of J. S. Bach

Johann Christian Bach

Johann Christian Bach (1735–82) wrote his first keyboard concertos while he was still living in Berlin with his elder half-brother Carl Philipp Emanuel and receiving instruction from him after the death of their father in 1750. These five concertos are in fact his earliest known works of undisputed authenticity.[23] Each invites a cadenza in its slow movement, while the first movements of nos. 1 and 5 contain tutti-reinforced cadential fermatas at the final solo cadences. In the first movement of the fourth concerto there is a pre-tutti cadential fermata at a subsidiary cadence in the relative minor at the end of the development section. Johann Christian was evidently familiar with many different ways of introducing cadential fermatas, even at this early stage in his career—the Berlin concertos include examples of pre-tutti, extended, as well as inserted cadenzas.

Most of his other keyboard concertos[24] were written for the English

---

[21] H. Fleischer lists 37 in the thematic catalogue included in his *Christlieb Siegmund Binder (1723–89)* (Regensburg, 1941).

[22] Ibid. 104 ff.

[23] It is known that they were written before he left for Italy in 1754. For an edn., see *Six Early Concertos*, ed. R. Maunder (details in n. 6 above).

[24] See C. Wolff, etc., *New Grove Bach Family* (London, 1983), 347 f. (revised offprint of articles on the Bach family contained in *Grove*, i) for a list of Bach's concertos, including those of doubtful authenticity.

market, and published in three sets of six: Op. 1 (1763), Op. 7 (1770), and Op. 13 (1777). They are on the whole lightweight works, many of them in two movements.[25] Just two concertos in each of the three sets contain three movements, and it is only in these concertos that cadential fermatas are to be found.

The first two sets are scored for an orchestra of two violins and bass only, and this, together with their dedication to Queen Charlotte, indicates the type of concerto and the type of market at which Bach was aiming—the light, divertimento concerto, well within the technical powers of amateurs. This impression is borne out by the use of rondo, minuet, or variation form for closing movements—Op. 1 No. 6 ends with a rondo on 'God Save the King'— all common features of the concerto aimed at the *Liebhaber* rather than the *Kenner*. Burney's description of Bach's keyboard music in general, that it was 'such as ladies can execute with little trouble',[26] seems apt at least for these concertos. The Op. 1 set contains no cadential fermatas at all: Op. 7 contains only three—they are found in the first two movements of No. 5 and the slow movement of No. 6.

Ex. 36.   *J. C. Bach, Concerto, Op. 13 No. 4, second movement, cadenza from Sieber edn.*

The Op. 13 set is scored a little more fully, with parts for two oboes/flutes and two horns in addition to the two violins and bass of the earlier sets. The fourth concerto, one of those consisting of three movements, is the only one in the set to contain a cadential fermata. Unlike the first edition (1777), published in London by Welcker, the Sieber edition (Paris, 1785) contains a written-out rhapsodic cadenza (see Ex. 36). Both its modest scale and its

---

[25] It has been suggested (*NOHM* vii. 484) that the two-movement form may have been influenced by the symphonie concertante; this seems unlikely, however, since the latter genre did not establish itself until the 1770s.

[26] Burney, *History*, iv. 482; ed. Mercer, ii. 866.

neutral (i.e. not affective) character are well-suited to the *galant* style of a concerto such as this, although it might appear a little out of place in one of the *empfindsam* concertos of C. P. E. Bach, or indeed in one of those five early and very different concertos written by Johann Christian Bach in Berlin.

Johann Christoph Friedrich Bach

Johann Christoph Fredrich Bach (1732–95) was another composer whose style of composition and of cadenza usage changed significantly in the course of his career. After visiting his younger brother Christian in London in 1778 he consciously adopted the lighter, more transparent, *galant* idiom of Christian's London works, having previously modelled his keyboard style on that of Carl Philipp Emanuel. Admittedly there is only one concerto which predates the journey, namely the E major Concerto of *c*.1765, but it is noticeable that, after calling for an ad libitum cadenza in each of its three movements, he only ever used a cadential fermata once in the later extant works.[27]

Hannsdieter Wohlfarth likens the E major Concerto to the type cultivated in Berlin under the influence of Tartini.[28] This seems particularly apt when one examines the notation of the cadenza in the first movement (Ex. 37). The use of a whole bar rest (a general pause in fact) is strongly reminiscent of Tartini's capriccios, and indeed 'Capriccio' followed by 'Cad' is written into the lower string parts at this point. The slow-movement cadenza occurs in the penultimate bar of the movement, with no tutti to follow; it seems that a repeat of the entire second section, including the cadenza, is intended here—the movement is written in binary form with repeat signs. The finale contains a straightforward pre-tutti cadential fermata, remarkable only in that it occurs at all in a concerto of this date.

It is not clear whether Friedrich is in fact the author of the set of six keyboard concertos published by Welcker in London under his name.[29] They are slight two-movement works, possibly written under the influence of

Ex. 37. *J. C. F. Bach, Concerto in E major, first movement*

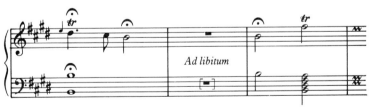

---

[27] F major Concerto, 1787, slow movement.
[28] H. Wohlfarth, *Johann Christoph Friedrich Bach* (Berne, 1971), 154 f.
[29] These are not mentioned by Wohlfarth. A publication date of around 1780 is suggested in the British Library Catalogue of Printed Music.

Johann Christian's London publications, and they contain no cadential fermatas. If they are by Friedrich, then it is perhaps unsurprising that he should have abandoned the cadenza altogether in these works—Christian after all did the same when writing his Op. 1 set. Perhaps more surprising is Friedrich's abandonment of the cadenza in his later concertos. Wohlfarth mentions that contemporaries spoke of Friedrich's brilliance at improvisation,[30] and he even speaks of solo cadenzas in the later concertos, but he actually seems to mean *Eingänge*, since most of these works contain no cadential fermatas. Wohlfarth also suggests a possible Mozartian influence;[31] while there is much in Friedrich's later music to suggest this, the influence does not seem to have extended as far as cadenza usage—Mozart's music is liberally supplied with cadential fermatas and obbligato cadenzas.

Mannheim

It has been pointed out that the concertos written by composers associated with the electoral court at Mannheim were relatively conservative in style.[32] Those features commonly associated with the 'Mannheim style'—bold dynamic effects, brilliant strokes of orchestration, extended crescendos, and the like—are exploited more in the symphonies than in the concertos of the Stamitz family and others.

On the other hand, it has also been claimed[33] that Mannheim acted as a centre of considerable influence on the later classical concerto, principally through the use of certain types of stereotyped thematic material, differentiated according to their function within the concerto movement. In view of the excellence of the orchestra at the Mannheim court, and the large number of outstanding virtuosi within its ranks, it is not surprising that the concerto was so widely cultivated there; nor perhaps is it surprising that the large number of concertos produced should have led to a proliferation of stereotyped ideas.

For the most part the virtuoso performers employed at Mannheim—Johann, Carl, and Anton Stamitz, Cannabich, Wendling, Ramm, Eichner —were not keyboard players, although a few small-scale keyboard concertos did appear in print under the names of one or other of the members of the Stamitz family. For the history of the keyboard cadenza the chief importance of the Mannheim composers was probably indirect, through the symphonie concertante, a genre which was well suited to exploiting the talent of the Mannheim performers. There was a fair amount of traffic between Mannheim and Paris, the principal home of this new genre (see Chapter 10), and from the

---

[30] Wohlfarth, *J. C. F. Bach*, pp. 153 f.   [31] Ibid. 161.
[32] P. Ward Jones, 'The Concerto at Mannheim, *c.*1740–1780', *Proceedings of the Royal Musical Association*, 96 (1969–70), 129 ff.   [33] *NOHM* vii. 456 ff.

outset Mannheim composers contributed significantly to the symphonies concertantes that were published and performed in Paris. The importance of the symphonie concertante for the present survey lies in its use of the ensemble cadenza.

One composer associated with the Mannheim court who was himself a keyboard player was Abbé Georg Joseph Vogler, a distinguished composer, pianist, and writer on music. He had a tremendous facility in improvisation, and his extemporizations were preferred by some to Beethoven's.[34] Thus it is not surprising to find cadenzas occurring quite frequently in his music. A particularly interesting publication to consider in this connection is his set of *Sechs leichte Clavierconcerte*, Op. 2 of 1779. Five out of the six are supplied with cadenzas of some kind, normally inserted cadenzas for first movements, although the second concerto contains what is technically a rondo cadenza, albeit a very small-scale one. These concertos were written for an amateur market, as Vogler himself points out when explaining why all but the fourth and sixth concertos are cast in two-movement form.[35] The prevailing style of

Ex. 38.   *G. J. Vogler, Concerto, Op. 2 No. 1, first-movement cadenza*

---

[34]   See J. Fröhlich, *Biografie des grossen Tonkünstlers Abt G. J. Vogler* (Würzburg, 1845), 55. Quoted in *Grove*, xx. 61.

[35]   G. J. Vogler, *Betrachtungen der Mannheimer Tonschule*, 3 vols. (Mannheim, 1778–81; facs. repr. Hildesheim, etc., 1974), ii. 36.

the concertos is that of early pianoforte writing—simple, *galant*, and cantabile with straightforward harmonic accompaniments, often Alberti basses. Most of the cadenzas make some reference to material from the movement, though since they are fairly small-scale it is not possible for them to treat the material at all extensively. These cadenzas are excellent models of short idiomatic keyboard cadenzas; they are well-shaped, pleasantly varied, interesting without being wayward, and importantly, in view of the destination of the concertos, not difficult to perform (see Ex. 38).

Whereas in the public concert life of London and Paris the cadenza seems to have been imported, in the German courts—Berlin, Dresden, Mannheim, and many others—it seems to have arisen naturally and without reference to foreign styles. While the vocal cadenza is Italian in origin, the keyboard cadenza seems to have appeared first in Germany, and only later to have spread with the German style to other parts of Europe. The German courts were its heartland in those early days, even though its heyday was lived in the musical capitals of Europe in the professional concerts which so dominated late eighteenth-century musical life. The one city within the German-speaking world which could claim to be a truly cosmopolitan musical capital was Vienna.

Vienna

The Viennese keyboard concerto was of an altogether different type from that cultivated in North Germany. While larger-scale forms were not entirely neglected, a great many Viennese concertos were virtually chamber works, written in a light divertimento idiom, frequently using binary forms with repeat signs (characteristically the opening tutti stood outside the binary structure), minuets, rondos, Alberti basses, all of which were quite foreign to the Berlin style. Larger scale works are also found, using a ritornello framework, but these occur more frequently from the 1770s onwards.

Keyboard concertos were being written in Austria as early as the 1730s. Some interesting cadenzas are included in an F major Harpsichord Concerto by Johann Michael Steinbacher, who was active in the period 1727–40 (see Ex. 39). They are short, single-part, and although they are notated metrically the effect is of an unbarred improvisation in each case, an effect that is strengthened by the fermata which articulates the opening of each cadenza. It can only be presumed that the stimulus behind this development came from the Italian opera or concerto, since it took place too early for the North German concerto to have exerted an influence in this part of the world.[36]

[36] Another instance of pre-1750 Austrian keyboard cadenzas is found in a concerto by M. G. Monn (D-B Mus ms 14630/6). The slow movement of this concerto contains both a subsidiary cadenza before the middle ritornello and a final cadenza which is a somewhat expanded version of the former.

Ex. 39. *J. M. Steinbacher, Concerto in F:* (a) *first-movement cadenza,* (b) *second-movement cadenza,* (c) *finale cadenza*

Georg Christoph Wagenseil was probably the most prolific composer of keyboard concertos in musical history. Helga Scholz-Michelitsch lists ninety-three concertos by him in her thematic catalogue, though not all of these are extant. They are mostly small-scale, often using an accompaniment of just two violins and bass. Many of the concertos are virtually chamber works; apart from some tutti reinforcement of cadences and perhaps a tutti introduction, they are divertimentos for harpsichord with string accompaniment. Others, especially those which survive in printed sources, are slightly more large-scale and use genuine ritornellos. It is not uncommon to find cadential fermatas in slow movements, usually occurring at the final solo cadence and easily omitted, but none of the concertos known to the author contains a cadential fermata in the finale; only one[37] requires a final cadenza in the firs movement. Occasionally one finds a subsidiary cadenza before a recapitula tion—another retrospective feature.[38] This style of concerto and cadenz; usage was very common in Vienna.[39]

It was principally in South Germany and Austria that the classical style grew to maturity. The dramatic articulation of the crucial events in the structure of a tonal composition by means of thematic differentiation, careful control of harmonic rhythm, of modulation, and of changes in scoring, texture, and rhythmic pace, was to reach its first peak of sophistication in Austria, and to spread from there to other parts of Europe. As a highly articulated form, the concerto benefited particularly from the increased resources which the classical style brought with it. The preference for the inserted cadenza over other types was one consequence of the growth of more dramatic articulation; another was the increasing incidence of first-movement cadenzas and the corresponding decline of slow-movement cadenzas.

That this is so is evident statistically from a study of the Viennese classical concerto; to account for it is not so easy. It may be that the first movement, being the weightiest of the three, tended to accumulate those features involving dramatic juxtaposition of tutti and solo of which the inserted cadenza is an example. An additional factor, however, is that slow movements and finales tended increasingly to be written in forms other than the ritornello-sonata scheme used in first movements. This was itself a consequence of the increasing weight of dramatically articulated sonata movements: the relief that was needed after a first movement was better provided by a less tightly structured form. While the use of a ritornello-sonata scheme was by no means a prerequisite for the insertion of a cadenza, it had come to be particularly associated with the cadenza, for it was at the important cadences of a movement structured in this way that the cadenza had evolved. A pattern which can be observed in the slow movements of Mozart's concertos and in his arias is that cadential fermatas are retained for as long as ritornello structures are retained, but that they virtually disappear once the looser forms of variation, rondo, ABA, etc., are substituted for the ritornello principle. Embellished fermatas and *Eingänge* are commonly found in the later arias and slow movements, but it was at the final solo cadences that Mozart had usually introduced cadential fermatas. There may also be aesthetic reasons for the change: the primacy of the slow-movement cadenza had been associated with the doctrine of the affections, and with the rhetorical approach to composition prevalent during the period of *Empfindsamkeit*. If a slow movement was

[37] SM 332. The source consulted was A-M V 862. Surprisingly, perhaps, it is an inserted cadenza.

[38] Found in the first movement of SM 326. The source consulted was D-Rtt Wagenseil 18.

[39] Another prolific Viennese composer of similarly lightweight concertos was Leopold Hofmann.

intended to convey an eloquent statement of a particular affection, it made sense to provide it with a climax in the form of a peroration at the cadence. If the emphasis was lyrical rather than rhetorical, on cantabile melody rather than on stylized expression, the result was that less importance was attached to this type of expressive climax at the end, and more to balance and symmetry.

Mozart was to adopt the first-movement inserted cadenza almost without exception once he began to compose original concertos. His contemporaries in Vienna were less consistent in this matter, but the trend towards providing first movements with inserted cadenzas is certainly noticeable.

Franz Anton Hoffmeister's concertos often require inserted cadenzas in first movements, but not in second movements or finales, while Dittersdorf sometimes calls for cadenzas in all three movements of a concerto. Ignaz Pleyel commonly requires an inserted cadenza in the first movement and sometimes a tutti-reinforced cadenza in the second movement, but none at all in finales. Outside Vienna itself, but still within the sphere of influence of the Viennese classical style, Johann Franz Xaver Sterkel usually calls for an inserted cadenza in his first movements, a cadenza of some kind in the slow movements, and in at least one instance in the finale also.[40]

The repertoire is large and such examples could be multiplied indefinitely, but the conclusions would remain much the same. It would be more instructive, perhaps, to consider a few examples of written-out cadenzas.

The three keyboard concertos by Antonio Salieri all date from 1773, after his arrival in Vienna but before his court appointment.[41] One is an Organ Concerto in C, which was composed 'per la Freule Paradis', that is to say, for the blind pianist Maria-Theresia Paradis. It may be that the two harpsichord concertos, in C and in B flat respectively, were also written for her, since the appearance of three concertos in a single year from a composer who seems not to have written any other keyboard concertos, suggests some particular occasion or commission. All three require cadenzas. In the case of the Organ Concerto and the B flat Harpsichord Concerto the cadenzas are written out at the end of the manuscript. Both are idiomatically written and in strict time for the most part, although the B flat cadenza is unbarred. The B flat cadenza makes considerable use of a figure '*x*' which suggests harpsichord style rather than organ or piano (see Ex. 40). The C major cadenza suffers from a certain shapelessness, the melodic line meanders through varying patterns of figuration, with little sense of direction and scarcely a breathing space. The B flat cadenza achieves a greater sense of urgency by its obsessive treatment of one or two small motivic ideas, and the return of the dominant note in the bass is well articulated.

One of the more prolific composers of classical piano concertos in Vienna during the period when Mozart lived there was the Bohemian Leopold

[40] Op. 26 No. 1.   [41] The autograph scores are in A-Wn Mus. Hs. 3726–8.

Ex. 40.   *A. Salieri, Concerto in B flat, first-movement cadenza (from A-Wn Mus. Hs. 3728)*

Ex. 40. – *Contd.*

Kozeluch.[42] A particularly large number of cadenzas is distributed among the sources of his concertos, and while few if any may be by Kozeluch himself, they provide an interesting cross-section of the types of cadenzas actually performed. Most of Kozeluch's piano concertos were written in Vienna during the 1780s, and many of them may have been intended specifically as concert pieces for his famous pupil Maria-Theresia Paradis, who may therefore be the author of some of the cadenzas contained in the Viennese sources.

Most of the concertos require ad libitum inserted cadenzas in the first movements. It is not unusual to find cadenzas in the slow movements, but no finale known to the author contains a cadential fermata. Written-out *Eingänge* are not uncommon, but Mozartian rondo cadenzas do not occur at all. If cadenzas are supplied, they are normally found on separate manuscript leaves loosely inserted into the bound copy.

The cadenzas found in the manuscript concertos housed in the Gesellschaft der Musikfreunde in Vienna[43] are probably the most accomplished, and they resemble Mozart's cadenzas more closely than any of the others. Both open thematically, and both elaborate the tripartite scheme that typically underlies Mozart's cadenzas (see Chapter 8), though the articulation of the sections is

---

[42] M. Poštolka lists 22 concertos in *Leopold Koželuh* (Prague, 1964), of which only about half have ever appeared in print.

[43] Q 16250 (VII 12281) and Q 16251 (VII 12282), in C and D respectively.

Ex. 41.   *L. Kozeluch, Concerto in C, P . IV: 17, cadenza from A-Wgm Q 16250 (VII 12281)*

Ex. 41. – *Contd.*

Ex. 41. – *Contd.*

clearer in the C major cadenza than in the D major one (the C major cadenza is reproduced in Ex. 41). Thematic fragmentation, shifts of mode, orchestral textures with right-hand tremolo, a 'composed rit.'—all these devices are familiar from Mozart's concertos, and while some of the figuration is a little awkward compared with Mozart's, and the piano writing less cantabile, the style is nevertheless close to his own. Poštolka has stressed the role played by Kozeluch in developing an idiomatic piano style and discouraging the use of the harpsichord.[44]

A most amusing cadenza is to be found inserted into the Götz edition of the concerto P. IV: 2 housed in the library of the Brussels Conservatoire.[45] It shows clearly how not all performers of the period were equally fluent at improvising cadenzas, and how some were forced to rely heavily on quotation. Not only does the first-movement cadenza quote a theme and some passage-work directly from the movement (a practice frequently employed by Mozart), but it actually quotes a dozen or so bars out of Clementi's 'Cadenza alla Kozeluch' from *Musical Characteristics*, Op. 19 (see Chapter 13). The 'composer' of the cadenza contributes nothing of substance at all. It should be said, however, that the pastiche is skilfully carried out. The transitions between Clementi and Kozeluch are smoothly achieved, and the tripartite division is well articulated. This is not the only borrowing from Clementi's Op. 19, for the last line of the longer of the two slow-movement cadenzas contained in this source comes from the 'Cadenza alla Clementi'.

Clementi's *Musical Characteristics* also contain parodies of the cadenza style of J. B. Vanhal, another Bohemian composer of keyboard concertos in the Vienna of Joseph II, and of J. F. X. Sterkel; for present purposes, however, by far the most important composer to feature in Clementi's parody was W. A. Mozart.

[44] *Grove*, x. 226.   [45] B-Bc 6115.

8

Mozart and the Cadenza

MOZART occupies a key position in this survey, both because of his outstanding contribution to the classical keyboard concerto, and also because of the substantial corpus of original ad libitum cadenzas that has survived.

It was Carl Reinecke who pioneered the revival of interest in Mozart's piano concertos in the late nineteenth century, after all but the D minor Concerto, K. 466, had virtually disappeared from concert programmes.[1] Reinecke put forward the view, until recently virtually unchallenged, that Mozart's ad libitum cadenzas were intended for the use of others of lesser ability and not for himself. He bases this assumption partly on the argument that Mozart's skill as an improviser would have made it unnecessary for him to write out cadenzas for himself, and partly on the argument that no other satisfactory explanation could be put forward for the undue simplicity of the cadenzas. This view seems to be coloured by the preconceptions of an age which took for granted the keyboard virtuosity required by Brahms and Liszt. Thanks to the greater historical awareness of the present age, brought about to no mean extent by the efforts of such as Reinecke, Mozart's cadenzas no longer seem inappropriately restrained. Although a collection of thirty-six 'cadenzas' by Mozart was published in 1878,[2] it seems that few performers saw fit to use them until the post-war interest in returning to original sources began to have an impact. Further discoveries of original cadenzas notwithstanding, there are still six late concertos for which no cadenzas by Mozart are extant.[3] Here the performer must either use some of the later cadenzas, for example by Hummel, Moscheles, and Reinecke, which might well be thought stylistically incongruous, or else must supply his own. In chapter 11 of their book *Interpreting Mozart on the Keyboard* (1957), entitled 'Cadenzas and Lead-Ins', Eva and Paul Badura-Skoda discuss Mozart's personal procedure in writing ad libitum cadenzas so that guidelines may be given to those who set out to imitate them when writing their own cadenzas.

The genesis of Mozart's cadenzas is connected not so much with the composition of the concertos as with the history of their subsequent performances in the composer's lifetime. A single concerto is often supplied with alternative cadenzas, sometimes quite different in style and date of composition from one another. It is often possible to deduce from the source material

---

[1] C. Reinecke, *Zur Wiederbelebung der Mozartschen Clavierconcerte* (Leipzig, 1891).
[2] *AMA* XXII: 18. Six of these are actually *Eingänge*.
[3] i.e. K. 466, K. 467, K. 482, K. 491, K. 503, and K. 537.

and from Mozart's correspondence the circumstances in which the cadenzas were written.[4] Christoph Wolff, writing in 1978, was the first to challenge the long-held view that they were written for others to perform, believing instead that they represent the ideal personal solutions of Mozart *qua* performer.[5] Wolff has worked out a rough chronology for the cadenzas, based partly on the evidence of source material and the correspondence, and partly on stylistic considerations. Tables 2 and 3 below offer a summary of the information provided by Wolff and by the introductions and critical reports of the *NMA*.

Table 2. *Cadenzas by Mozart for use in his mature concertos*

Concerto	Movement	Date of Cadenza	Number in K^6 626a I*
K. 175	i	Feb. 1783	2
K. 175	ii	Feb. 1783	4
K. 382		Feb. 1783	26
K. 175	i	Mar. 1783?	1
K. 175	ii	Mar. 1783?	3
K. 382		Mar. 1783?	25
K. 238	i	1777/8 or before	5
K. 238	ii	1777/8 or before	6
K. 238	iii	1777/8 or before	7
K. 242	i	Feb. 1776	—
K. 242	ii	Feb. 1776	—
K. 246	i	1777/8	8
K. 246	ii	1777/8	11
K. 246	i	*c*.1777/8	9
K. 246	ii	*c*.1777/8	12
K. 246	i	after Apr. 1782	10
K. 246	ii	after Apr. 1782	14
K. 271	i	1784	15
K. 271	ii	1784	17
K. 271	i	1777	16
K. 271	ii	1777	18
K. 365 (316a)	i	Nov. 1781	23
K. 365	iii	Nov. 1781	24
K. 413 (387a)	i	1783?	37
K. 413	ii	1783?	38
K. 414 (385p)	i	1782/3?	28
K. 414	ii	1782/3?	31
K. 414	iii	1782/3?	35
K. 414	i	1785/6	27
K. 414	ii	1785/6	32
K. 414	iii	1785/6	34

---

[4] All the concertos, together with their cadenzas, have been published in the *NMA*, the seven early arrangements in vol. x: 28/ii, and the twenty-three original concertos in the eight vols. of series v: 15. The introductions to each volume discuss in detail the source material for both concertos and cadenzas, and references from the correspondence are fully documented.

[5] C. Wolff, 'Zur Chronologie der Klavierkonzert-Kadenzen Mozarts', *M-Jb* (1978–9), 244. Frederick Neumann, in *Ornamentation and Improvisation in Mozart* (Princeton, 1986), 257 f., objects that Wolff's thesis cannot be proven. Neumann suggests that the cadenzas are records of Mozart's actual improvisations, kept so as to be shown to students.

Table 2. – *Contd.*

Concerto	Movement	Date of Cadenza	Number in K⁶ 626a I*
K. 415 (387b)	i	1783?	39
K. 415	ii	1783?	40
K. 449	i	1784?	42
K. 450	i	1784?	43
K. 450	iii	1784?	45
K. 451	i	June–July 1784	46
K. 451	iii	June–July 1784	47
K. 453	i	June–July 1784	48
K. 453	i	June–July 1784	49
K. 453	ii	June–July 1784	50
K. 453	ii	June–July 1784	51
K. 456	i	1784?	54
K. 456	iii	1784?	57
K. 456	i	after no. 54	53
K. 456	i	after no. 53	52
K. 456	iii	after no. 53	56
K. 459	i	1785–9?	58
K. 459	iii	1784–90?	60
K. 488	i	Mar. 1786	61
K. 595	i	Jan.–Mar. 1791	62
K. 595	iii	Jan.–Mar. 1791	64

* The number 626a is assigned to Mozart's ad libitum keyboard cadenzas in K⁶. The editors have divided the cadenzas into two groups, those in Group I being intended for use in the mature concertos. These cadenzas are numbered consecutively from 1 to 64, but not all are included here; thirteen of them are *Eingänge*, and no. 33 is simply a fragment of no. 32. To these are added the two cadenzas for K. 242, absent from K⁶.

Table 3. *Cadenzas by Mozart for use in concertos by other composers and in his early concerto arrangements*

Cadenza from K⁶ 626a II*	Estimated date	Concerto movement	Description
A	after 1772	K. 107 No. 1, i	
B	after 1772	K. 107 No. 1, ii	
C	1773	K. 40, i	
D	1779	Schroeter, Op. 3 No. 4, i	incomplete
F	1779	Schroeter, Op. 3 No. 6, i	incipit
G	—	Schroeter, Op. 3 No. 6, ii	incipit
H	1779	Schroeter, Op. 3 No. 1, i	incipit
N	1779	Schroeter, Op. 3 No. 3, i	
O	1779	Schroeter, Op. 3 No. 3, ii	
K	1773	Beecke, ?, ii	
—	1767	K. 40, i?	incomplete?

* The cadenzas in K⁶ 626a II are all intended for use either in the early concerto arrangements or else in the concertos of other composers; they are labelled with letters of the alphabet.

The Position of the Cadenza in Mozart's Piano Concertos

In each of the twenty-three mature piano concertos[6] Mozart invites an inserted ad libitum cadenza in the first movement. The same is true of his concertos for other solo instruments with the exception of the Clarinet Concerto and the first two Horn Concertos,[7] where no first-movement cadenza is invited at all. For all the mature piano concertos up to and including K. 459, original cadenzas are extant. Of the remaining eight concertos, original cadenzas are extant for only two, K. 488 and K. 595.

In most cases the cadenzas are preserved separately from the sources of the concertos. While some probably date from the time of composition of the concertos, it is known that others were written considerably later, especially in the case of those concertos for which alternative versions of the cadenzas are extant. Only in K. 242, the Concerto for Three Pianos (both in its original form and in the later arrangement for two pianos), and in K. 488 are cadenzas written into the autograph score.[8] The former was written to be performed by Countess Lodron and her two daughters; since the three ladies could not be expected to compose, least of all to improvise cadenzas for themselves, it is not surprising to find cadenzas written into the score. Mozart's reasons for including a cadenza in the autograph of K. 488 present more of a puzzle and are considered below.

The bar in which the cadential fermata occurs is normally notated in the concerto sources in a manner such as that shown in Ex. 42, quoted from the autograph of K. 459/i.[9] There is little unanimity with regard to the precise notation of these bars, even among different sources of the same concerto; clearly the actual notation used at this point is no more than a convention, and

Ex. 42.   *W. A. Mozart, Concerto in F, K. 459, first movement*

---

[6] i.e. all those composed after the seven early arrangements, beginning with K. 175. The figure includes the Concerto for Two Pianos, K. 242, and the Concerto for Three Pianos, K. 365 (316a).

[7] K. 412 (386b) and K. 417.

[8] See Wolff, 'Chronologie', p. 236. The passages in K. 271/iii to which Wolff also refers are *Eingänge*, and are thus excluded from the present discussion.

[9] See *NMA* v: 15/v, *Kritischer Bericht*, p. e/59.

would not have been interpreted literally.[10] While it has been noted that in C. P. E. Bach's concertos the uppermost right-hand pitch of the penultimate, as notated in concerto sources, normally matches the opening pitch of the corresponding original cadenza, this is seldom the case in Mozart's concertos, for the simple reason that most of his cadenzas are intended to begin after a caesura which separates them from the penultimate. Mozart's cadenza for K. 459/i begins and ends as shown in Ex. 43, and this is no doubt a typical example of the way in which such notation as that of Ex. 42 would have been interpreted.

The ending given in Ex. 43 is entirely characteristic of Mozart's written-out keyboard cadenzas. They normally end with a long trill on the supertonic in the right hand (usually lasting one bar, but occasionally two), harmonized by a dominant seventh chord in the left hand which enters half-way through the trill, thus providing a signal to the orchestra to prepare for their entry.[11] This formula is so commonly found that Eva and Paul Badura-Skoda base a part of their argument for the inauthenticity of two cadenzas on the use in these cadenzas of an alternative formula in which the trill and the dominant seventh chord begin simultaneously.[12] This aspect of their argument is unconvincing, however. The coincidence of right-hand trill with left-hand chord may be uncharacteristic, but it does occur occasionally in cadenzas of undoubted authenticity, such as K^6 626a I: 54 and 17.[13]

Ex. 43.   *W. A. Mozart, cadenza 58*

Most of the slow movements in the mature concertos that are written in the form characteristic of concerto first movements, i.e. with ritornello structures, require inserted ad libitum cadenzas, just as the first movements do.

---

[10] The apparently exceptional notation found at this point in K. 491/i, in which the place of the expected dominant chord is taken by a rest, has a simple explanation. The autograph score leaves the piano staves completely blank between the final solo cadence in bar 473 and the 'Dal Segno' with which Mozart indicates bars 492–506, simply adding 'cop' to indicate that the left hand should play 'col basso'.

[11] But see Ch. 3 above for a discussion of the endings of Mozart's rondo cadenzas.

[12] *NMA* v: 15/v, *Kritischer Bericht*, p. e/6. Reference is made to K^6 626a I: 49 and 51, which are attributed to Mozart in both the following edns. of Mozart's cadenzas: *Cadences originales* (Vienna, Artaria, 1801), and *Cadences ou points d'orgue* (Offenbach, André, 1804).

[13] Wolff ('Chronologie', p. 245) considers it likely that all the cadenzas printed by André and Artaria were prepared for publication from Mozart's autographs.

The slow movement of K. 453 is, however, the last to be written in this form, later ones being more loosely constructed in ABA form, or around a lyrical refrain, or as variations. It is no coincidence that the slow movement of K. 453 is also the last to require a cadenza, although there are embellished pauses of various other kinds in some of the later slow movements. As mentioned earlier, there is a close correlation between the use of cadenzas in eighteenth-century music and the use of ritornello structures of some kind. Mozart's early concerto arrangements, characteristically for small-scale works of the 1760s and 1770s, use a ritornello-sonata layout for almost every movement[14] (which is scarcely surprising, since they are for the most part arrangements of sonata movements). Of the mature piano concertos, K. 175, the first, written in 1773, is the only one to do so in all three movements.

The finales of Mozart's subsequent concertos are either rondos (admittedly incorporating elements of the sonata in most of the later examples) or variations (K. 453 and K. 491), or both (K. 382). It is significant that K. 382 was composed as a substitute for the original finale of K. 175 when Mozart performed this concerto in Vienna in 1782. Whereas the slow movements contain no further provision for cadenzas once they cease to be written in ritornello form, a little over half of the rondo finales in Mozart's concertos continue to invite cadenzas. This can perhaps be explained by the prominence of ritornello and sonata elements alongside those of rondo. The finale cadenzas differ in two important respects from those of first and second movements, however. Firstly, while they are usually introduced by a tutti passage, it is not normally a structural tutti (K. 466/iii is an exception), but simply a tutti reinforcement of the preceding bars. Secondly they normally end not with a trill cadencing into a tutti as described above, but rather as if they were *Eingänge*, leading into a thematic statement from the soloist; that is to say, they are rondo cadenzas.

Original cadenza material is available for all the slow movements that require cadenzas, and for all except three of the rondo finales which require cadenzas (K. 466, 467, and 482).

The cadenzas in the mature concertos are all of the inserted variety: even the rondo cadenzas are invariably preceded by a tutti passage. The same cannot be said of the seven concerto arrangements. The first, K. 37, does not require a first-movement cadenza at all, in which respect it is unique among Mozart's piano concertos; the first movements of the other arrangements all require inserted cadenzas in the normal way. The slow movement of K. 107 No. 1 and the finales of K. 37 and K. 41, however, require pre-tutti cadenzas, a type to which Mozart never returned in his mature piano concertos. Even in his arias Mozart seldom used pre-tutti or even extended types, preferring the more dramatic inserted cadenza (see below). This seems to have been largely a personal preference. It is certainly true that the inserted cadenza was becom-

---

[14] The exceptions are the finales of each of the later set of arrangements, K. 107.

ing more common, and the other types less so, but in view of the exceptional and almost exclusive use of inserted cadenzas in Mozart's music, it seems likely that he made a conscious choice to avoid the other types.

Mozart's Arias

It is interesting to observe a parallel between Mozart's abandonment of the cadenza in the slow movements of his concertos and a similar development in his arias. The early operatic works contain a fair number of da capo arias requiring a cadenza in both the main section and the middle section, making three in all in the course of the aria. In other arias the da capo scheme is not followed, and there may be only a single cadenza, or perhaps a second in a concluding fast section. Quite exceptional is the aria 'Jener Donnerworte Kraft' from *Die Schuldigkeit des ersten Gebots* (1767), in which the 'Posaunen- schall' of the Last Judgement is represented by a trombone obbligato. Not only are there the three cadenzas customary in a da capo aria, in this case duet cadenzas for voice and trombone, but there are a further three for solo trombone, one in the opening ritornello, and one in the ritornello which concludes the main section both first time round and in the da capo. It is rare to find provision for cadenzas in comic operas, although *La finta semplice* does require one.[15] The early *opere serie* contain an abundance of cadential ferma- tas, as might be expected, yet even in the *seria* works it is rare to find a cadential fermata in an aria written after 1780. *Idomeneo* contains only four cadential fermatas, as opposed to twenty-three in *Mitridate* (including all the da capos): *La clemenza di Tito* contains none at all.

A similar pattern may be observed in the individual concert arias which Mozart wrote fairly continuously throughout his life—the cadential fermatas virtually disappear after 1780. Most of the church music was written before 1780 in any case, but here too there are further examples of arias containing cadential fermatas. A late example is found in the 'Et Incarnatus' of the C minor Mass, K. 427 (417a, 1782–3) where Mozart supplies an obbligato vocal cadenza accompanied by a wind trio.[16] The overwhelming majority of

---

[15] It occurs at a subsidiary cadence in Fracasso's aria 'Nelle guerre d'amore'. It is interesting that Mozart originally intended to introduce a short ensemble cadenza for the three ladies at the end of the first number in *Die Zauberflöte*. See *NMA* II: 5/xix, p. 371, where the cadenza has been reconstructed, and also ibid. xvi f. Mozart's decision to abandon this 'cadenza in tempo' is in keeping with the general trend observed here.

[16] An even later example is found in the oratorio *Davide penitente*, K. 469 (1785), most of which consists of arrangements of movements from the C minor Mass. There are, however, two newly-composed arias, and one of these (no. 8) contains an inserted cadential fermata. Perhaps this is the exception which proves the rule. The short newly-composed passage for three solo voices inserted towards the end of the final chorus (no. 10) is often called a cadenza; it must be said, however, that there is a distinct lack of clear cadential preparation. Admittedly the change to solo voices draws attention to the insertion in this instance.

Mozart's vocal cadential fermatas are, like those of his concertos, of the inserted variety.

There are a number of reasons for the virtual disappearance of cadential fermatas from Mozart's arias around 1780. It was partly a matter of taste: da capo structures, extended ritornellos, and long cadenzas were becoming increasingly unfashionable in operatic circles, under the influence of the same ideals of dramatic verisimilitude which were responsible for the Gluckian reform and the rise of comic opera. There were also technical reasons; the abandonment of ritornello structures involved the removal of the most natural context for the insertion of cadenzas, and it is here that a parallel with the slow movements of concertos may be observed. It must also be said that the growth in scale which was taking place at around this time in both the ensemble cadenza and the keyboard cadenza could not possibly be emulated by a single unaccompanied voice; it is significant that by the time of composition of the C minor Mass Mozart was apparently thinking in terms of ensemble cadenzas in preference to unaccompanied solo cadenzas.

Mozart's Use of the Cadenza in Other Genres

If the most natural setting for a cadenza is in a ritornello framework, it might be expected that examples outside the aria/concerto repertory would be relatively rare. In Mozart's music, though, there are several genres which borrow certain elements of concerto style, the cadenza being one element that is occasionally borrowed. A case in point is the last of the organ sonatas, K. 336 (336d) in C, which closely resembles a one-movement concerto and even invites an ad libitum cadenza. Cadential fermatas are also found occasionally in some of the orchestral serenades involving solo instruments. Early examples of obbligato ensemble cadenzas occur in each of the first two movements of the Concertone, K. 190 (186E, 1774), and in the third movement of the Posthorn Serenade, K. 320, written five years later.[17] The Musical Joke, K. 522, is also provided with a written-out cadenza, this time for unaccompanied violin, and it is in fact the only solo violin cadenza by Mozart that is extant. Unfortunately it can hardly serve as a model to be imitated by those who seek to provide cadenzas for the violin concertos: Mozart makes the most of the opportunity to parody the efforts of violinists whose invention and intonation is not up to the task of improvising cadenzas —the last five bars, quoted in Ex. 44, illustrate the point.

Chamber music occasionally introduces concertante elements; for example, the Oboe Quartet, K. 370 (368b), requires an ad libitum cadenza in the slow movement, while the Quintet for Piano and Wind, K. 452, contains an

[17] As Walter Senn observes in the foreword to *NMA* IV: 12/v, p. xiv, the third and fourth movements of this serenade may be detached and performed as a symphonie concertante in their own right.

Ex. 44.   *W. A. Mozart, Musical Joke, K. 522, third movement*

obbligato cadenza for all five soloists in the finale. Obbligato rondo cadenzas are also found in the finales of the D major Violin Sonata, K. 306 (300l), and of the Piano Sonata in B flat, K. 333 (315c).

One genre that is quite unlike the concerto, but in which Mozart sometimes provides obbligato cadenzas nevertheless, is the variation for solo piano.[18] The function of the cadenza within variation form is at least partly to provide relief from the regular succession of equal rhythmic units, each following a more or less identical harmonic design. (This same function is sometimes fulfilled by extended finales, such as that found in Haydn's F minor Variations, Hob. XVII: 6.) Cadenzas provide an opportunity for a markedly freer display of virtuosity than can normally be achieved elsewhere in a set of variations. They also provide an opportunity for the composer to use contrasting material; whereas the majority of Mozart's concerto cadenzas, excepting one or two early ones, are thematically integrated into the movements to which they belong, the cadenzas found in his sets of variations seldom make any reference to the theme, which by this stage should be very familiar to the listener. The material of these cadenzas tends instead to be largely neutral passage-work (see below for a more detailed discussion).

[18] Cadenzas are included in the variations on 'Lison dormait', K. 264 (315d, 1778), on 'Salve tu Domine', K. 398 (416e, 1783), on 'Unser dummer Pöbel meint', K. 455 (1784), and on 'Ein Weib ist das herrlichste Ding', K. 613 (1791).

Why Did Mozart Write Ad Libitum Cadenzas?

Mozart's reasons for writing ad libitum cadenzas are not entirely clear. As noted earlier, Wolff takes issue with the widely held belief that they were written primarily for pupils or with a view to publication. The weight of evidence, he argues, suggests that they were written for Mozart's own use. It is true that didactic considerations were involved in certain cases, as for example in cadenzas 8 and 11 for K. 246, the 'Lützow' Concerto. Mozart wrote these cadenzas for the benefit of his pupil Therese Pierron, who performed the concerto in Mannheim in February 1778.[19] In the case of the multiple concertos, K. 242 and K. 365 (316a), the cadenzas had to be written down since cadenzas of this complexity could not be simultaneously improvised. There remain, however, a number of cadenzas written by Mozart for use in concertos which he reserved for himself to play and which he never prepared for publication, for example those to K. 450, K. 451, K. 459, and K. 595.

It is clear from the correspondence that he made a practice of sending copies of the concertos to his family in Salzburg, and also, though usually at a later date, copies of cadenzas and *Eingänge* to go with them. He was happy enough that the concertos should be performed by Nannerl, even though he often protected them scrupulously from wider circulation. It cannot have been necessary for him to send her cadenzas as well; unlike some of her brother's pupils, she would have been perfectly capable of supplying her own, and if she had needed any help, her father would have been there at hand. Mozart often delayed sending the cadenzas, and apologized in his letters for this, pleading an extremely busy schedule. In spite of this he found time to write down and dispatch cadenzas to his family eventually. By the 1780s cadenzas had reached proportions sufficient to allow the expression of a fair degree of individuality by the performer; the mere fact of Clementi's publication in 1787 of cadenzas in the styles of Mozart, Haydn, Vanhal, Kozeluch, Sterkel, and himself is evidence of this. It is likely, then, that Mozart regarded his cadenzas as personal property, even more so than the concertos, and that he wished to share them with his sister, but with no one else. If this explanation is correct, it is hard to account for the absence of cadenzas for six late concertos; Wolff's suggestion that the missing cadenzas may once have existed, and are simply lost,[20] seems plausible. Most of the extant manuscript sources of cadenzas can be traced back to Mozart's widow or to his family in Salzburg: a wider circulation would have been expected had they been written for pupils. The fact that some of the alternative cadenzas are evidently revisions of earlier versions suggests that Mozart had copies to hand. If the cadenzas had been tossed off lightly for the benefit of pupils, it is unlikely that Mozart would have been so anxious to preserve them and to protect them from wider circulation.

---

[19] He also provided a rudimentary realization of the continuo part to this concerto for her.
[20] 'Chronologie', p. 245.

The Content of Mozart's Piano Concerto Cadenzas

Eva and Paul Badura-Skoda concern themselves with the analysis of Mozart's written-out cadenzas specifically in order to extrapolate guidelines for the pianist who is faced with the task of supplying his own cadenzas to those concertos for which none by Mozart survives. Hence their aim is to discuss the most common features, the rule rather than the exception. They concentrate on thematic treatment and harmonic plan, since these are the crucial problems with which the intending composer-soloist has to deal. Since it is mostly in first movements that original cadenzas are missing in Mozart's piano concertos, the emphasis in the Badura-Skodas' book is on first-movement cadenzas.

The schema which they extrapolate from Mozart's original cadenzas, and which they recommend to those attempting to imitate them, is tripartite. An opening section, based either on an important theme from the concerto, or on the figure heard during the cadential preparation, or else on virtuoso passage-work which may or may not be derived from the movement, leads to a second section consisting of a thematic statement in the tonic, usually of a cantabile second subject. The transition from the first to the second sections is frequently marked by a fermata. The cantabile theme is not presented in its entirety, but is broken off at some point (i.e. it is 'fragmented') and extended sequentially, or perhaps with new harmonies, leading eventually to a return of the penultimate in the bass. The third section is devoted to virtuoso passage-work, frequently of a rhapsodic nature. The Badura-Skodas do not treat the return of the penultimate as an invariable indication of the start of the third section, presumably because the passage-work sometimes begins earlier, and the return of the penultimate often occurs late. Since it is such a common feature, however, it is convenient for present purposes to treat it as the start of the third section.

Harmonically the opening of the cadenza is usually presented over a tonic 6–4, and it works its way round to tonic 5–3 harmony for the second section. Examples are quoted by the Badura-Skodas of pedal-points and of descending bass-lines in opening sections.[21] The surprise continuation of the theme in the second section often involves unexpected harmonies, though the tonic is the only key to be firmly established at any point.[22] Attention is drawn to characteristic harmonies in the later part of the cadenza, such as a turn to the dominant of the dominant, or, alternatively, a move via a diminished seventh to the subdominant area. Finally a survey is made of Mozart's general harmonic vocabulary, primarily, it seems, because a frequent fault of nineteenth-century and later cadenzas written for Mozart's concertos is to overstep the limits customarily observed by Mozart in his choice of har-

---

[21] Badura-Skodas, *Interpreting Mozart*, pp. 219 ff.
[22] See J. P. Swain, 'Form and Function of the Classical Cadenza', *The Journal of Musicology*, 6/1 (Winter 1988), 37.

Ex. 45.   *W. A. Mozart, cadenza 62*

monies. The scheme is illustrated by ample references to the cadenzas under discussion, deviations from the pattern are mentioned, and extensive quotations are made. The whole of one of Mozart's mature first-movement cadenzas, namely no. 62, written for use in K. 595/i, is quoted here (Ex. 45) in order to provide an illustration of the tripartite scheme. The beginning of the second section is clearly recognizable (it is labelled 'X'); the return of the penultimate is indicated at the point 'Y'.

About half of Mozart's first-movement cadenzas, including most of those written in Vienna, can in fact be described fairly accurately in terms of the schema proposed by the Badura-Skodas. A more general historical survey, however, conducted without a specific practical aim, needs to take more account of deviations from this scheme, of the differences in character to be found in cadenzas belonging to slow movements and finales, and of Mozart's changing preferences from the time of his earliest-known cadenzas up to those of his Viennese years.

The Cadenzas of K^6 626a II

Since the cadenzas listed in Table 3 above have received little attention in previous critical literature, they will be considered first, and in rather greater detail than the more familiar examples. They are all included in *NMA* x: 28/ii, those written for the concerto arrangements appearing at the appropriate points in the scores of their respective concertos,[23] and the others in an appendix.[24]

Table 3 gives details of chronology and of the work for which each cadenza was intended, in so far as this is known. Cadenza C, for the first movement of K. 40, and cadenza K, for the slow movement of an unknown concerto by Beecke, survive in autographs, and were originally written on a single sheet of paper, later cut into two pieces and sold separately by Konstanze. Ernst Fritz Schmid[25] has dated these cadenzas to the summer or autumn of 1773, which predates the composition of any of the cadenzas listed in K^6 626a I. It is interesting that both are written without bar-lines, although cadenza C is written as if in common time throughout.[26] Lasting only ten 'bars' it is shorter than most of Mozart's later cadenzas. After the opening run (the only thematic reference in this cadenza) the remainder proceeds with uninterrupted semi-quaver figuration. The patterns used are simple enough and include some hand-crossing—a feature commonly found in Mozart's later cadenzas too, but more often than not in reference to figuration found in the concerto. Unlike most of the later examples, cadenza C is not articulated into separate sections. Although written some six years after the arrangement itself, it still predates the earliest of Mozart's original concertos, K. 175. For its date it is quite advanced in its use of idiomatic keyboard figuration, although there is as yet little sign of the ingenuity of the mature cadenzas.

Cadenza K is perhaps more interesting in that a measured (although unbarred) opening leads via a diminished seventh pause chord to a 'Recitativo'. The conclusion consists of a brilliant upward sweep of right-hand figuration, crowned with an expressive harmonized cadence. Since the concerto for which this cadenza was written appears to be lost, it is impossible to know whether the recitative is a reference to the parent movement, although Schmid[27] indicates that Beecke was known for his use of instrumental recitative, almost certainly learnt from C. P. E. Bach. So whether it is a direct reference to the movement or not, it seems likely at least to be a reference to Beecke's style. The only other instance of instrumental recitative in Mozart's cadenzas occurs in K^6 626a I: 17 and 18, where it is indeed a reference to

---

[23] pp. 101, 175, and 182.   [24] pp. 227 ff.

[25] E. F. Schmid, 'Schicksale einer Mozart-Handschrift', *M-Jb* (1957), 52.

[26] The *NMA* actually supplies editorial bar-lines.   [27] 'Schicksale', pp. 48 f.

an idea from the parent movement (the slow movement of K. 271 in both cases).

The only cadenza by Mozart which appears to be of still earlier date is that which appears last in Table 3—it is not listed in K^6.[28] Eduard Reeser[29] reports that it is found on the back of the last written page of the autograph of the concerto arrangement K. 40 (which suggests 1767 as its date of origin), originally written in pencil (apparently by Mozart) and partly written over by Leopold in ink. It is indeed curious; unbarred, it switches from three-crotchet groups to four-crotchet groups; although no key signature is indicated, it appears to move between D minor and D major, cadencing in the latter key. Largely because of its irregular metre Reeser assumes that it cannot have been intended as a cadenza for K. 40, and assigns it instead to an unknown concerto. Yet there seems to be no reason why a cadenza written in 1767 should observe the metre of the parent movement; as has been observed, even cadenza C written six years later contains no bar-lines, while cadenza K, also written in 1773, seems to begin in duple metre, in so far as its measured opening suggests any metre at all, rather than the triple metre of the parent movement.[30] As late as 1778, in the finale of the violin sonata, K. 306, Mozart writes an obbligato cadenza in a different metre from the parent movement. Given the location of this early cadenza on the back of the autograph of K. 40, it seems most probable that it was indeed intended for use in the first movement of this concerto (the other movements do not contain cadential fermatas).

The most awkward problem is not the irregular metre but the confusion of mode. Not only does it vacillate between the major and minor forms of the tonality, but it begins with a diminished seventh on G sharp. It was most unusual at this stage for a cadenza to begin with a harmony other than that of the penultimate. Possibly what we have here is an incomplete cadenza, lacking the beginning. If this is the case, then the problem of mode is solved—it would be quite in keeping with the harmonic idiom of the early classical period to explore the minor side of the tonality in the middle of the cadenza, although to do so at the beginning would be unusual. Unusual, but not entirely unknown, for C. P. E. Bach draws attention to a trap for the unwary accompanist whereby composers sometimes approach the cadenza in a piece written in the major mode by way of the minor mode.[31] In such cases the cadenza itself would be in the minor mode, but the chord of resolution after the cadential trill needs to be in the major mode. In the keyboard concerto repertoire, this procedure seems to have been very rare indeed, and it is certainly uncharacteristic of Mozart. A link with C. P. E. Bach does exist here, however. Not only is the style of the cadenza wild and improvisatory,

[28] It is quoted on p. 227 of *NMA* x: 28/ii as no. 1.   [29] *NMA* x: 28/ii, p. xiv.
[30] The approach to the penultimate is supplied in the source of the cadenza, from which it is evident that the movement was in 3/4.   [31] *Versuch*, ii. 264 f., *Essay*, p. 384.

suggesting Bach's fantasia idiom, but the finale of K. 40 is actually an arrangement of a short piece by Bach.[32] So it could well be that Mozart was using Bach's keyboard style as a model here.

Cadenzas A and B, written for the first two movements of K. 107 No. 1, are almost certainly later in date than the arrangement itself, now thought to date from 1772. Since the autographs of these cadenzas are lost,[33] attempts to establish the date of their composition must be based on stylistic considerations. It is thought that Mozart performed these concerto arrangements repeatedly,[34] and that the cadenzas were written for use in some of the later performances: it was frequently Mozart's practice to write new cadenzas when he revived a concerto, even when he had already composed cadenzas for the concerto in question.

Cadenza A opens metrically, but gives way to rhapsodic writing towards the end. The only reference to material from the movement occurs at the arrival of tonic 5–3 harmony in bar [4]. Although the material quoted is not a cantabile second theme but a passage in 'orchestral' style, it seems to mark an important division in the cadenza, in that it occurs at the first change of bass-note and of figuration. Hence it would be possible to describe cadenza A in terms of the Badura-Skodas' tripartite schema, although it lacks the clear articulation of the more mature cadenzas.

Cadenza B contains two references to the material of the parent movement: it opens with a transformation of an idea from the middle section, now in a new harmonic context, and it uses a tutti theme to articulate the return of tonic 6–4 harmony towards the end. The technique of fragmentation is used in bars [6]–[7] in a manner which suggests increasing assurance in Mozart's handling of the cadenza, and foreshadows certain traits familiar to us from Mozart's later cadenzas. Perhaps it was for concerto performances during the Mannheim–Paris journey of 1777–8 that Mozart wrote these cadenzas. At that time he had composed only four mature concertos, and he frequently had occasion to play and to teach these concertos to his pupils. The style of cadenzas A and B seems close to that of some of the cadenzas written for the original concertos around this time (e.g. nos. 5–7, 16, and 18), but they do not seem quite so advanced as those written during the early Viennese period.

The remaining cadenzas from K[6] 626a II are all thought to have been written for certain of the six concertos by Johann Samuel Schroeter published as Op. 3 in 1774.[35] G. de Saint-Foix claims that cadenzas D, F, G, and H were intended for use in 4/i, 6/i, 6/ii, and 1/i of the set respectively.[36] The use of themes or quotations from the movements named in the first three instances seems to confirm Saint-Foix's assertion beyond reasonable doubt. The suggestion that cadenza H belongs in 1/i, however, is somewhat puzzling, for the

---

[32] La Boehmer, H. 81.   [33] See *M-Jb* (1957), 57, Anm. 1.
[34] *NMA* x: 28/ii, p. xviii.
[35] J. S. Schroeter, *Six Concertos for the Harpsichord, or Piano Forte . . . Opera III* (London, Napier, 1774).   [36] See K[6], pp. 734 f.

movement named does not contain a cadential fermata. Since the publication of the incipits of cadenzas F, G, and H in K^3, the autographs have been lost and only the incipits remain.[37] The incipit given for cadenza H is unmetrical and athematic, unlike the openings of D, F, or G, but it is quite possible that a reference was made during the remainder of the cadenza to the material of 1/i from Schroeter's Op. 3. Since Saint-Foix had access to the autograph, his testimony must be respected, although the unusual circumstances mentioned must at least place a question mark over his assertion. While the autograph of cadenza D has survived, and can be dated *c*.1779 on the basis of sketches contained on the reverse, it is incomplete, breaking off during the second section. The first two sections, however, are clearly articulated, and the second, which quotes the second theme of the movement, is extended in a manner suggestive of Mozart's practice in the later cadenzas.

The most mature of the cadenzas from K^6 626a II are unquestionably N and O, which Reeser assigns to the first and second movements of the concerto Op. 3 No. 3 by Schroeter.[38] Cadenza N falls clearly into three parts, relying on a figuration borrowed from the development in the first section, and on the second theme of the movement in the second section. Cadenza O begins with a thematic reference, but soon wanders into flat keys, exploring rich chromatic harmonies and unusual dynamic contrasts. Its predominantly lyrical, flowing style renders a tripartite analysis less appropriate, as is often the case with slow-movement cadenzas.

It seems a shame that this attractive pair of cadenzas should be consigned to virtual oblivion simply because the concerto for which they were written is so seldom performed. The concertos from Schroeter's Op. 3 are pleasant enough, and it is easy to understand their great popularity at the time they were written. The existence of these cadenzas by Mozart seems as good a pretext as any for the revival of at least Op. 3 No. 3, the only one for which complete cadenzas are extant.

The Cadenzas of K^6 626a I

K. 242

The earliest cadenzas to be written for any of the mature concertos are the pair intended for use in K. 242, the Concerto for Three Pianos: they are included in the autograph score, and can thus be dated to 1776 with some confidence.[39] They contain little by way of thematic development, but they do rely heavily on quotation, a common feature of Mozart's later cadenzas. Bars [2]–[4], the second half of bar [5], and the first half of bar [6] in the slow-movement cadenza are taken almost note for note from the parent movement. In the first-movement cadenza, bars [4]–[7], while not an exact quotation, use a

---

[37] See *NMA* x: 28/ii, p. xiv.   [38] See *NMA* x: 28/ii, p. xiv.
[39] They are not actually listed in K^6 626a I.

pattern of figuration that features prominently in the development section, albeit altered here to suit a new harmonic context. This use of figuration borrowed from the movement is another characteristic of Mozart's cadenzas: figuration has the advantage of being adaptable to many different harmonic contexts. Some of the figuration in this cadenza, however, is new: the opening pattern, bars [1]–[3], and the closing material, bars [15]–[17]. Being ensemble cadenzas, these two are in a class apart from most of the others, and this may account for the lack of rhapsodic passage-work and the unusually heavy dependence on quotation. It is interesting to note that Mozart makes little or no use of thematic development here, although this was to be such a common feature of the later cadenzas.

K. 238

The next cadenzas to be written were nos. 5–7, one for each movement of K. 238, and these deserve a mention if only because their connections with the parent movements seem so far to have passed unnoticed. The broken-thirds figure in bars [2] and [5] of the first-movement cadenza is probably a reference to bars 183–4 in the movement. This might seem far-fetched were it not for the close proximity of the two passages: the cadenza begins in bar 191. It is of course common for a cadenza to open with a figure borrowed from the tutti immediately preceding it—here the figure is taken from just a little further back. The slow-movement cadenza does not, as the Badura-Skodas suggest,[40] open with a theme that is quite new, but with the characteristic rhythm of the transitional tutti, bars 41–4, a rhythm which also dominates the cadential preparation, so that the listener is likely to make the connection. If the melodic shape is unrecognizable, it is because the harmonic context at the beginning of the cadenza is new: the rhythm is so characteristic that it retains its identity irrespective of melodic shape. It also audibly resembles the rhythm of the second subject, bars 18 ff. Bars [6]–[8] of the slow-movement cadenza are a quotation of bars 50–2 of the movement with a new harmonization, reproducing the remarkable juxtaposition of triplet quavers with normal semiquavers. The finale cadenza again begins with a thematic reference —here it is a decorated and slightly modified version of the theme heard in bars 55–9 and in bars 207–11. The continuation is new, and the conclusion rhapsodic. It is probably Mozart's earliest rondo cadenza. All three cadenzas are between eleven and thirteen bars in length. They are slight indeed and can hardly be compared with the much more ambitious cadenzas of the 1780s. Nevertheless, certain features of Mozart's thematic techniques are here anticipated—notably quotation and harmonic transformation.

It is clearly neither possible nor appropriate in a book of this kind to discuss every Mozart cadenza individually. A useful insight into the development of

[40] *Interpreting Mozart*, p. 216.

his cadenza style during the 1780s, however, may be gained by studying some of the alternative sets, and noting the different ways in which often similar material is treated.

K. 246

There are three pairs of original cadenzas for the so-called 'Lützow' Concerto, two dating from the late 1770s and one from the 1780s.

Cadenzas 8 and 11, written for Therese Pierron and each lasting only four bars, make no use of material from their respective movements; cadenzas 9 and 12 are completely unbarred, again making no reference to the concerto material. The first-movement cadenzas, 8 and 9, are virtually solos for the right hand, while the slow-movement cadenzas, 11 and 12, are more idiomatically written for the keyboard. Brevity, right-hand predominance, lack of reference to material from the movement, and absence of bar-lines are common features of cadenzas written by other composers in the 1770s and even later. With the exception of some of the cadenzas written for K. 246 and some of the cadenzas listed in K^6 626a II, however, these characteristics are seldom found in Mozart's concerto cadenzas.

Cadenzas 10 and 14 are quite different from the above group. Both can be analysed in terms of the Badura-Skodas' tripartite schema, although no. 10 fits more conveniently into this pattern. It opens with a transformation of an idea used by the soloist as transition material, here, of course, presented over initial tonic 6–4 harmony. After a brief passage of dominant preparation, the second theme of the movement is introduced with its original harmonization, until a surprise diminished seventh chord at the end of bar [18] begins a move away from thematic quotation. The third section begins in bar [23], after a silent bar, with a literal quotation of three bars of passage-work taken from bars 177–9,[41] again differently continued, leading to some fast scales and the cadential trill.

When the difference between earlier and later sets is less marked than is the case with K. 246, it is possible to observe how Mozart has taken an earlier cadenza as a starting-point and reworked it. Wolff[42] discusses this process in order to arrive at criteria for establishing the relative chronology of alternative cadenzas in cases where source study provides no clue. The kinds of alterations made then serve as the basis for his deductions about Mozart's increasingly thematic approach to cadenza writing. It can be illustrated usefully with reference to the cadenzas for K. 271.

---

[41] This is closing material, originally stated in the dominant in bars 81–3.
[42] 'Chronologie', pp. 240 ff.

K. 271

The two cadenzas written for the first movement, nos. 15 and 16 (16 being the older), open in a similar fashion. The first section treats two ideas from the opening tutti in turn, but whereas no. 16 leads from this into eleven bars of amorphous passage-work using new material entirely, no. 15 follows the tripartite schema characteristic of the later cadenzas. A clearly articulated increase and decrease in rhythmic animation leads via a fermata to a statement of the cantabile second theme, which is extended in an unexpected flat sixth area after an interrupted cadence. An augmented sixth chord is used to return to a tonic 6–4, after which virtuoso runs usher in the conventional trill.

The slow-movement pair, 17 and 18 (18 being the older), stand in a similar relation to one another. Again there are slight improvements of detail in the later version but, more importantly, it is considerably longer and the dramatic element is made much more convincing. The parent movement is an impassioned C minor Andantino, containing some instrumental recitative which is quoted in both cadenzas. Where cadenza 18 uses a rather perfunctory run and a syncopated, chromatically rising chain of trills in bars [4]–[5] in order to effect a transition from the initial chromatic idea (previously unheard) to the quotation of recitative, no. 17 prolongs both the run and the chain of trills into much more powerful dramatic gestures. In no. 18 the trill chain occupies a single bar of a contrasting metre (common time instead of 3/4) and a contrasting tempo ('adagio' instead of 'andantino'); in no. 17, however, this single bar is expanded into four, the prevailing tempo and metre are maintained, the trills and the syncopations are presented successively rather than simultaneously, and the net result is a most effective acceleration and intensification of the rising chromatic line. If the rising chromatic idea in no. 18 was intended to mirror the descending chromatic line of the opening of the cadenza, it does so much more noticeably in the later version: in the earlier cadenza it seems to exist solely in order to effect a link with the ensuing recitative quotation. The recitative is also handled much more effectively in the later version, in which the intensity of the rising chromatic passage is followed by a moment of relief: during a prolongation of dominant harmony the second theme is stated, and this might be said to constitute the second section of the tripartite schema. The Neapolitan harmony of the recitative quotation then bursts in in bar [14] with a renewal of intensity. Its continuation is longer and again more dramatic than the equivalent passage in no. 18.

Ex. 46. *W. A. Mozart, cadenza 17*

Where the latter uses simple imitation and repetition to lead to the climax, cadenza 17 develops figure 'x' (Ex. 46) through various harmonies, and approaches the climactic diminished seventh in bar [23] via two others in the two preceding bars.

K. 456

Revision did not always involve expansion. Of the three cadenzas written for the first movement of K. 456, the second, no. 53, is considerably shorter than the first, no. 54, which contains a number of substantial quotations from the movement. Most of these are expunged from cadenza 53, in which new opening figuration and a fair amount of rhapsodic material is substituted, and only the second theme is retained out of the wealth of allusive material contained in cadenza 54. Wolff discusses the changes made to this second theme both in no. 53 and in the later no. 52. It is in fact on the basis of a comparison of the three forms of this passage that Wolff arrives at the relative chronology given here. Cadenza 53 is clearly based on no. 54 at this point, the passage being extended by an acceleration of harmonic rhythm through descending chromatic harmonies. The version of this passage found in no. 52 is extended even further. Bars [3]–[8] of cadenza 52 borrow the opening figuration of no. 53; at forty-one bars this latest cadenza is the longest of the three, and unlike no. 53 it contains numerous thematic references and borrowed figuration in addition to the theme common to all three cadenzas.

Both in the alternative cadenzas for K. 271/ii and in those for K. 456/i there are examples of material common to different cadenzas but absent from the movement itself. In the former case it is the syncopated trill chain, and in the latter the opening figuration of cadenzas 53 and 52. If cadenza 18 had not been discovered, it would be hard to account for bars [5]–[8] of cadenza 17, which would probably be dismissed simply as 'non-thematic', whereas they are in fact a reworking of material from an earlier cadenza. It must be said that most of the Viennese concerto cadenzas rely heavily on the parent movement for material. None the less, exceptions exist, of which the most striking is no. 61, the cadenza of K. 488/i, one of the few cadenzas to be included in the autograph of the parent concerto.

K. 488—An Interchangeable Cadenza?

The opening, Ex. 47a, has been thought to be a reference to some passage-work occurring early in the development section (bars 158–9 and 162–3, see Ex. 47b).[43] No other reference is made in the cadenza to material from the movement, and this particular reference is far from exact, involving a scrap of passage-work which occurs only twice, occupying a total of four bars early in the development. It should be pointed out that the opening of cadenza 61 also

---

[43] Badura-Skodas, *Interpreting Mozart*, p. 260.

Ex. 47. W. A. Mozart, (a) *cadenza 61*, (b) *Concerto in A, K. 488, first movement*, (c) *cadenza 27*

resembles a passage in cadenza 27 (see Ex. 47*c*) written for the first movement of K. 414 (385p), the other A major concerto. Cadenza 27 is known to have been written at around the same time as K. 488.[44] Comparison of Exx. 47*a*, 47*b*, and 47*c* reveals that Exx. 47*a* and 47*b* each have more features in common with Ex. 47*c* than they have with each other.

[44] A sketch for the clarinet parts in the later concerto occurs as an addendum to the autograph of cadenzas 27, 32, and 34.

It would be straining the evidence somewhat to suggest that Ex. 47*c* was consciously used by Mozart as a source for both Ex. 47*a* and Ex. 47*b*, given that there could be no possible reason for doing so. It does not seem too far-fetched, however, to suggest that having written cadenza 27, the figure from Ex. 47*c* remained on his mind, and that both Exx. 47*a* and 47*b* owe their particular morphology to this haunting idea. It is suggested, accordingly, that Ex. 47*a* should not be considered as a reference to material from the movement at all, but simply as an instance of some characteristic Mozartian figuration.

It might be thought that in writing the cadenza into the score, Mozart was asserting the authority of the composer by prescribing an obbligato version of the cadenza. But there are problems with this interpretation. The work was apparently written for Mozart to perform himself at a subscription concert, probably in March 1786. We know from Mozart's correspondence that the concerto, one of five offered to Prince Josef Maria Benedikt of Donaueschingen, had not been widely circulated, and that Mozart did not wish it to be released.[45] Nor was it published during Mozart's lifetime, and it appears therefore that far from wishing to impose a particular cadenza on those who performed the work, he did not wish it to be publicly performed at all, other than by himself. The autograph of the score predates the correspondence with the prince of Donaueschingen, so there can be no question of the cadenza having been included for his sake. When other performers began to play the concerto after Mozart's death, they did not hesitate to supply their own cadenzas.

The lack of any reference to material from the movement may provide a clue to Mozart's reasons for including cadenza 61 in the autograph score of K. 488. It is just possible that Mozart originally intended to offer the concerto for sale, included the cadenza in the score for the benefit of potential amateur purchasers, and later changed his mind. In the absence of any documentary evidence to support this hypothesis it must remain extremely tentative, but it does at least offer an explanation both for the inclusion of the cadenza in the score and for its non-thematic construction. If, as suggested earlier, Mozart customarily reserved his cadenzas for the intimate family circle, it makes sense that a cadenza offered to the public should be in a less personal style, conforming more to the prevailing taste.

If the majority of Mozart's cadenzas for his Viennese concertos can legitimately be said to refer to material from the parent movements, it is necessary to distinguish between the different ways in which this borrowed material is treated. Paul Mies draws attention to the contrast between Mozart's approach and Beethoven's.[46] Where Beethoven concentrates on a single principal motivic idea, subjecting it to rigorous and extended developmental treatment,

---

[45] See *NMA* v: 15/vii, p. vii.   [46] *Krise*, pp. 54 ff.

Mozart draws on a wide range of secondary ideas, often avoiding his main theme altogether. His technique is more often one of quotation and juxtaposition than of development, although the latter is certainly found as well. Juxtaposition is not only used for surprise effect. The opening of cadenza 57 to K. 456/iii presents in smooth succession a detail from the rondo theme and a quotation from the end of the last solo. This illustrates well the fluency with which Mozart was able to construct cadenzas out of a variety of borrowed material.

The Beethovenian concentration on a single idea, extensively manipulated, is more characteristic of Mozart's rondo cadenzas, however, and nowhere more clearly than in cadenza 60 to K. 459/iii. Admittedly the main theme does not appear until half-way through, but from this point it is absent for scarcely a bar, appearing even underneath the cadential trill. In cadenza 64 to K. 595/iii the opening idea is also treated at length, and combined with an idea heard previously only in an (ad libitum) *Eingang*[47]—a further example of Mozart's use of ideas derived from other ad libitum insertions in addition to those taken from the parent movement. Imitative entries, such as those which open cadenza 24 to K. 365/iii, and the fugato from cadenza 47 to K. 451/iii are among the devices which may be newly applied in a rondo cadenza. It would be unusual to find such intensive thematic treatment in one of Mozart's first-movement cadenzas.

Slow-movement cadenzas are less likely than first-movement cadenzas to fall into the tripartite schema, if only because virtuoso runs and passage-work, the usual articulating material of the schema, would be out of place in a slow-movement cadenza. Thus there tends to be greater continuity between one section and another; while some slow-movement cadenzas, such as no. 17 to K. 271/ii, discussed in detail above, could be said to fall into a tripartite plan, in others the joins between sections are so smooth as to render this analytical model inappropriate.

There remains the question of metre in Mozart's mature cadenzas. As has been pointed out, very few do without bar-lines altogether. There are some which retain metrical freedom to the extent that they contain isolated bars in a different time-signature from the remainder of the cadenza—nos. 2 and 18 are examples. Significantly both of these cadenzas exist in later versions (nos. 1 and 17) which avoid the change of metre by judicious reworking of the passage in question. The trend to be observed is towards greater metrical integration with the parent movement. None the less, the later cadenzas make more use than the earlier ones of rhapsodic material and of fermatas. There are two reasons for this: an impression of improvisatory freedom is thereby retained, but at the same time these passages serve to articulate the tripartite division so characteristic of the later cadenzas—spontaneity and coherence are thus combined.

---

[47] K[6] 626a I no. 63.

The very fact that it has been possible here to discuss the style of Mozart's mature concerto cadenzas in general terms illustrates the essential truth of the assumption made by the Badura-Skodas, namely that a degree of standardization obtains in the procedures used, as a result of which it is possible to imitate Mozart's cadenza style. It should be stressed that the standard pattern which the Badura-Skodas describe applies principally to first-movement cadenzas written in Vienna, and to a somewhat lesser extent to slow-movement and rondo cadenzas from the same period. It has been shown that the earlier cadenzas tend not to follow this pattern. Nor in fact do the cadenzas written for works in other genres. It may be salutary to survey these briefly, lest such 'exceptional' cadenzas as the non-thematic no. 61, or the predominantly 'in tempo' pair of cadenzas for K. 242 with their heavy reliance on quotation, be thought more unusual than in fact they are.

The Content of Mozart's Obbligato Cadenzas outside the Keyboard Concerto Repertory

As mentioned earlier there are obbligato ensemble cadenzas in each of the first two movements of the Concertone, K. 190, and in the third movement of the Posthorn Serenade, K. 320. Characteristically for ensemble cadenzas, each of these examples is in tempo throughout (there is just a brief pause over a rest in K. 190/i and K. 320). The cadenza in the Posthorn Serenade is unique in Mozart's work for its use of full orchestral forces: both the string ripieno and the wind concertino take part. Like several other written-out ensemble cadenzas, it is unusually long (over a fifth of the length of the movement) and consists largely of exact quotations from the movement. The opening (itself a quotation of bars 19–22) takes the form of a point of imitation with five entries at one-bar intervals—one for each of the solo woodwind instruments. This in itself makes for a degree of metrical regularity seldom found in a solo cadenza, and it is a direct consequence of the relatively large number of participating soloists. The finale cadenza in the Quintet for Piano and Wind, K. 452, also begins with a point of imitation which produces a similar effect of metrical regularity.[48] Unlike the quintet cadenza, however, in which an improvisatory effect is maintained by the avoidance of thematic allusions, the cadenza in the serenade includes a quotation of the main theme of the movement in its original form (apart from one or two details, such as a pizzicato instruction in the lower strings!). In a curious way this cadenza seems to foreshadow the integrated finale cadenzas of Viotti's late violin concertos, with their orchestral participation, and the inclusion in most cases of a statement of the rondo theme about half-way through (see Chapter 11).

Metrical regularity, insistent imitation of a brief motivic idea, and a

---

[48] This cadenza also lasts for over a fifth of the movement.

substantial element of direct quotation may be observed even more clearly in the obbligato cadenza for voice and wind trio in the 'Et Incarnatus' of the Mass in C minor, K. 427. The imitations occur during the first half of the cadenza: a scalic figure which had appeared earlier as part of a vocal melisma is stated eleven times, with no alteration in shape. It forms a rising sequence, and then descends again over a tonic pedal which itself joins in the imitations. There follows a long quotation (bars 101–9 in the wind parts are virtually identical to bars 7–15), to which a vocal counterpoint is added, and this leads straight to the cadential trill.

One obbligato cadenza that uses entirely new material is found in the rondo finale of the D major Sonata for Violin and Piano, K. 306. This work was written in Paris in 1778, and it seems to betray the influence of some of the rather mechanical ensemble cadenzas popular in Paris at the time in the works of Rigel and others (see Chapter 10). It is another long cadenza, lasting for forty-five bars of common time (i.e. over a fifth of the length of the movement). It is not even written in the same metre as the movement, which alternates between 2/4 and 6/8. Rather empty patterns of figuration, including numerous runs in thirds and even a chain of trills in thirds, fill these forty-five bars in what can best be described as a scintillating and light-hearted display of virtuosity. This was the last of a set of six sonatas which Mozart published in Paris—it shows him as ever to be a master at reproducing a newly encountered idiom. The cadenza in the Quintet, K. 452, makes no reference to material from the movement either, but it is saved from the monotony of the cadenza in the Violin Sonata by its greater harmonic and contrapuntal interest.

If the somewhat diffuse non-thematic cadenza of the Violin Sonata, K. 306, has few counterparts among the cadenzas discussed so far, it stands much closer to those which occur in the sets of piano variations. Two instances, found in the variations on 'Lison dormait' and in those on 'Salve, tu Domine', are not even metrical, least of all thematic. Lasting respectively four and a half and six lines of music (roughly equivalent in each case to about thirty bars), they are quite lengthy, extremely brilliant, and perhaps closer to a genuinely improvisatory style than any of the ad libitum cadenzas written for the concertos.

The cadenza occurring in the variations on 'Unser dummer Pöbel meint', K. 455, is the longest of all Mozart's cadenzas, lasting for sixty-one bars, of which the first six are in common time and the remainder in 3/8, the metre of the preceding variation. The opening six bars constitute an introductory flourish; the change of time-signature brings with it a return to the 3/8 version of the theme, now presented as a one-bar rhythmic motive, and extensively developed through various flat keys. The length of this cadenza matches the overall proportions of the work. If all repeats are included, the piece is over 400 bars long, and some relief is needed from the metrical and harmonic regularity intrinsic to the variation form. This cadenza is introduced in a similar way to that of the Concert Rondo in D, K. 382, itself effectively a set of variations, the only justification for the label 'rondo' being the repetition of the theme between each variation. In both cases, the cadenza occurs during an extension of a 3/8 variation, and constitutes the only departure from the regular succession of equal rhythmic units characteristic of the variation form.

Some obbligato cadenzas do develop thematic material in the manner characteristic of the ad libitum keyboard cadenzas, however. The example which comes closest to keyboard concerto style is the rondo cadenza from the finale of the Piano Sonata in B flat, K. 333, composed in the early Viennese years. The whole movement is written in deliberate imitation of concerto style, and it contains quasi-orchestral passages which articulate the various solo episodes just as if the piece were a reduction of an orchestral score. Thus it is not surprising that the cadenza should be constructed along the same lines as those of the Viennese concertos. Uncharacteristically for a rondo cadenza, it dismisses the rondo theme fairly soon, after this has been stated successively over tonic major and tonic minor 6–4 harmony; the intensive motivic treatment customary in rondo cadenzas is reserved for a three-quaver rhythmic figure borrowed from the quasi-orchestral passages in the rondo. This figure makes its first appearance in the cadenza during a five-bar quotation of just such a passage, which is followed by motivic development of the three-note figure. The conclusion of the cadenza illustrates well the distinction between a first-movement cadenza and a rondo cadenza. The conventional trill with which a first-movement cadenza would normally have ended is carried an octave higher by a demisemiquaver run, but instead of repeating the trill in this register and cadencing into a tutti, Mozart introduces a four-note descending figure, repeated over and over again, a step lower each time in gradually longer note-values, in order to lead to a simple solo thematic restatement.

Non-thematic cadenzas, then, occur rather more frequently outside the concerto repertory than within it. While cadenza 61 may be unusual in its lack of thematic allusion, it appears less so when considered in the context of the Viennese compositions in other genres. Mozart's ensemble cadenzas differ in a number of respects from those written for solo keyboard concertos; points of imitation give rise to a higher degree of rhythmic regularity, and when this is combined with an intensive preoccupation with a single idea, largely unaltered in shape, such as is found in the cadenza to the Posthorn Serenade or that of the 'Et Incarnatus' from the C minor Mass, the result is highly patterned and anything but spontaneous. The closest counterparts of these ensemble cadenzas in the keyboard cadenza repertory are those written for the multiple concertos, namely K. 242 and K. 365. In these a more regular construction than is normally found in Mozart's concerto cadenzas is achieved by means of quotation, the use of borrowed figuration, and (in the finale cadenza) successive imitative entries. The textural freedom of keyboard writing does, however, allow Mozart a certain amount of rhapsodic passage-work, and even, in no. 24 to K. 365/iii, some genuine motivic development. Perhaps the most important lesson to be learnt from this brief consideration of Mozart's obbligato cadenzas outside the keyboard concerto repertory is the great variety of his approach, which may serve as a corrective against too general a categorization of his cadenza style. Between the extremes of the wild rhapsodic 'Salve tu Domine' cadenza, which is labelled in the score 'Cadenz Capriccio', and the patterned regularity of the cadenza to the Posthorn Serenade, made up almost exclusively of quotations, practically all intermediate stages can be found.

Conclusions

Mozart's work represents the heyday of the classical cadenza. The ensemble cadenza and the idiomatic keyboard cadenza both feature prominently in his output. Whereas most of C. P. E. Bach's keyboard cadenzas suggest the idiom of transcription in their limited scope, Mozart's are genuinely pianistic and correspondingly larger in scale. Nevertheless the higher-level function of the cadenza—the articulation of a structural cadence—is never obscured. The limited tonal range of Mozart's cadenzas ensures that the underlying harmonic progression is clarified. The character of an insertion is always preserved by clear articulation at the beginning—witness the overwhelming preference for inserted cadenzas over pre-tutti ones—and in most cases also by a long cadential trill at the end, although the rondo cadenzas, which are followed by a thematic statement, are less clearly articulated at this point.

The virtual disappearance of cadential fermatas from Mozart's vocal works after 1780 is matched by a consolidation of thematic technique in his concerto cadenzas. In other words his instrumental cadenzas became more substantial than it was possible for the unaccompanied vocal cadenza to be. The vocal cadenza had had its heyday a little earlier and was now becoming unfashionable, as newer dramatic ideals derived from comic opera and the Gluckian reform began to influence even works to Metastasio's libretti, such as *La clemenza di Tito*. Yet no such considerations of dramatic verisimilitude interfered with the use of ritornello structures and extended cadenzas in the concerto—so it was possible to continue the older operatic tradition in instrumental music.

Mozart's cadenzas range from wild rhapsodic virtuoso flourishes to ingeniously worked out thematic constructions. The general trend to be observed, however, from the earlier examples to the later Viennese ones, is of an increasing emphasis on thematic construction and regular metre. Rhapsodic passages are not altogether excluded, at least not from the keyboard examples, where they help to preserve the effect of improvisation. Rather than destabilizing the structure, these passages serve to clarify it. The increasingly common tripartite division ensures that improvisatory virtuosity can coexist with thematic development, borrowed figuration, quotations, and new juxtapositions, within an ordered scheme that provides an effective peroration.

At the same time, however, thematic integration marked the beginning of the end of the classical cadenza. If Mozart never asserted the claims of the composer over those of the soloist to the extent of prescribing an obbligato cadenza in a solo concerto, the use of thematically integrated ad libitum cadenzas pointed in this direction. Viotti's and Beethoven's much more closely integrated cadenzas tended to obscure the character of insertion, and made the eventual abandonment of the ad libitum cadenza inevitable.

9

Haydn and the Cadenza

MOST of Haydn's keyboard concertos were written quite early in his career, and many of them are slight works, case in a *galant* idiom close to that of the concertos of Wagenseil or Hofmann. Consequently, received opinion has not rated him highly as a composer of concertos. While a manuscript alleged to contain original ad libitum cadenzas for use in these concertos is located in the library of the Gesellschaft der Musikfreunde in Vienna,[1] its authenticity is considered doubtful.[2] It might be expected, therefore, that Haydn could be of little interest to such a survey as this. In fact what makes him interesting is not so much his use of the cadenza in concertos, but rather his adventurous use of concerto-like gestures in other works, which not infrequently include cadenzas or cadenza-like passages. Lesser composers, or those with less interest in trying out unusual formal procedures or playing tricks on the listener, are less likely to attempt such devices as introducing a cadenza unexpectedly.

There are, for example, a number of cadenzas in Haydn's symphonies. The best-known is probably the one occurring in the slow movement of Symphony No. 7, 'Le Midi', a movement in which the solo violin and the solo cello are treated in a concertante manner throughout. Since this movement is preceded by an instrumental recitative for solo violin and orchestra, it is strongly suggestive of a recitative and aria, and it is in this context that the duet cadenza is best explained. It is quite long for its date (1761), but in the circumstances this too is easily explained: Haydn had only recently been appointed Kapellmeister to the Esterházy court at Eisenstadt, and in the three descriptive symphonies nos. 6–8 ('Le Matin', 'Le Midi', and 'Le Soir'), he was deliberately taking the opportunity to display both his own versatility and skill and that of his new orchestra.

Concertante writing in symphonies was something to which Haydn returned from time to time throughout his life. The slow movement of no. 102 offers a late example—it contains an elaborate and expressive part for solo cello—although in this instance there is no cadenza. The slow movement of no. 24, however, is written as a flute solo, just as if it were the slow movement of a concerto, complete with cadential fermata. Rather more unusual, perhaps, is the slow movement of Symphony No. 54, in which an obbligato cadenza is apparently performed not by a soloist or soloists, but by the entire

---

[1] Q 13156 (VII 16810). See *JHW* xv: 2. 200.
[2] See H. C. R. Landon, *Haydn: Chronicle and Works*, ii. *Haydn at Esterháza: 1766–1790* (London, 1978), 571 f.

violin section.[3] There are actually two cadenzas in this movement (the longest
slow movement in any of Haydn's symphonies):[4] a subsidiary cadenza lasting
five bars before the 'middle ritornello' and a final cadenza lasting seventeen
bars before the 'final ritornello'. An obbligato cadenza for wind soloists is
found in the slow movement of no. 87, while that of no. 96 contains an
obbligato cadenza in which the whole orchestra participates.

It must suffice to mention in passing some of the places where cadenzas are
used in other non-concerto genres. The string quartets contain a number of
cadential fermatas, although there do not appear to be any written-out
cadenzas. The fermatas occur mostly in movements where the first violin has
received markedly soloistic treatment, and it is significant that as many as five
out of the six quartets from Op. 9, the set written soon after Haydn's arrival at
Eisenstadt where Tomasini would have played the first violin part, contain
cadential fermatas in the slow movements. The latest example occurs in the
aria-like slow movement of the Quartet Op. 33 No. 6. The baryton trios
contain a number of cadential fermatas as well as some obbligato cadenzas.
The challenge presented to Haydn by this uninspiring medium, in which he
had to compose such a huge quantity of music, led him to explore various new
techniques and novel procedures, including the incorporation of concerto-
like features such as the cadenza. Both cadential fermatas and written-out
cadenzas are found in some of the earlier keyboard sonatas, and here it seems
reasonable to point directly to the influence of C. P. E. Bach. Haydn is known
to have been greatly stimulated by those of Bach's keyboard sonatas which he
discovered as a young man in Vienna during the 1750s.[5] Isolated later
examples of cadential fermatas in his piano sonatas are normally found in
movements modelled directly on concerto form (e.g. Hob. XVI: 46/ii, 39/ii).

With regard to vocal cadenzas a similar pattern may be observed to that
discussed in connection with Mozart; that is to say cadential fermatas occur
frequently in the earlier more old-fashioned da capo arias, but seldom in the
later arias which show a greater influence from the sonata style and make less
use of ritornello structures. This may be illustrated particularly clearly by a
comparison between the original version of Haydn's first oratorio, *Il ritorno di
Tobia* (1774–5), in which every aria contains at least one cadential fermata,
and *The Creation*, written over twenty years later, in which there are none at
all. (There are in any case significantly fewer arias in *The Creation*.) The
revisions made to *Il ritorno* for the 1784 performance already indicate the way

[3] Landon, however, suggests that the parts may have been played soli throughout (*Haydn at
Esterháza*, p. 308). That solo violins were not the norm in the Esterháza orchestra is nevertheless
quite clear from the scoring of the last movement of the Farewell Symphony, written only two
years before no. 54. Here the violins divide into four, and it is intended that only two solo violins
should remain at the end, effecting a noticeable reduction from the full violin section.
[4] Landon, *Haydn at Esterháza*, p. 308.
[5] See *Haydn: Two Contemporary Portraits*, ed. and trans. V. Gotwals (Madison, 1968), 12,
95 f.

that the tide was turning.[6] Haydn abbreviated the score in numerous places, shortening ritornellos and very often omitting both the cadential fermata and the preceding tutti.[7] He also wrote a pair of alternative cadenzas for each of two tenor arias in a manuscript which contains some highly ornamented versions of the arias in question.[8] The motive for the alterations was not so much a desire to eliminate the cadenza as to reduce the number that were performed, so that those remaining would function more effectively as virtuoso climaxes. The indiscriminate use of the cadenza in every aria in the original version had weakened the dramatic impact of individual cadenzas.

It is clear from an examination of the works discussed so far that Haydn was familiar both with the cadenza and with the conventions surrounding its use, and that the use of extended cadenzas with some harmonic variety was part of his style. He was also familiar with the various methods of placing the cadential fermata which were current at the time; whereas all three movements of the Concerto in D for Corno di Caccia and Orchestra (1762) contain inserted cadential fermatas, most of the examples from his keyboard concertos are either of pre-tutti or tutti-reinforced cadenzas of some kind. This should serve as a warning against overhasty conclusions about Haydn's relatively sparing use of cadenzas in his keyboard concertos.

Haydn's Use of the Cadenza in Keyboard Concertos

In the three harpsichord concertos (Hob. XVIII: 3, 4, and 11) there is a tutti-reinforced cadential fermata in each of the first two movements. The G major Concerto (Hob. XVIII: 4) also contains a hidden cadenza in the finale beginning in bar 214 (see Ex. 4). While this seems to be the only example of an obbligato cadenza in any of the keyboard concertos, it does not appear particularly exceptional when viewed in the context of Haydn's other music. Numerous examples of obbligato cadenzas have been noted elsewhere in Haydn's work; and the concertos for *lira organizzata*, written for the King of Naples (*c*.1786), also contain extended 'cadenzas in tempo'.

It is interesting to note that at least one near-contemporary of Haydn failed to recognize this passage as a cadenza, and actually interpreted the fermata in bar 256 as an invitation to supply an ad libitum cadenza. Horst Walter's edition of these concertos includes in an appendix an assortment of cadenzas found in manuscript sources of the concertos;[9] a Kroměříž source of the G

---

[6] See E. F. Schmid, 'Haydn's Oratorium "Il Ritorno di Tobia", seine Entstehung und seine Schicksale', *Archiv für Musikwissenschaft*, 16 (1959), 292 ff.

[7] These revisions are indicated in the score, ed. E. F. Schmid, *JHW* XXVIII: 1 (Munich, 1963).

[8] 'Quando mi dona un cenno' and 'Quel felice nocchier'. See *JHW* XXVIII: 1 and Schmid, 'Haydn's Oratorium'. [9] *JHW* XV: 2. 159 ff.

major Concerto contains cadenzas for all three movements! Given the fact that the cadenza has already occurred at this point, the only form of improvisation that might be appropriate here would be a very simple embellishment of the two cadential chords.

The only instances of cadential fermatas in any of the authentic organ concertos[10] are found in the slow movement of the C major Concerto, Hob. XVIII: 1, and in each of the first two movements of Hob. XVIII: 6, the Double Concerto for Organ and Violin.[11]

The cadenzas quoted by Walter in the *Joseph Haydn Werke* edition vary considerably in scope and length, and afford an interesting illustration of the great variety of solutions that were evidently adopted within a few decades of the composition of the concertos.[12] Some are long and rambling, others are much more tightly constructed. Most of the first-movement cadenzas for the D major Concerto make some use of motivic material from the parent movement.

Mention should also be made of the manuscript of keyboard cadenzas 'del Sigr. Giuseppe Hayden' shelved in the Gesellschaft der Musikfreunde in Vienna as Q 13156 (VII 16810). This manuscript contains ten cadenzas, without any indication of the works or movements for which they were intended. It seems likely that cadenza 7 in A major was intended for the slow movement of Hob. XVIII: 11, since the opening figure so closely resembles the main theme of the movement, although cadenza 3 is also in A major and is therefore a possible alternative.[13] Only one cadenza, no. 4 in B flat, cannot be matched with any authentic concerto movement by Haydn in the same key.

The average length of these cadenzas is between seven and eight lines of music. They exhibit a pleasing variety of pace, figuration, harmony, and metre, achieved in spite of the lack of any obvious thematic references. Many different types of idiomatic keyboard figuration are used, and the invention flags only occasionally, when slightly mechanical patterns are extended for a little too long.

If these cadenzas are by Haydn, they are not unworthy of him. One possible argument against their authenticity would be that there is no sign here of Haydn's delight in the art of the surprise, the unexpected silence, the sudden rhythmic or harmonic twist: is it not likely that Haydn would have made

---

[10] i.e. Hob. XVIII: 1, 2, and 6—see the work-list supplied by G. Feder for the article 'Haydn' in *Grove*.

[11] Two pairs of 18th-cent. cadenzas for this concerto are preserved in manuscript copies, and they are reproduced in *Konzert in F-Dur*, ed. H. Schultz (Kassel, etc., 1959), 36 ff.

[12] Dating these cadenzas is virtually impossible, since they are preserved separately from the concertos. Stylistically none of them appears to have been written more recently than the early 19th cent.; moreover it is most unlikely that these concertos would have continued to be performed for long after Haydn's death.

[13] It was in fact cadenza 3 which was chosen for inclusion in the Eulenburg miniature score of this concerto (London, 1949; repr. 1977). The Peters edn. of the concerto arranged for two pianos (Leipzig, 1931) contains cadenzas 3, 5, 7, and 10.

particularly striking use of such devices had he been the composer of these cadenzas? Even Clementi's 'Cadenza alla Haydn' (see Ex. 58) is a little more 'Haydnesque' in its insistence on a tiny rhythmic cell which is carried through various chromatic harmonies in the passage leading to the return of the penultimate. Yet perhaps it is wrong to expect Haydn's cadenzas to be like this. Unlike Mozart, Haydn was not an outstanding performer and is likely to have felt that the style of the ad libitum cadenzas performed in his concertos was not his concern, but that of the performers. For anyone to imitate his personal style might have affronted or amused him, but it is hardly likely that he would have expected it. It is indeed difficult to see for what reason he might have written ad libitum cadenzas for his concertos, unless he did so for pupils or amateur performers. Numerous instances have been discussed of Haydn's use of surprise in the way that he introduces cadential fermatas, and here he is on home territory, acting *qua* composer and not *qua* performer. Might it not have been trespassing on the territory of the performer to write ad libitum cadenzas in a markedly personal style?

10

Outside Germany and Austria

Italy

MUSICAL life in Italy, unlike that in France and England, was not centred around a single capital city with a flourishing concert industry. Nor did Italy possess a centre of music publishing comparable with London or Paris through which the works of Italian composers could be widely disseminated. The keyboard concerto was not an indigenous genre, and while it was not entirely neglected, it received far less attention from Italian composers than from German, and the potential audience was far smaller than in London or Paris, where concert-going was an established tradition. Many of the extant keyboard concertos by Italian composers were in fact written and published outside Italy.

Little wonder then, that relatively little space is devoted to the Italian keyboard concerto in histories of the genre.[1] It must be admitted that not only the quantity, but also the general quality of these works is not particularly high. At their best the Italian concertos are as good as many of the lighter South German and Austrian examples. Indeed one of the concertos long held to be by Galuppi is in fact by Haydn.[2]

One consequence of the paucity of published source material in the area of the Italian keyboard concerto is that it is hard to date the concertos which are extant. Almost certainly some of those by Padre Martini, conveniently dated by the composer, are among the earliest. He wrote at least five keyboard concertos, of which the D major Concerto edited in *I classici musicali italiani*[3] was written in 1746. It is the G major Concerto, however, which invites a cadential improvisation, and it does so at the final solo cadence in the first movement—a bar of dominant harmony. In one recent edition of this work[4] a highly anachronistic editorial cadenza is supplied,[5] with no indication that the cadenza is editorial. Whatever view is taken as to the style of cadenza that is appropriate in modern performances of these works, it must surely be agreed the some clear indication is necessary when a cadenza is published that is not

---

[1] e.g. in H. Engel, *Das Instrumentalkonzert*, 2 vols. (Wiesbaden, 1971–4), the Italian keyboard concerto is discussed in a little over one page.
[2] Hob. XVIII: 2.   [3] Vol. ii, Milan, 1943.   [4] E. Desderi (ed.), Padua, 1971.
[5] It is too harmonically active and too thematic for a concerto written as early as 1752, and it ends with a series of double trills on various degrees of the dominant 7th chord, concluding with trills on C and D simultaneously.

contained in any of the sources. Unfortunately, though, unacknowledged editorial suggestions and interpretations are very common where cadenzas are concerned.

Other Italian composers who wrote keyboard concertos include Galuppi, Jommelli, Gazzaniga, Paisiello, Pellegrino, Rutini, and Felici.[6] Cadential fermatas appear to be equally distributed between first and second movements, and to occur rather less frequently in finales, though more often than was found to be the case in German concertos.

It has been claimed that two solo sonatas by Galuppi contain 'cadenzas', namely Op. 1 No. 2 in D minor and Op. 2 No. 3 in E minor,[7] which were published by Walsh in 1756 and 1759 respectively. In the case of the former, this seems simply to refer to some bravura semiquaver figuration which is used at various points in the movement, but the latter does indeed contain a remarkably brilliant insertion towards the end. Dramatically prepared, by means of a series of interrupted cadences in which the music is wrenched out of C major into D minor and thence to E minor, it is launched from a Phrygian cadence in E minor, with a fermata marked over the B major chord, followed by a rest. Toccata-like, it consists entirely of semiquaver figuration, mostly arpeggiated, exploring sequences, suspensions involving ninth chords, and a number of diminished seventh harmonies, without ever ranging far from E minor. Twenty-eight bars in common time are followed by nine in 3/4, after which a ritornello-like statement of the opening theme brings the work to a close. The patterned nature of the figuration, the harmonic interest, the size of the insertion, and especially the change of metre towards the end, all point towards the tradition of the capriccio rather than that of the cadenza. Galuppi was a Venetian, and would therefore certainly have been familiar with Vivaldi's concertos, and probably with Locatelli's as well. The cadential fermatas in Galuppi's concertos could scarcely be interpreted as invitations to supply outbursts such as this; once again the use of the term 'cadenza' to describe the passage proves to be misleading.

England

The keyboard concerto in England during the eighteenth century was strongly influenced by the towering figure of Handel. Not until the arrival of several continental *galant* composers during the last third of the century did Handel's influence abate at all noticeably. It seems, though, that keyboard cadenzas in England, while greatly stimulated by the example of the *galant* foreigners, were not unknown to the older native tradition.

---

[6] The harpsichord concerto attributed to Boccherini in D-Dlb Mus 3490-O-7 is actually by F. X. Pokorny. The autograph is D-Rtt Pokorny 149.

[7] W. S. Newman, *The Sonata in the Classic Era*, 2nd edn. (New York, 1972), 198.

The Native Tradition

An interesting example is found in the last of a set of six concertos by Thomas Sanders Dupuis, published in 1760 as Op. 1.[8] Here the orchestral parts suddenly break off towards the end of the fourth movement (a fugue), and the instruction 'ad libitum—lead off on the close' follows during a blank bar. At the corresponding point in the solo part comes the passage quoted in Ex. 48. Since the arrival of the dominant penultimate is not articulated but the 'cadenza' emerges simply as a result of a non-metrical continuation of the preceding figuration, it is evidently an example of the deceptive cadenza. There is a trill at the end to alert the orchestra to be ready for their entry, of the

Ex. 48.   *T. S. Dupuis, Concerto, Op. 1 No. 6, fourth movement*

[8] GB-Lbl g. 76c (parts); h. 2732m. (1)—keyboard.

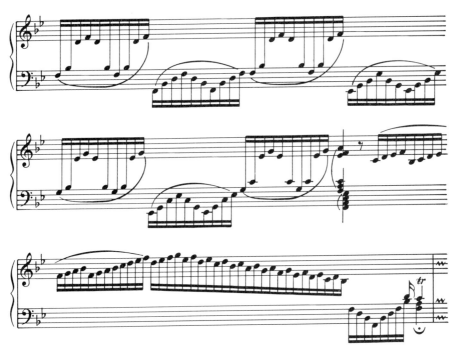

kind which Burney describes in his account of Handel's improvisations (see Chapter 5). This passage illustrates conveniently the transition between the Handelian improvisation of complete episodes 'in tempo' and the rhapsodic cadential improvisations used by some of Handel's imitators.

This set of six concertos by Dupuis is only one of an enormous number of English publications of organ concertos from this period to be based on the Handelian model. Just as Claude Balbastre was to lead the vogue for the organ concerto in the Paris of the 1750s and 1760s (see below), so Handel set a trend which a great many English composers of instrumental music in the period were to follow. Thus it is that the concertos of William Felton, Matthias Hawdon, Henry Burgess, and John Stanley often share certain characteristics with Handel's concertos, marking them apart from the contemporary continental concerto: there may be an irregular sequence of movements, frequently opening with a Largo followed by a fugal Allegro, as in the older concerto da chiesa of Corelli and Geminiani, or Phrygian cadences at the ends of movements, with perhaps a slightly archaic musical language for the 1750s and 1760s. Unlike Handel's concertos they do contain one or two cadential fermatas, especially after 1760, but these are relatively rare. Handel's concertos are unlikely to have acted as a stimulus to their use, and it is far more likely that Italian opera was the direct cause. The earliest traced so far seem to be those contained in a manuscript of a concerto by William Hayes, thought to

Ex. 49.   *W. Hayes, Concerto in G major, second-movement cadenza*

date from *c*.1740.[9] The presence of two cadenzas in the second movement,[10] one before the third tutti (reproduced in Ex. 49), cadencing in the dominant, and one before the fourth and final tutti, cadencing in the tonic, is itself perhaps a pointer towards the aria, for subsidiary cadenzas were more characteristic of the aria than of the concerto.

Cadential fermatas without written-out embellishments occur in one or two quasi-vocal passages in the concertos of William Felton, a prolific composer of keyboard concertos,[11] but more characteristic, perhaps, are one or two perfidia-like passages that occur towards final solo cadences.[12] Such passages probably illustrate an older tradition of virtuosity in the keyboard concerto reaching back to Handel, which makes use of a more idiomatic type of keyboard figuration than the vocal-style cadenza illustrated in Ex. 49.

Mention should also be made of some surprisingly early English cadenzas occurring outside the concerto repertory, but in a genre which borrows certain gestures from the concerto, namely the organ voluntary. John Stanley's first published set of voluntaries, Op. 5 (1748), does not contain any cadenzas or cadential fermatas, just one or two perfidia-like pedal-points and adagio cadences of the kind encountered in many of Felton's concertos. The second published set, Op. 6 (1752), however, contains a single written-out cadenza,[13] while the last set, Op. 7 (1754), contains no fewer than four.[14] All these cadenzas are barred in common time, even though Voluntaries 3 and 6 from Op. 7 are written in 3/4. Quantz, of course, felt that it was better not to introduce cadenzas into movements in triple metre (see Chapter 2). Stanley appears to have had no scruples over this particular point, although he evidently felt that triple metre was not workable during a cadenza. None is longer than five bars, and they are all written in a single-part texture over a stationary bass (see Ex. 50 for the cadenza from Op. 7 No. 3). Stanley's approach was somewhat stereotyped—the cadenza to Op. 7 No. 4 is almost identical to Ex. 50. Nevertheless it reveals a fluency in handling the cadenza

---

[9] GB-Ob Ms. Mus d. 82.

[10] i.e. the E minor Andante. The 8-bar Adagio introduction to the first Allegro is a later addition.

[11] Thirty-two concertos by Felton appeared in print between 1744 and 1760.

[12] Examples are found in the first movements of the second and sixth concertos from Felton's Op. 7 set, published in 1760.

[13] i.e. in the G minor Voluntary, no. 3.   [14] i.e. in Voluntaries 1, 3, 4, and 6.

Ex. 50. *J. Stanley, Organ Voluntary, Op. 7 No. 3*

which suggests that among the keyboard improvisations that were never recorded something akin to cadential improvisation may have been practised in England before written evidence for it becomes frequent.

The *Galant* Concerto

If the cadenza was something of a rarity in the native English concerto tradition, it was much more common in the *galant* concerto that a number of immigrant continental composers brought to England. These included such familiar names as Johann Christian Bach (whose concertos are discussed in Chapter 7) and Carl Friedrich Abel, as well as Tommaso Giordani, Johann Christian Fischer, and Johann Samuel Schroeter. The pattern established by J. C. Bach with his three published sets—slight, mostly two-movement works with no viola parts in the orchestra—was to be followed by many other composers working in England. Variations on popular tunes became increasingly common in the English concerto at this time; examples are provided by Bach in the finale of Op. 1 No. 6 which uses 'God Save the King' and in that of Op. 13 No. 4 which uses 'The Yellow-Hair'd Laddie'.

The concertos of Abel, Giordani, and Fischer contain rather more cadential fermatas than do those of Bach. They are found in almost all first movements, many slow movements, and some finales. The manner of preparing cadential fermatas in these and other *galant* concertos published in England at this time follows the conventions and uses many of the stereotyped turns of phrase (e.g. string syncopations, dotted rhythms, chromatic bass-line) found in the *galant* concerto on the Continent. While these composers did not introduce the cadenza to England, it may safely be said that their work helped to establish it, and to establish the conventions which surrounded its use on the Continent.

It is worth drawing attention to one or two English publications by foreign composers of collections of cadenzas which appeared at about this time. The earliest was Tessarini's *Accurate Method*, published by Welcker in 1765.[15] The title-page promises instruction in 'how to make proper cadences' and indeed the third part contains on page 11 nine model violin cadenzas, each one line in length, unthematic, and unbarred. Their somewhat patterned style is not far removed from Tartini. Tommaso Giordani published a set of twenty keyboard cadenzas in 1777,[16] and he included eight in a rather more advanced style in his 'Fourteen Preludes or Capricios and Eight Cadences', Op. 33, less than ten years later.[17]

Those included in the first set use idiomatic keyboard figurations, although there is relatively little for the left hand to contribute. The material is for the most part neutral and figurative, as befits the interchangeable context which such cadenzas had to serve. Among the twenty cadenzas are to be found examples in all the most frequently encountered keys, with three each for the particularly common tonalities of D major and B flat major. Most are written in fast tempo, but a few are designed for use in Andante or Largo movements.

The eight cadenzas contained in the later publication are longer and more complex, each involving polyphonic textures and changes of tempo. There are major–minor juxtapositions, some dynamic contrasts, and more frequent changes of figuration than were found in the earlier set. None of the cadenzas in either set contains much breathing space, however; compared with Mozart's they are somewhat relentless, and the changes in figuration seem gratuitous. This fault is more marked in the later cadenzas than in the earlier, where the relative brevity renders the lack of variety in pace a less urgent problem.

Just as there were many native English composers who took their lead from Handel's organ concertos, so too there were many who adopted the lighter *galant* idiom of Bach, Abel, Giordani, and Schroeter. One of the most popular English concerto composers was James Hook, appointed organist at Vauxhall Gardens in 1774, who performed a concerto every evening during the season there for almost half a century. None of his published concertos contains any cadential fermatas. There are one or two pauses for *Eingänge* during rondos (many of the concertos are simply two-movement works with a rondo as the second movement), but that is all. Virtuoso improvisation would hardly be suited to a pleasure garden, of course, where what is needed is tuneful background music.

In 1769, Philip Hayes published a set of six concertos which have been described as the best English concertos of the period,[18] while the third of the set, according to Charles Cudworth,[19] may have been the first English concerto for the pianoforte. Hayes mixes old and new in this collection. While the more up-to-date three-movement fast–slow–fast scheme is used for each

---

[15] GB-Lbl h. 210i (3). This work may have been a trans. of Tessarini's *Nouvelle méthode* (Liège, 1760), but its origin is not entirely clear.

[16] GB-Lbl e. 223.   [17] GB-Lbl f. 133k. (1).   [18] *NOHM* vii. 486.

[19] C. Cudworth, 'The English Organ Concerto', *The Score*, 8 (1953), 55.

concerto, and four of the slow movements contain cadential fermatas to which the word 'cadenza' is added, nevertheless an active bass-line, a few Phrygian cadences, and an occasional reliance on sequence show traces of the older Handelian tradition.

Another native composer who mixes old and new elements is Thomas Augustine Arne, whose 'Six Favourite Concertos' appeared posthumously in 1787. In the variable number and sequence of movements, as well as the occasional organ fugue or fantasia-like linking movement, these concertos stand closer to Handel's style than do those of Hayes, but they do contain more cadential fermatas than Hayes's set (seven in all), some of them prepared by a dramatic unison passage that points towards the continental style.[20] The less distinguished native composers were naturally more derivative, and tended to adopt wholesale either the Handelian style (Hawdon, Boyton) or else the *galant* idiom (Thomas Haigh).

John Stanley deserves a mention and is a particularly interesting composer to study because his two sets of keyboard concertos were separated by some thirty years. The first set of six concertos (Op. 2, *c*.1745)[21] belongs firmly within the Handelian tradition, with no cadential fermatas at all. The second set of six concertos (Op. 10, 1775), however, contains several. Clearly Stanley was able to move with the times.[22] From the evidence of his published sets of organ voluntaries (see above) it would appear that he became familiar with the use of the cadenza within ten years of the publication of Op. 2.

It is appropriate to imagine cadenzas resembling those of Giordani's first set being performed in the more up-to-date concertos of this period, although it is important to remember that many of the sources contain written-out single-breath cadenzas in a single-part stationary-bass texture. The more archaic the style of the concerto, the more likely it is that a cadenza of this kind would have been expected. Slow movements, of course, tend to require single-part cadenzas because of their frequent aria-type texture, and it is not without significance that the more archaic the style of the concerto, the more likely it is to invite cadenzas in slow rather than fast movements.

Later in the century, of course, the idiomatic free-voiced keyboard texture asserted itself more and more; the four cadenzas included by Joseph Dale in his *Introduction to the Piano Forte*,[23] three of which are by Schroeter, are idiomatic, and they modulate, but they do not develop themes and are

[20] Further evidence of Arne's familiarity with continental cadenza usage is found in his oratorio *Judith* (1761), which contains an obbligato cadenza for two solo cellos in the final ritornello of the aria 'No More the Heathen Shall Blaspheme'.
[21] These concertos for organ and strings are arranged from the original set published as *Six Concerto's in Seven Parts*, Op. 2 (London, 1742).
[22] See O. Edwards, 'The Cadenza in Eighteenth-Century English Concerto Fugues', *The Music Review*, 36 (1975), 92 ff., for a discussion of the differences in cadential articulation between Stanley's Op. 2 and his Op. 10. It should be noted that what Edwards tends to call 'cadenzas' would be classed as 'perfidias' according to the terms used in the present survey.
[23] London, 1797.

thus freely interchangeable; in other words, they resemble the cadenzas of Giordani's second set.

The prominence of London as a musical capital attracted many virtuoso performers, especially after the Revolution in France when a large number of virtuosi such as Viotti fled from Paris. Thus it is that several of the composers of the generation of the 'virtuoso concerto' lived, worked, and published in London. Since most of the virtuoso pianist-composers who lived and worked in England around the turn of the nineteenth century were non-native composers—Dussek, Clementi, Steibelt, J. B. Cramer—it seems more appropriate to postpone consideration of their work until a later stage. By the era of the virtuoso concerto, the language of the concerto had become largely international, and a classification according to country of origin would be meaningless even if the extensive travels of the virtuosi did not make it impracticable.

France

Here cadenzas are all the rage: there is one after every air in the solos. *I* do not care for them at all; not only are there too many of them, but they are always the same. It makes me inclined to laugh when I see some fat castrato blowing himself up like a balloon to give off a score of roulades one after another, up and down the scale without taking breath.[24]

Such were the impressions of Charles de Brosses, writing in 1739–40 about his experiences of music in Italy. This kind of distaste for the trappings of the Italian *aria di bravura* was to remain a constant theme of eighteenth-century musical criticism in France. Coupled with a strong preference for vocal over instrumental music, this attitude was clearly unfavourable to the development of the cadenza.

 Yet France could not remain aloof from the influence of Italian music indefinitely. The Guerre des Bouffons broke out in 1752, and in the previous year the first volume of the great *Encyclopédie* of Diderot and d'Alembert appeared. Rousseau, who contributed the articles on music in the latter work, was an impassioned and outspoken advocate of the superiority of Italian music over French, and while it was primarily the *opera buffa* that the anti-nationalist party in the Guerre des Bouffons upheld, their more partisan members were prepared to prefer all forms of Italian music to French. As

---

[24] Président Charles de Brosses, *L'Italie il y a cent ans ou lettres écrites d'Italie . . . en 1739 et 1740*, 2 vols. (Paris, 1836; 2nd edn., 1858), ii. 382 (letter L). Trans. taken from Burney, *Musical Tours*, i. 290 n. 3.

early as 1747 a concerto by Tartini had been performed at the Concert Spirituel,[25] and while, according to Burney, the violinist Pagin who played it 'had the honour of being hissed . . . for daring to play in the Italian style, and this was the reason of his quitting the profession',[26] the music of Tartini, Vivaldi, and Locatelli was nevertheless gaining a foothold in Paris. The programmes of the Concert Spirituel indicate that a growing number of French composers were writing concertos, and although much of the music is lost (not one of the innumerable organ concertos composed and performed by Claude Balbastre between 1755 and 1772 has survived), it seems at least plausible that some of these concertos may have included cadential improvisations.

That the keyboard cadenza was not entirely unknown in France around the middle of the century is evident from an isolated early example which is written out in Jacques Duphly's 'La Damanzy', a character piece included in his 'Second livre de pièces de clavecin', announced in the *Mercure de France* in 1748. It is single-part, unmetrical, and the bass is stationary throughout. One can only guess at the stimulus behind it. It is probably a reference to Italian style, and it indicates that this must have been known in Paris, even though the greater part of the musical public tended to resist it.

Twenty years later, Rousseau was to provide the following article under the heading 'Cadenza'[27] in his *Dictionnaire de Musique*.

An Italian word by which is meant an unwritten 'point d'orgue', which the author leaves to the will of him who is performing the principal part so that he may produce those passages, according to the character of the air, which are the most suitable for his voice, his instrument, or his taste.

This 'point d'orgue' is called *Cadenza* because it is normally made on the first note of a final cadence, and it is also called *Arbitrio*, because of the liberty granted to the performer to abandon himself to his ideas and to follow his own taste. French music, especially vocal music which is utterly wretched, does not grant any such liberty to the singer, who would in any case be quite perplexed about how to use it.

Where vocal music is concerned it is clear that Rousseau is describing a practice found in Italian music but not in French; in the case of instrumental music, however, it is hard to be sure whether his definition applies only to imported music, or whether the cadenza was also a feature of native French music by the time of writing: he does not specifically include French instrumental music in the category of 'wretched' music which does not grant such a liberty to the performer. The article does, however, undoubtedly

---

[25] C. Pierre, *Histoire du Concert Spirituel 1725–1790* (Paris, 1975), 113, 254.

[26] Burney, *Musical Tours*, i. 28.

[27] Rousseau uses the Italian term 'cadenza', although the more usual term in French is 'point d'orgue'.

suggest that cadenzas were becoming more familiar to French audiences, even if this was still principally via imported music.[28]

Be that as it may, the cadenza was certainly a familiar phenomenon to French composers and audiences by the early 1770s, when the first symphonies concertantes began to appear in print. The growth of the ensemble cadenza was perhaps the most distinctive French contribution to the development of the cadenza, largely because of the extensive cultivation of the symphonie concertante in Paris in the last thirty years of the century. In the 1760s and 1770s, moreover, a large number of German concertos began to appear in print in Paris,[29] and to be included in concert programmes.[30] From this time onwards the style of the French concerto became noticeably more cosmopolitan, and the fluency with which it now incorporated cadenzas was one aspect of this growing internationalism. In this way the ground was prepared for Giovanni Battista Viotti to lead the French to a position of European dominance in the violin concerto in the last years of the century with his series of twenty-nine violin concertos, of which the first nineteen were probably written in Paris. Viotti's contribution to the history of the cadenza is of some importance, and deserves to be treated separately in Chapter 11.

The Keyboard Concerto in France: 1755–1772

The following review of the Concert Spirituel which took place on 25 March 1755 appeared shortly afterwards in the *Mercure de France*:[31] 'M. Balbâtre played an organ concerto of his own composition, that surprised and charmed the entire assemblage; his brilliant playing made this instrument sound in an authoritative manner, and made the impression that he alone has the right to lead all others. One cannot praise too highly . . . the singular talent of M. Balbâtre.'[32] This was the first time that an organ concerto had been performed at the Concert Spirituel, but it was by no means the last. Balbastre was evidently popular, for he appeared on more than a hundred occasions performing organ concertos of his own composition in addition to giving many performances of arrangements of opera overtures, etc. Following his lead, a number of other organist-composers, including Beauvarlet-Charpentier, Séjan, and Damoreau, began to compose and perform organ

---

[28] More than 20 years after Rousseau's *Dictionnaire* was published, Nicolas-Étienne Framery (1745–1810) commented on the 'Cadenza' article: 'As far as instrumental music is concerned . . . [cadenzas] were . . . common at the time when Rousseau was writing his dictionary, and he should have said so. Accustomed to denigrate French music, he refused to take account of the progress it was making, which was already considerable in the field of instrumental music.' See *Encyclopédie méthodique: Musique*, ed. N.-É. Framery and P. L. Ginguené, 2 vols. (Paris, 1791–1818). It is not easy to decide which of these writers is the more trustworthy.

[29] See C. Johannson, *French Music Publishers' Catalogues of the Second Half of the Eighteenth Century* (Malmö, 1955).

[30] Pierre, *Histoire*, pp. 292 ff.　　　[31] May 1755, pp. 180 f.　　　[32] *Grove*, ii. 60.

concertos at the Concert Spirituel. Organ concertos continued to be heard there until 1772, when the organ in the Salle du Concert Spirituel was sold.[33]

Very little information is available about the organ concertos which were so popular in Paris during those twenty years, largely because so few sources survive. Not a single concerto by Balbastre is known today. It seems probable, however, that improvisation and display contributed towards the popularity of his concertos. Balbastre was renowned for the improvisations on Christmas noëls with which he used to attract huge crowds to Midnight Mass in the church of St Roch, where he was organist, until in 1762 he was forbidden by the Archbishop of Paris to play the organ at Midnight Mass. Balbastre not infrequently played 'Concerts mêlés de Noëls' at Christmas Eve or Christmas Day performances at the Concert Spirituel.[34]

Only a few printed sources of organ concertos by French composers from before 1770 are extant. Michel Corrette's 'VI concerti a sei strumenti, cimbalo o organo obligati', Op. 26 (Paris, 1756), does not contain any cadential fermatas.[35] One or two of the concertos by foreign composers (e.g. Wagenseil, Schobert) which were published in Paris in the 1760s contained cadential fermatas, and it may be that a precedent was set here for the dramatic use made of the cadenza in some of the early symphonies concertantes in the following decade. Mention might also be made of Henri-Joseph Rigel (originally Riegel) and Ernst Eichner, both Germans, each of whom published a concerto in Paris *c*.1770 which made use of the dramatic formula of the inserted cadenza. Rigel settled in Paris in 1768.

It is possible that the capriccios of Locatelli provided a further stimulus to the French cadenza. They were certainly known in the 1760s, since Rousseau refers to them in the *Dictionnaire*,[36] and they may have been introduced to Parisian audiences by Pagin. The sonatas for violin and continuo, Op. 4, by Guillaume Navoigille (Paris, 1768) contain a capriccio concluding with a cadenza in each slow movement,[37] and it seems reasonable to attribute this to the influence of Locatelli.

Conclusions about the importance of cadenzas in the French concerto before 1770 are necessarily tentative since the musical sources contain so little evidence concerning them. The strongest indication that they did indeed take place is the article 'Cadenza' in Rousseau's *Dictionnaire*, although even here it is hard to be sure how far Rousseau was speaking of French music and how far

---

[33] Pierre, *Histoire*, p. 44.

[34] Concertos for other solo instruments also made occasional use of noëls at Christmas concerts. Pierre notes that a violin concerto by Gaviniès, performed by the composer on 25 Dec. 1762, contained 'comme cadences, des variations sur des noëls connus' (*Histoire*, p. 282).

[35] In a recent edn. of the Sixth Concerto, however (M. Corrette, *6ᵉ concerto en ré-mineur*, reconstructed by F. Oubradous, Paris, 1957), a cadenza is inserted at a cadence in the dominant immediately before the final tutti in the finale.

[36] See the article 'Caprice'.

[37] See B. S. Brook, *La Symphonie française dans la seconde moitié du XVIIIᵉ siècle*, 3 vols. (Paris, 1962), i. 296 ff.

he was speaking simply of imported music. Given the international prestige which Paris began to acquire in mid-century for its concert life, conditions were certainly favourable by this time to the growth of the 'public phenomenon' of the cadenza. Be that as it may, clear evidence that the cadenza had 'arrived' in indigenous French music by the early 1770s is provided in a symphonie concertante by Jean-Baptiste Davaux, published by Bailleux *c.* 1772 as the second of a set of two, Op. 5.

The Ensemble Cadenza

What is striking about the cadenza in Davaux's Symphonie Concertante No. 2[38] is that it appears to be the work of a composer fully conversant with the dramatic placing of the cadenza during the final ritornello, and it is already of a considerable length (fifteen bars) with three changes of tempo. The appearance of the same work in 1775 arranged as a trio for harpsichord or piano, violin, and ad libitum bass[39] brings this cadenza into the keyboard repertoire

Ex. 51. *J.-B. Davaux, Symphonie concertante No. 2, arranged as a trio, first-movement cadenza*

---

[38] The numbering adopted is that of D. H. Foster's thematic catalogue of symphonies and symphonies concertantes by Davaux given on pp. xxxi ff. of series D, vol. 5, *The Symphonie Concertante* (New York and London, 1983), in the Garland series *The Symphony 1720–1840*.

[39] *Les IV Simphonies Concertantes . . . arrangés . . .* (Paris, 1775). The violin part is missing both in the Paris source (F-Pn Vm⁷ 5620) and in the Cambridge source (GB-Ckc). In Ex. 51 the violin part has been reconstructed from the original version of the work.

Outside Germany and Austria

Ex. 51. – *Contd.*

at an early date—the cadenza is retained in the arrangement, and is quoted in full in Ex. 51.

The close resemblance between this cadenza with its dramatic preparation and those of South German and Austrian concertos of this period—the syncopations in upper strings, the bass progression from tonic down to submediant and thence via the sharpened fourth scale degree to the dominant penultimate, the appearance of the word 'cadenza' in the symphonie concertante source, and the single bar's rest in the accompanying parts for the entire duration of the cadenza—all this suggests that Davaux may have modelled the passage on some German concertos known to him. No precedent has been found in French music, and it is likely that the influx of German music and German musicians at this time provided the stimulus for the adoption of the dramatic form of cadenza placing in French music.

Whatever the source of its inspiration, the formula quickly established itself in Paris, not only in the symphonie concertante, but also in indigenous solo concertos, including those for keyboard instruments, and those for harp—another Parisian speciality.[40] At first, however, only a small proportion of symphonies concertantes contained written-out cadenzas. Of the twelve extant works in the genre by Davaux, only two contain written-out cadenzas,[41] while among the fifty-one extant examples by Giuseppe Maria Cambini, the most prolific composer of symphonies concertantes, only four

---

[40] Concertos were sometimes declared on their title-pages to be written 'per l'harpa o cimbalo'. It was in any case common practice to leave the choice of solo keyboard instrument open, presumably with a view to promoting sales, and at times it was claimed on title-pages that the concertos could equally well be performed on the harpsichord, organ, piano, or harp! Johann Baptist Krumpholtz and Franz Petrini seem to have been the most prolific composers of concertos written specifically for the harp among those whose music appeared in Paris at this time. Inserted cadenzas are required more often than pre-tutti cadenzas, although both are found. A number of Petrini's cadenzas are written out, as is one by Pollet. Compared with the keyboard examples, these cadenzas are much more regularly patterned. The one by Pollet is monophonic. Petrini's concertos and their cadenzas date from the late 1780s; the cadenza by Pollet, however, was written *c.*1802.

[41] See *The Symphonie Concertante*, p. xxv.

contain written-out cadenzas.[42] If the pioneers of the French symphonie concertante made only limited use of the obbligato cadenza, their followers were to leave many more examples, however. Increasing numbers of ensemble cadenzas appeared, particularly in symphonies concertantes for a mixed wind ensemble. The present concern rests more specifically with those symphonies concertantes which have a keyboard instrument among the soloists, and those which exist in arrangements involving a keyboard instrument.

One work in the former category was the 'Concerto Concertant' Op. 20, by Henri-Joseph Rigel (1786), scored for solo harpsichord and violin with an accompanying orchestra of strings and optional pairs of oboes and horns. Both the first and second movements of this work contain written-out measured cadenzas lasting seventeen and fourteen bars respectively. The cadenzas contain not only a number of tempo changes but also changes of metre. Like the Davaux example quoted in Ex. 51, they are effectively duets for right hand and violin, with a supporting bass in the left hand, although the latter has a slightly more independent role here than in the earlier example. A favourite device, and one used at the opening of the first-movement cadenza, is to give a short phrase to one of the solo voices, then to repeat it a third higher with the other voice joining in at the original pitch (Ex. 52). Both cadenzas are made up entirely of short phrases such as that in Ex. 52, with a tendency to emphasize the notes of the tonic chord. Every phrase or fragment heard is immediately repeated at least once, perhaps with voice-exchange, octave-displacement, an added voice as in Ex. 52, or just a third higher or lower. While the frequent pauses and changes of tempo or metre break up what could easily become monotonous, adding a constant element of surprise in spite of the stationary harmony, the charge of monotony is not entirely avoided; since neither cadenza is particularly virtuoso, the deficiency in content cannot be

Ex. 52. *H.-J. Rigel, Concerto Concertant, Op. 20, first-movement cadenza*

---

[42] They are listed as C3, C6, G6, and E29 in the thematic catalogue by A. D. Parcell, jun., contained in *The Symphonie Concertante*, pp. xlvii ff. I am indebted to Professor Parcell for kindly supplying this information, which supersedes his statement that only three symphonies concertantes by Cambini contain written-out cadenzas (ibid., p. xliii).

attributed to the display element, which was not in any case particularly prominent in the symphonie concertante. Yet these two cadenzas should not be considered unsuccessful; rather, they suit the ephemeral nature of the genre to which they belong. On a first hearing, they would have appeared charming enough, full of surprises of an unsophisticated but effective kind, and would have been admired as much for the timbre of the violin–harpsichord combination as anything else. The enjoyment of colour in various solo combinations was after all a major factor in the popularity of the symphonie concertante. All those repetitions and chains of thirds and sixths which look so uninteresting on paper would have held the attention of the audience and would no doubt have delighted them.[43]

It cannot be claimed that Italy, England, or France played a leading role in the development of the cadenza. Yet in each of these countries the cadenza was known and cultivated, and towards the end of the eighteenth century national boundaries took on less importance, thanks to travelling virtuosi. One of these in particular had an important part to play in the final stages of the history of the classical cadenza, one who spent time in Italy, France, and England—the violinist Giovanni Battista Viotti.

---

[43] It is worth adding at this point that Rigel was one of the first composers in Paris to write out a cadenza in a solo keyboard concerto, namely the second of 'Deux Concertos périodiques', Op. 11, dating from *c*.1776, where a 6-bar cadenza is inserted into the concluding ritornello of the first movement. It is made up of neutral, but pleasantly varied keyboard figurations.

11

Viotti and the Cadenza

AN Italian by birth and upbringing, Giovanni Battista Viotti went to Paris in 1782 and achieved an instant success at the Concert Spirituel. While a few of his twenty-nine violin concertos may have been written before his arrival in Paris, as display pieces for use during the concert tour that he made with his teacher Pugnani in 1780–1, it was in Paris that he won for his concertos the acclaim which was to be the basis of their international reputation. By 1783 he had had ten concertos published in Paris, and by the time he left for London in 1792 he had composed nineteen.

Viotti's importance for the present survey derives principally from his pioneering use of integrated, accompanied cadenzas in the finales of violin concertos written during the 1790s, after his escape from revolutionary Paris, but also from the arrangements that were made of fifteen of his violin concertos as piano concertos.[1] The violin concertos will be examined first.

Violin Concertos

A little over half of the first movements require an inserted ad libitum cadenza; most of these belong to concertos written in the periods 1782–3 and 1792–7 during which Viotti made frequent concert appearances in Paris and London respectively. His concert appearances were a spectacular success, and it is not surprising to find the dramatic form of cadenza placing occurring so frequently in these first movements. The remaining first movements contain no cadential fermatas at all. None of the original printed sources contains a written-out first-movement cadenza.

Two-thirds of the slow movements require cadenzas. Each of the different types of placing is encountered here, but in view of the brevity of most of the concluding tuttis it is sometimes difficult to distinguish between inserted and extended types. With the exception of a flourish of thirty-one notes in Wh. I: 28, none of the original printed sources contains a written-out second-movement cadenza.[2]

---

[1] See C. White, *Giovanni Battista Viotti (1755–1824): A Thematic Catalogue of his Works* (New York, 1985). The arrangements are listed as Wh. Ia: 1–14 and Wh. Ia: 20.

[2] Viotti's revision of Wh. I: 19 also contains a written-out slow-movement cadenza in the form of a single-line flourish of 29 notes. The revised version was published by Janet et Cotelle *c.*1818, and may be consulted in F-Pn Vm²⁴ 294. See also C. White, 'Viotti's Revision of his 19th Violin Concerto', in R. Weaver (ed.), *Essays on the Music of J. S. Bach and Other Divers Subjects: A Tribute to Gerhard Herz* (Louisville, 1982), 223 ff.

The finales of concertos Wh. I: 1–21 do not contain cadenzas at all, whereas each of Wh. I: 22–9 does. These eight concertos were all composed after 1792, the year of the move to London. In each case[3] the cadenza is fully written out and accompanied by the orchestra. Wh. I: 22 in A minor, the best-known of all Viotti's concertos for a number of reasons, including Brahms's particular liking for it, its frequent use as a didactic piece, and the appearance of several modern editions,[4] was the first to contain a cadenza of this kind. It will be discussed here in some detail.

The Finale Cadenza in Violin Concerto Wh. I: 22

The parent movement is a rondo; perhaps Mozart is the model here, for although the rondo lacks the subtlety of Mozart's combined ritornello-sonata-rondo structures, there are few other precedents for including an extended cadenza in a rondo finale. Whereas Mozart's rondo cadenzas normally occur during the tutti after the 'recapitulation', it is impossible to speak of a recapitulation here in the same sense. The structure of the movement is ABA'CA″, with the cadenza occurring during A″. A and A' each consist of a statement of the rondo theme in the tonic by the soloist, followed by tutti material, whereas A″, which is rather longer than the other tonic-key sections, begins with a tutti thematic statement; this leads into conventional cadential preparation, dramatically articulating the arrival of the 6–4 penultimate with the help of chromatic bass movement under an inverted pedal in the upper strings.

The arrival of the penultimate, then, is clearly articulated. The cadenza which follows (reproduced in Ex. 53) is orchestrally accompanied and in tempo from the outset; it contains not a single rallentando, rhapsodic passage nor even a fermata.[5] It begins with sequential treatment of the idea heard in the bass during the preparation (itself derived from the five-note figure '*x*' which had formed a part of the tutti material in the opening section), now given a new extension; after the second statement of this idea, the five-note figure '*x*' appears in inversion, and is used in order to effect a return to A minor, in which key the violin begins a passage of legato semiquavers, wandering through various dominant-tonic progressions in nearly related keys, and wending its way back to A minor for a solo statement of the theme. This is deflected after only six bars, and figure '*x*' is used to carry the music towards the dominant chord. The remainder of the cadenza consists of dominant preparation for the final tutti, although it is only eight bars before the end that the 6–4 is clearly re-established.

---

[3] The apparently exceptional case of Wh. I: 27 is considered below.

[4] e.g. Eulenburg miniature score, ed. A. Einstein (London, 1929; repr. 1972), and Peters edn., ed. F. Hermann (Leipzig, n.d.).

[5] Not even the penultimate carries a fermata sign, but it is prolonged by means of a 'composed fermata': the chord is held for two and a half bars before the soloist begins.

Ex. 53. *G. B. Viotti, Concerto Wh. I: 22, finale cadenza (solo violin part only)*

Ex. 53. – *Contd.*

The dissimilarity between this passage and most of the cadenzas which have been examined so far is only too obvious; apart from the articulation of its opening, it proceeds in a manner virtually indistinguishable from a normal solo episode, texturally, harmonically, melodically, and rhythmically. The closest comparable type encountered so far is the ensemble cadenza in tempo, which would have been familiar to Viotti from his time in Paris during the 1780s, although the use of orchestral accompaniment in this instance integrates the cadenza much more fully into the work. In order to illustrate just how fully integrated this cadenza is, it is useful to consider its structure in terms of the tripartite schema used by Mozart.

The derivation of the opening from a new extension of the idea used in the cadential preparation is a familiar enough device;[6] but Viotti, unlike Mozart,

---

[6] It is a common procedure in the cadenzas of C. P. E. Bach; Mozart's cadenza 43, written for K. 450/i, offers another familiar example.

handles the phrasing in a remarkably four-square manner, so that the end-result does not sound like an improvisation. With the same caveat, a resemblance could be argued between the passage of 'wandering semiquavers' in Viotti's cadenza and the virtuoso figurations that often bring the first section of a Mozart cadenza to its conclusion. Viotti's lack the cumulative tension of Mozart's, but this is characteristic of his much more leisurely approach to the shaping of the cadenza. At the point where Mozart might quote a lyrical thematic idea, Viotti returns to the opening theme (see bar 313). The deflection after six bars could be compared with the fragmentation applied to the theme at this point in Mozart's cadenzas, although once again Viotti handles this with much less tension, and with much more predictable phraseology. The same could be said of the dominant preparation, the return of the 6–4, and the cadential trill, for which comparable (usually rhapsodic) passages exist in many of Mozart's cadenzas. The broad outlines are familiar, but in the working out of them Viotti has 'tamed' the cadenza, so that it scarcely stands out from its surroundings.

What of its relation to the rest of the movement? Lasting for seventy bars (a fifth of the entire movement) the cadenza is unusually long for a solo concerto. The disruptive effect on the balance of the movement of omitting the passage, if such a thing were possible, would be enormous.

In *The Rhythmic Structure of Music*, Cooper and Meyer speak in the following terms of the relation of the cadenza to its surroundings:

A case of interrupted continuity that comes readily to mind is found in the classical concerto, in which the resolution of a I 6/4 chord onto a V chord may be delayed for several minutes by the insertion of a cadenza . . . there is a certain unreality about the interruption. It is not part of the 'real' piece, which will resume as though nothing had happened whenever it is allowed to.[7]

In other words, the cadenza normally functions as what Meyer would call a 'parenthesis', that is to say, its omission would not impair the coherence of the movement. Yet the cadenza in the finale of Viotti's Concerto Wh. I: 22 is not a 'parenthesis', because it possesses considerable structural importance in relation to the rest of the movement. It gives the necessary length to section A″ so that it may balance A and A′. Without it the soloist would be silent throughout the (very short) final section of the rondo. While the specifically harmonic tension set up in the cadential preparation and the 6–4 chord is not fully resolved until the beginning of the final tutti—and it is this which defines the extent of the cadenza—a number of other structural tensions are actually resolved during the cadenza. The thematic statement beginning in bar 313 and the dominant preparation beginning in bar 324 are both of crucial importance for the overall thematic symmetry of the movement—they are required to balance a number of passages occurring long before the cadenza.

---

[7] L. B. Meyer and G. Cooper, *The Rhythmic Structure of Music* (Chicago, 1960), 149.

So this passage could not be omitted without impairing the coherence of the movement. In this respect Viotti's accompanied cadenzas foreshadow their nineteenth-century counterparts and particularly the cadenza in the 'Emperor' Concerto.

Other Finale Cadenzas

Viotti was to repeat this pioneering form of cadenza in each of his subsequent concerto finales.[8] The cadenza in the finale of Wh. I: 27[9] is unlike any of the others in that it begins rhapsodically for unaccompanied violin. The movement is a rondo once again, with the structure ABA′ CA″ DA‴ (see Table 5 below); the cadenza begins at the start of the D section with a written-out rhapsodic passage. This comes to an end on a rather weak tonic cadence (Ex. 54) which is insufficient to resolve the cadential 6–4. Consequently, the following accompanied solo must also be considered part of the cadenza. This

Ex. 54.   *G. B. Viotti, Concerto Wh. I: 27, finale cadenza*

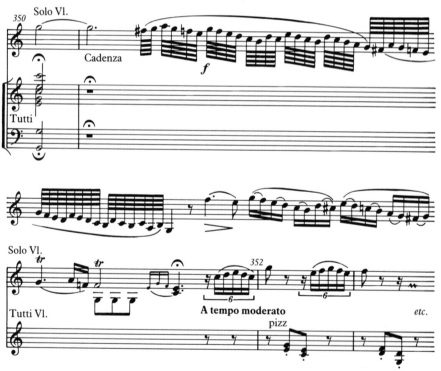

    [8] Some are labelled 'cadenza' e.g. Wh. I: 22; in other cases the passages are simply labelled 'solo', but are unquestionably 'hidden' cadenzas.
    [9] This work is available in a modern edn., namely *G. B. Viotti: Four Violin Concertos*, ed. C. White (Madison, 1976), no. 4.

measured section of the cadenza (bars 352–422) begins by extending the opening sextuplet figure by means of which the key of A flat (the Neapolitan of the dominant G) is temporarily established, soon to be followed by dominant preparation for the C major solo statement of the rondo theme that begins in bar 384. Instead of leading directly into the C major tutti that had followed it on its three previous statements, this theme leads to extended dominant preparation culminating in a trill. In bar 423 the tutti re-enters and the tonic returns. It is here, then, that resolution of the cadential 6–4 occurs conclusively, and thus it is here that the cadenza comes to an end. As always it is the opening of the passage which establishes that it is a cadenza, and, as in the case of the cadenza from the finale of Wh. I: 22, it is no mere parenthesis, but an essential part of the composition. Unlike the earlier example, however, it comes from a work which also exists in an arrangement as a piano concerto (see below).

Brief mention might also be made of the finale cadenza in Wh. I: 29, of interest because it is launched not from a 6–4 but from a diminished triad. The word 'cadenza' is used, and the similarity of the passage to those of the previous seven finales is enough to establish that it is a further example of the same phenomenon. It will be realized, however, that this cadenza is closer to the romantic cadenza than to the classical, being integrated harmonically as well as thematically, texturally, and rhythmically.

Piano Arrangements

Only one of the piano concertos is known to have been arranged by Viotti himself,[10] and it is likely that none of the others was. The title-pages of two publications by Boyer and Naderman of 'piano concertos' by Viotti claim that the works in question were originally composed for the piano and not for the violin, but Chappell White has argued convincingly that this is not the case.[11] Comparisons between the arrangements and their originals, then, shed light not so much on Viotti's own cadenza usage as on that of the arrangers—for example Dussek, Steibelt, Cramer—as well as on the continuing freedom that was widely granted to the arranger/performer in this matter.

In some cases a cadenza is written out by the arranger where none had been supplied in the original; in one case a cadential fermata is added where none had been present in the original;[12] and in several cases a cadential fermata present in the original is omitted in the arrangement. The addition or

[10] Wh. Ia: 14—the arrangement of the outer movements of Wh. I: 24. Autograph F-Pn Mss 1422 and 1423.

[11] C. White, 'Did Viotti Write any Original Piano Concertos?', *JAMS* 22 (1969), 275 ff. The concertos in question are Wh. Ia: 7 and Wh. Ia:8.

[12] The slow movement of Wh. Ia: 1. This simply involves the addition of two bars of music, of which the first serves to extend the final solo cadence and the second bears the cadential fermata.

omission of cadential fermatas is not simply a matter of notational detail, however, since in the works under consideration it involves a degree of recomposition. No longer is the inclusion or omission of a cadenza a detail which can be decided in performance, as in the days of C. P. E. Bach.

The first movements of Wh. Ia: 7, Wh. Ia: 8, Wh. Ia: 9, Wh. Ia: 10, and Wh. Ia: 12 do not contain the cadential fermatas present in the originals. In most of these examples the piano arrangement leads straight from the final solo cadence into the final tutti (i.e. the one which had followed the cadenza in the original), so that both the cadenza and the preparatory tutti are omitted. In Dussek's arrangement of Wh. I: 25 as Wh. Ia: 10 a cut is made after the fourth bar of the preparatory tutti to the fifth bar of the final tutti, with a similar effect. In Steibelt's arrangement of Wh. I: 19 as Wh. Ia: 9, however, a new tutti altogether is introduced after the final solo cadence, based on the opening theme of the movement. In the slow movements of both Wh. Ia: 9 and Wh. Ia: 11 the short final tutti of the original is rewritten so as to exclude the cadential fermata.

Four of the piano concertos were arranged from violin concertos with finale cadenzas, namely Wh. Ia: 7, Wh. Ia: 10, Wh. Ia: 13, and Wh. Ia: 14 (see Table 4). The last-named is the only one of the four in which the cadenza is preserved in the piano arrangement. It is interesting that this is the arrangement made by Viotti himself. In the other cases, arranged by Dussek and Cramer, this section of the movement is rewritten so as to avoid any suggestion of a cadenza. In Dussek's arrangement of Wh. I: 23 as Wh. Ia: 7, the alterations are very slight indeed; the approach is extended by one bar so as to arrive not on a 6–4 but on a dominant seventh underneath the fermata. Since the cadenza began with a thematic statement from the soloist, the effect of this alteration is to change the penultimate into an ordinary pause chord which may or may not be embellished by means of an *Eingang*; the thematic

Table 4. *Alterations in the distribution of cadenzas/cadential fermatas in the piano concerto arrangements of Viotti's violin concertos*

Violin Concerto*	Piano Concerto arrangement	Movements in which cadenzas or cadential fermatas are omitted (or otherwise as noted)
I: 6	Ia: 1	ii, cadential fermata added
I: 23	Ia: 7	i, iii
I: 20, 8	Ia: 8	i
I: 19	Ia: 9	i, ii
I: 25	Ia: 10	i, iii
I: 10, 14, 12	Ia: 11	ii
I: 21	Ia: 12	i
I: 27	Ia: 13	iii
I: 24	Ia: 14	cadenzas retained

* More than one violin concerto is listed when the arrangement uses movements from two or three different concertos.

statement follows, and in the absence of the conventional signal that a cadenza was about to take place, the music which had formerly functioned as a cadenza seems here indistinguishable from a normal solo episode. The cadential trill is extended by four bars in Dussek's arrangement: otherwise it is virtually a literal transcription.

Cramer's arrangement of Wh. I: 27 as Wh. Ia: 13 involves rather more alteration (see above for a discussion of the original); the third thematic statement (A''), the cadential preparation, and the start of the cadenza (D) are all omitted. Cramer abandons Viotti's text during section C, and rejoins the original text during the passage which has been described above as the measured second section of the cadenza, more specifically at the beginning of A''' (see Table 5). From here onwards, with only minor alterations, needed in order to give a fuller statement of the theme to compensate for the one omitted earlier, Cramer follows Viotti's text quite closely. The result is a considerably simpler structure, ABA' CA'' instead of ABA' CA'' DA''', and one that is perhaps more closely matched to the lighter style of the virtuoso concerto.[13]

Dussek's treatment of the finale cadenza of Wh. I: 25 in his arrangement of the work (Wh. Ia: 10) was similar. A cut is made before the preparatory tutti (a thematic statement) and Dussek resumes Viotti's text towards the end of what had been the cadenza. The conclusion of the passage is slightly rewritten. The result is that the movement is considerably shorter than the original, and no cadenza actually takes place, although some of the music that had formerly belonged to the cadenza is retained.[14]

The ease with which the arrangers were able to retain most of the music

Table 5.   *Structural overview of Cramer's arrangement (Wh. Ia: 13) of the finale of Viotti's Violin Concerto No. 27 (Wh. I: 27)*

Bar nos.	1–72	73–156	157–201	202–316	317–350		351–384 ⊙ 351–352–	385–437 –422
							CADENZA	
Viotti	A	B	A'	C	A''		D	A'''
Cramer	A	B	A'	C abbr.	——	[cut]	——	A'''

Note: Bar numbers, quoted according to Viotti's original, do not correspond exactly with those of Cramer's arrangement which amplifies or abbreviates transitional passages and thematic statements. The cut from C to A''' is Cramer's only substantial alteration.

[13] This arrangement, like many that were made of Viotti's violin concertos, tends to prolong the closing passages, especially cadential trills, by extending the bravura passage-work, thus drawing the work into the category of virtuoso concerto.

[14] It should be noted that a certain number of cadential fermatas are retained in the arrangements—principally in slow movements, where the arrangers occasionally supply cadenzas. It would not be true to say that cadential fermatas are rare in the arrangements, although they are rarer here than in the originals.

contained in Viotti's cadenzas, while adapting them so that they ceased to be cadenzas, conveniently illustrates just how well integrated they were, and how close to the nineteenth-century cadenza. The reduction in the overall number of cadential fermatas, and the obscuring of the cadential articulation in the finales also illustrates the trend away from 'set-piece' cadenzas and towards a more even distribution of virtuosity. This of course was characteristic of the virtuoso concerto.[15]

The importance of Viotti and his followers for their influence on Beethoven and on the subsequent history of the nineteenth-century concerto has frequently been noted.[16] As far as the history of the cadenza is concerned Viotti's single most important achievement was the transformation of the ensemble cadenza in tempo, familiar in France owing to the great popularity of the symphonie concertante, into the structurally integrated, accompanied cadenza of his late concerto finales. It seems likely that these cadenzas served as an inspiration to Beethoven, particularly in the 'Emperor' Concerto, the first movement of which resembles the Viottian model most closely, and also to the romantic composers, for whom structurally integrated cadenzas were to become the norm.

[15] Five written-out cadenzas have been found among the sources of the piano concerto arrangements. Wh. Ia: 3/i contains a cadenza in tempo for the two soloists, B-Bc 11541 (a source of Wh. Ia: 5) contains a separately preserved manuscript cadenza for the slow movement, Wh. Ia: 13 contains an extensive slow-movement cadenza by Cramer, Wh. Ia: 7 contains a slow-movement cadenza by Dussek, as does Wh. Ia: 10.

[16] See e.g. A. Schering, *Geschichte des Instrumentalkonzerts* (Leipzig, 1905), 171 f., and B. Schwarz, 'Beethoven and the French Violin School', *MQ* 44 (1958), 431 ff.

12

Beethoven and the Cadenza

BEETHOVEN'S cadenzas have received more critical attention than any others from the classical period. This may be partly because for him the cadenza posed compositional problems which, arguably, he was never able to solve. His approach to cadenza-writing was to change considerably in the course of his career until 1809, the year in which the 'Emperor' Concerto was composed, after which he never wrote another cadenza nor did he complete another concerto.[1] It has been suggested that Beethoven's whole approach to the improvisatory genres of cadenza and fantasia, and indeed to the concerto, underwent a crisis at about this time: a crisis which would only be resolved much later, in the synthesis of improvisatory freedom and compositional control which characterized his late works.[2]

The aim of this chapter is to focus particularly on the changes that occurred in Beethoven's use of the cadenza, from his earliest examples until 1809, and to situate this development within the broader context of the history of the classical cadenza. It would be beyond the scope of the present work to attempt a thorough analysis of the cadenzas themselves, or of their relation to their parent movements. More detailed analytical studies of the cadenzas may be found listed in the Bibliography.

The Position of the Cadenza in Beethoven's Concertos

Beethoven's practice in this matter is broadly similar to Mozart's. In addition to the Triple Concerto, Op. 56, there are seven complete solo piano concertos: the early E flat Concerto of 1784, WoO 4, the five numbered concertos, and the arrangement for piano and orchestra of the Violin Concerto, Op. 61. The Triple Concerto does not contain any cadential fermatas, the 'Emperor' Concerto is a special case, but the first movements of all the other concertos require inserted ad libitum cadenzas (see Table 6). The position regarding slow movements is more variable. Three slow movements do not require cadenzas at all, namely those of the C major Concerto, the 'Emperor' Concerto, and the violin concerto arrangement (although the last named requires an *Eingang* to lead into the finale). The slow movement of the early E

---

[1] It is well known that the first movement of the 'Emperor' Concerto contains an instruction to the soloist not to supply an ad libitum cadenza.

[2] P. Mies, *Die Krise der Konzertkadenz bei Beethoven* (Bonn, 1970), 49 ff.

Table 6. *The incidence of cadenzas and cadential fermatas in Beethoven's piano concertos (not including* Eingänge)

	1st movt	2nd movt	3rd movt
WoO 4	inserted ad lib	inserted ad lib	
No. 1	inserted ad lib		inserted obbligato (senza cadere)
No. 2	inserted ad lib	inserted hidden	
No. 3	inserted ad lib (senza cadere)	pre-tutti obbligato	
No. 4	inserted ad lib (senza cadere)	pre-tutti deceptive	inserted ad lib (senza cadere)
Violin Concerto arrangement	inserted ad lib		inserted ad lib (senza cadere)
No. 5, 'Emperor'	inserted obbligato		

flat Concerto requires an inserted ad libitum cadenza, but the three remaining slow movements all contain obbligato cadenzas of some kind. These are often left out of account in critical studies of Beethoven's cadenzas, but they are in fact of great importance for an accurate assessment of the historical development of Beethoven's cadenza treatment. The slow-movement cadenza in the C minor Concerto is pre-tutti; the other two slow-movement cadenzas, from the second and fourth concertos, are both somewhat unusual.

That of the B flat Concerto is a hidden inserted cadenza with orchestral participation, and it begins in bar 74. The passage is not labelled, nor is there a cadential fermata in bar 74, yet the cadential preparation in bars 72–3 and the sustained orchestral 6–4 in bar 74 provide a clear signal that a cadenza is about to follow. The hidden cadenza takes the form of an instrumental recitative, a device which Beethoven was to use frequently in his later music. From this point onwards the piano plays only a single line in the right hand, while the orchestra punctuates the soloist's utterances with pianissimo statements of the opening idea of the movement. Although a recitative, the cadenza is notated metrically, but the markings 'con gran espressione' and 'ad libitum' suggest that a slightly freer manner of performance is desirable. The final phrase in the piano part ends on the leading note, and the orchestra is left to complete the cadence. This example is one of several in which it is hard to say where the cadenza ends; the completion of the cadence in bar 88 is not a clearly articulated moment, as it occurs within a continuous tutti passage of five bars during which the cadence is stated three times (see Ex. 55). The single-part

Ex. 55.   *L. van Beethoven, Piano Concerto No. 2, second movement*

solo cadenza in the slow movement of the C minor Concerto also comes to an end on a dominant harmony, but the tutti completes the cadence immediately afterwards.

The slow movement of the G major Concerto contains at the end of the last, longest, and most expressive of the short solo utterances a partly rhapsodic prolongation of dominant ninth harmony which is resolved by the entry of the tutti in bar 64. The approach (see Ex. 56) to the penultimate, with its syncopations and chromatic bass movement, is not unlike cadential preparation, although it leads on this occasion to a dominant harmony rather than to a tonic 6-4 as usual.[3] This is the one passage in the movement where the soloist is given a loud dynamic, a fortissimo in fact, and it is undoubtedly the expressive and dramatic climax of the movement. The fermatas over the trills in bar 55 help to give the passage the character of an insertion, although for

---

[3] There is a tonic 6-4 four bars earlier in bar 51; it could be argued that the cadential prolongation begins here. This serves only to underline the lack of clear articulation in the passage, characteristic of the deceptive cadence, and matching the lack of clear articulation at the endings of many of Beethoven's cadenzas (see below).

Ex. 56.   *L. van Beethoven, Piano Concerto No. 4, second movement*

present purposes the passage must be classified as a deceptive cadenza.[4] Brahms seems to have been influenced by this passage in writing the slow movement of his own first piano concerto, where an unbarred prolongation of dominant harmony is actually labelled 'Cadenza' (see Chapter 4).

Beethoven's concerto finales are all rondos, and most include pauses for *Eingänge*, either obbligato or ad libitum. The finales of the C major and G major Piano Concertos and of the Violin Concerto contain inserted cadential fermatas; in the case of the C major Concerto the cadenza is obbligato, while in the other two it is ad libitum. Each of these is an instance of what Beethoven, referring to a cadenza for the first movement of the G major Concerto,[5] described as 'cadenza, ma senza cadere'—a cadenza which does not cadence. This does not simply refer to the procedure observed in some of the slow-movement cadenzas whereby the soloist ends on a half-close, leaving the tutti to complete the cadence; in these instances it seems as if the cadential trill has arrived, but instead of cadencing onto the tonic, it moves in an unexpected direction, with the result that the resolution of the cadence underlying the cadenza is delayed until rather later. Beethoven makes the listener think that the cadenza is about to be concluded, but then he deliberately thwarts this expectation, just as Mozart and Haydn had thwarted the listener's expectation that a cadenza was about to begin in the 'false-start' cadenzas discussed in Chapter 1.[6] Whenever conventions of this kind are established, there arises the possibility of deliberately ignoring them for surprise effect.

Not only is this procedure a good illustration of Beethoven's tendency to obscure the articulation of his concerto movements, a matter with important implications for the future of the cadenza, but it also provides a good example of the novel and expressive uses to which he put the trill. The trill is a particularly useful ornament in a piano cadenza, as it provides a means of sustaining a note indefinitely, of introducing both crescendos and diminuendos, and of subtly altering the colour of the note by changing a tone trill for a semitone trill, or vice versa, something which Beethoven does frequently in his cadenzas. (Expressive and even thematic treatment of trills was of course to be a favourite device in much of Beethoven's late music.)

As an illustration of Beethoven's deceptive resolution of what appear to be cadential trills, let us consider the finale of the C major Concerto; here the trill on D in bars 458–61 moves unexpectedly to a trill on D sharp, harmonized by a 6–4 on F sharp. After a brief spell in B major, during which the rondo theme is played by the soloist, there follows a modulation back to the tonic, and in

---

[4] It is interesting that Mies includes this passage in his list of cadenzas by Beethoven, although he does not include any other obbligato cadenzas (*Krise*, pp. 11 f.). Each of the other cadenzas listed by Mies is found in *BW* VII: 7.

[5] Cadenza 7. See frontispiece of *BW* VII: 7 for a facsimile reproduction of the first page of the autograph.

[6] See Swain, 'Form and Function', for a different interpretation of the label 'cadenza, ma senza cadere'.

bar 486 the tutti bursts in with the rondo theme in C major. Harmonically the resolution of the cadenza arrives only at this point.

Just before the end of this movement there comes another passage labelled 'cadenza', but this time it is of a rather different kind. In a number of works by Beethoven[7] the headlong rush towards the final cadence is preceded by a Haydnesque pause for breath, a reflective, wistful, sometimes humorous phrase or two in a slower tempo, with pause signs. In the present case, the first of two such phrases (bars 562–3) takes the form of a rhapsodic prolongation of a cadence from dominant to tonic—technically a cadenza, but better understood as a parody of the earlier cadenza: its significance is purely local.

Deceptive resolutions of what appear to be cadential trills are found not only in the three finales mentioned, but also in the first movements of the C minor and G major Concertos. In each case the tutti re-enters during or immediately after the trill, but in a purely accompanimental role, for the soloist continues playing.[8] It would be possible to interpret the cadenzas in each of these movements as follows: the first section, which is unaccompanied and, in all but the first instance, ad libitum, ends on a trill which creates an expectation that the cadenza is about to end. Resolution is delayed, however, until after a second, obbligato, and accompanied section of the cadenza. (The similarity between this procedure and that of the finale cadenza in Viotti's concerto Wh. I: 27 will not have passed unnoticed.) According to this view, the point at which each cadenza ends is the point at which the tonic is finally re-established, and in many cases this is also the point at which the tutti takes over from the soloist.

This interpretation makes Beethoven's procedure in the first movement of the 'Emperor' Concerto appear as a natural extension of his earlier practice, rather than a sudden change of direction. In the first movement of the 'Emperor' Concerto, at the point in bar 497 where the cadential fermata arrives, there occurs the famous instruction 'Non si fa una Cadenza ma s'attacca subito il seguente'[9]—'Do not play a cadenza, but proceed directly with the following'. 'The following' is in fact an obbligato cadenza. After eight bars the piano works its way onto an extended trill on B flat (the dominant), which changes from a tone trill into a semitone trill, thus preparing the ground for a statement of the second theme of the movement in the tonic minor. It could be argued that the appearance of this theme marks the end of the

[7] e.g. the first movement of the 'Waldstein' Sonata, the finale of the Fourth Symphony, and the finale of the B flat Quartet, Op. 18 No. 6.

[8] It is interesting to note that in the first movement of the G major Concerto the ending of the ad libitum cadenza closely parallels the endings of the exposition and the recapitulation solos; here too the cadential trill is denied the expected resolution, and the tutti begins during a dominant 7th harmony. In this movement the sectional articulation is consistently obscured, so that the cadenza is not only integrated locally but fits neatly into the overall structure.

[9] Or 'sequente', as in the 1st edn. (Leipzig, 1811).

cadenza.[10] At the end of bar 516 the horns enter with a tonic major version of the theme which the soloist has just played. For thirteen bars soloist and orchestra combine until the soloist withdraws briefly during the loud tutti affirmation of the tonic in bar 530. By analogy with the instances of delayed resolution discussed above, it could be argued that it is this moment which marks the actual conclusion of the cadenza. Rather more important than the particular point at which the cadenza is considered to come to an end, however, is the fact that its ending is obscured, and that it blends so smoothly with the orchestral coda.

The cadenza in the first movement of the 'Emperor' Concerto appears to resemble closely the pattern discussed above in which an unaccompanied section that is ad libitum or rhapsodic is followed by an accompanied, obbligato section. The principal differences are that the unaccompanied section in the 'Emperor' cadenza is relatively short, it is neither ad libitum nor rhapsodic, but obbligato and metrical, and the entry of the orchestra is not in this case articulated by means of a long trill on the supertonic, hence the listener is not led to believe that the cadenza is about to conclude. Although Beethoven had written an obbligato cadenza with orchestral accompaniment before (see Op. 19/ii), he had not done so in the first movement of a concerto, nor had he previously integrated any of his cadenzas quite so closely into the coda.

After the Trill

In the first movements of each of the third, fourth, and fifth concertos, and of the Violin Concerto, the soloist continues playing after the cadenza[11] right up to the closing bars of the movement. The closing orchestral tutti, a hallmark of the earlier concerto, is absent here. It is true that an orchestral passage is found in each case between the final solo cadence marking the end of the recapitulation and the start of the cadenza—i.e. the cadenzas are 'inserted' —but in other respects the older formal articulation between solo and ritornello at the end of the movement is discarded. Mozart had anticipated this development in the first movement of his C minor Concerto, K. 491, to which Beethoven's C minor Concerto—the first in which the soloist continues after the cadenza—has often been compared. Yet the two cases are very different. In the Mozart concerto the trill resolves conventionally into a loud

---

[10] Although cadential trills do not normally occur on the dominant note, a precedent exists in Beethoven's Concert Rondo in B flat, WoO 6, thought to be the original finale for the Op. 19 concerto. Here the brief cadenza comes to rest on an extended trill on the dominant note, underneath which the orchestra enters with the rondo theme. For an edn. based on Beethoven's autograph of this work see *Beethoven: Supplemente zur Gesamtausgabe*, iii, ed. W. Hess (Wiesbaden, 1960). The version printed in the old *Gesamtausgabe* is based on Czerny's revision, and differs considerably from Beethoven's original at the point where the cadenza is introduced.

[11] The soloist also continues into the closing bars of most finales, but this was less unusual.

tutti, and it is only after this tutti that an epilogue in the form of a *pp* series of solo arpeggios to light orchestral accompaniment rounds the movement off over a tonic pedal. In Beethoven's C minor Concerto, though, the trill does not resolve conventionally, so that the tension of the movement is not fully dissipated by the cadenza, and the energy remaining in the piano part carries it through after the trill right up to the closing bars. The piano continues to make important contributions to the music, and enters into dialogue with the orchestra. All four of the first movements listed above end in a similar way with a crescendo to at least fortissimo accompanied by surging scales and arpeggios in the piano part until the last three fortissimo chords.

So soloist and orchestra combine in a grand sweep forward which continues beyond the final solo cadence and beyond the cadenza into the closing bars. This very fact robs the cadenza of part of its effect and renders it less climactic. In the earlier classical concerto the movement would have been considered to be virtually over by the end of the cadenza, the subsequent tutti serving merely to round off the movement, satisfy the requirements of formal balance, and provide a foil for the brilliance of the preceding cadenza; in many instances it was rendered inaudible by the applause which greeted the soloist's cadenza. In Beethoven's hands the cadenza becomes a part of the coda, no longer either a complete resolution in itself of the tensions of the movement, nor a mere 'parenthesis' (see Chapter 11). This may be seen as another reason why eventually the ad libitum cadenza had to be abandoned. If it was conceived as only a part of a larger section, it made little sense for the composer to relinquish responsibility for the content of the passage. A cadenza needs to function as a parenthesis if it is to be ad libitum.

Cadenzas or Codas?

The pattern which emerges from a study of Beethoven's use of the cadenza within the concerto is one of increasing integration. This process manifests itself partly in the thematic derivation of all but one[12] of his ad libitum cadenzas—a common enough procedure by the turn of the century—but also in the frequent blurring of the articulation of the ending, as a result of which it becomes difficult to distinguish between cadenzas and codas. In many respects Beethoven's ad libitum cadenzas resemble codas, a point which Tovey[13] and Mies both emphasize, but the converse is also true.

The first movement of the Triple Concerto, Op. 56, does not contain a cadenza at all, but its coda uses some of the gestures characteristic of cadential preparation. The multiple trills at the final solo cadence resolve onto a surprise harmony of A flat (bar 462) at which point a tutti begins, which seems to signal the approach of a cadenza. It reaches a dominant harmony instead of a 6–4,

---

[12] No. 11. For a discussion of the content of the cadenzas see below.
[13] D. F. Tovey, 'Prefaces to Cadenzas for Classical Concertos', *Essays and Lectures on Music* (London, etc., 1949), 315 ff.

however, and the soloists re-enter (bar 470); they participate throughout the remainder of the coda right up to the closing bars. In this instance Beethoven does no more than hint at a cadenza—it cannot strictly be claimed that this movement contains one.

An interesting work to consider in connection with the overlap of function between cadenza and coda is the 'Waldstein' Sonata. Several writers have commented on the cadenza-like character of the codas in the outer movements of this exceptionally brilliant and concerto-like sonata. According to the definitions adopted throughout the present survey, however, it is not possible to regard either passage as a cadenza, in view of the lack of clear articulation at the beginning of the passages. Yet, as Barry Cooper has shown, the word 'Cadenza' actually appeared in Beethoven's sketches for the first movement at an early stage,[14] and Cooper goes on to suggest that the initial idea of a cadenza survived as bars 259–94 of the movement.

According to this interpretation, bars 249–59 correspond to the tutti cadential preparation, beginning on a surprise harmony of D flat but working towards the dominant at bar 259 where the cadenza begins, while bars 295 to the end correspond to the closing tutti. Each of these passages bears a certain resemblance to the corresponding section of a concerto movement. Surprise harmonies at the final solo cadence are not uncommon in Beethoven's concertos (see the first movements of the Triple Concerto, the Violin Concerto, or the G major Concerto), and they even have precedents in the concertos of Mozart and C. P. E. Bach;[15] moreover, the acceleration in harmonic rhythm, the fortissimo marking in bar 257, and the chromatic approach towards the dominant in the bass are all characteristic of cadential preparation. Similarly, the closing 'tutti' with its thematic opening and its huge crescendo from pianissimo to fortissimo is reminiscent of the endings of some of Beethoven's concerto movements. Many of the techniques used in the 'cadenza' itself are familiar from Beethoven's ad libitum cadenzas (e.g. virtuoso figurations, fragmentation and manipulation of the main theme, recollection of the second theme). The difficulty with this interpretation, however, is the lack of articulation at the beginning of the passage in bar 259: in the absence of a recognizable signal the listener is not led to regard the passage as an insertion. The evidence of the sketches supports the view that the coda of this movement may have been originally conceived as a cadenza surrounded by a pair of tuttis, a pattern to which it does bear certain resemblances, but this does not alter the fact that the end product is pure coda and not a cadenza.[16]

---

[14] B. Cooper, 'The Evolution of the First Movement of Beethoven's "Waldstein" Sonata', *Music and Letters*, 58 (1977), 175.

[15] See the final solo cadences in the first movements of Mozart, K. 453, and C. P. E. Bach, H. 473 and 475 (see Ex. 33 above).

[16] Cf. the codas into which the arrangers of Viotti's late violin concertos sometimes transformed his obbligato finale cadenzas. See Ch. 11.

Although the evidence of the sketches provides no comparable clues in the case of the last movement, it is possible by analogy with the first movement to point out a resemblance to tutti preparation in bars 441–65, to a cadenza in bars 465–514, and to a closing tutti from bar 515 to the end. Again, however, the articulation in bar 465 is not clear enough to indicate more than a resemblance.[17] It is true that the harmonic character, the thematic treatment, and particularly the use of trills in the passage between bars 465 and 514 cause it to resemble Beethoven's cadenzas closely, but, as has been noted, many of Beethoven's cadenzas closely resemble his codas. The two overlap so much in his music that in the end they can be distinguished from one another only by their articulation.

At this point it is interesting to consider an earlier C major Piano Sonata which also betrays the influence of concerto form, namely Op. 2 No. 3. The first movement, uniquely among Beethoven's solo piano sonatas,[18] contains a genuine cadenza, fully written-out, clearly articulated by a 6–4 with a cadential fermata, set off from its surroundings by its rhapsodic character, and resolving conventionally via a supertonic trill and a chromatic scale into a passage resembling a closing tutti. If the analogy were to be pursued, it would be possible to compare the sudden *ffp* in bar 218 with a tutti entry (once again on an unexpected harmony), and the passage between bar 218 and the fermata in bar 232 with tutti cadential preparation. Harmonically it does indeed have the character of cadential preparation, although texturally it is not at all orchestral in character.

The finale of the sonata, strictly speaking, does not contain a cadenza, but the passage beginning in bar 281 suggests one at least as strongly as do the corresponding passages from the 'Waldstein' Sonata discussed above. The two previous bars are a clear reference to the gestures of tutti cadential preparation, and the extended trill accompanied by thematic allusions and followed by a double and then a triple trill is a feature found in many of Beethoven's genuine cadenzas.

Yet the most interesting feature of this passage is the failure of the trill to resolve conventionally. Instead, the trill on D changes to a trill on D sharp. After a general pause with a fermata, there follows a thematic allusion in A major, then another in A minor, each followed by a rest with a fermata, in the

[17] The extent to which the 'cadenza' in the finale of the 'Waldstein' Sonata lacks clear articulation at the opening is well illustrated by the differences of opinion concerning the point at which it actually begins. Tovey (*Beethoven* (London, 1944), 113), interprets bar 465 as the start of the passage, whereas Knödt ('Zur Entwicklungsgeschichte', p. 419) and Mies (*Krise*, p. 44) place the start of the 'cadenza' in bar 403. Referring to the first-movement 'cadenza', Knödt claims that it begins 'gradually' after the abrupt change of harmony in bar 249.

[18] An early chamber work which also includes an obbligato cadenza is the Sonata in F for Cello and Piano, Op. 5 No. 1 (first movement, bars 347–85). At 38½ bars, this appears to be Beethoven's longest clearly articulated obbligato cadenza. It is a genuine ensemble cadenza, barred throughout, and one of his most conventional. A thematic section and a virtuoso section are separated by six bars in adagio tempo.

manner of the wistful 'pause for breath' discussed above; it is the fortissimo *Tempo primo* which carries the music forward to the final bars, at which point the cadence is eventually resolved. In this movement Beethoven seems to be trying out for the first time the technique which he was to use in many of his later concertos, in which the trill does not resolve conventionally, but merges with what follows.

At the cadential fermata in the finale of the G major Concerto is found the instruction 'la cadenza sia corta'—'let the cadenza be short'. It is, in Tovey's words, 'an incident in one of Beethoven's greatest codas'.[19] A consequence of the absorption of the cadenza into the coda was that the ad libitum section could, and indeed should, be shorter than it had previously been. Beethoven's ad libitum cadenzas vary in length from 5 to 126 bars (see Table 7); his obbligato cadenzas on the other hand are always fairly short, because they are usually integrated into the coda, and they do not seem to be intended, as some of his longer ad libitum cadenzas do, to fulfil the function of an entire coda in themselves. The unaccompanied section of the cadenza in the first movement of the 'Emperor' Concerto is remarkably brief, a feature which is in some ways even more striking than either its obbligato character or its unobtrusive ending, since it contrasts so markedly with the trend towards great length observable in both the obbligato and the ad libitum cadenzas of contemporary composers of concertos.

So what are the features common to the ad libitum cadenza and the coda in this music? A stimulating account of the processes involved in Beethoven's codas is contained in a short article by Joseph Kerman.[20] Kerman argues that in addition to their harmonic function, the emphatic affirmation of the tonic, they possess an important thematic function which is not adequately expressed by such terms as 'second development'. That is to say, some hitherto unresolved 'aberrance' in the main theme is finally ironed out during the coda. Thus the chromatic C sharp in the opening bars of the Eroica Symphony is fully resolved not in the recapitulation, where it is merely reinterpreted, but in the coda, thereby allowing the theme at last to be presented in an undiluted diatonic form in bars 631–62. Similarly, the main theme of the first movement of the first symphony is restated one scale degree higher in both the exposition and the development—in the coda it is restated on successive steps of the C major triad. Kerman describes this technique as 'thematic completion', and claims that it is the principal theme of the movement which normally receives this treatment and therefore features most prominently in the coda. When subsidiary themes are used as well it is often in the manner of a 'distant recollection'.

Kerman adds a brief discussion of certain cadenza-like features in Beethoven's codas, which, as he admits, is characterized by a lack of any clear

[19] 'Prefaces', p. 320.
[20] J. Kerman, 'Notes on Beethoven's Codas', in A. Tyson (ed.), *Beethoven Studies*, iii (Cambridge, 1982), 141 ff.

definition of what a cadenza is.[21] One of the points made by Kerman is that the manner in which secondary material is used, more akin to recollection than to development, is common to both.[22] He also points out that both are principally concerned with the main theme of the movement, subjecting it to various developmental techniques, and presenting it in keys not previously used. This is almost a complete reversal of the original purpose of including thematic references in cadenzas—confirmation of the prevailing *Affekt* through recollection of material.

It is hardly possible for ad libitum cadenzas to fulfil the function of 'thematic completion' described by Kerman in connection with Beethoven's codas, because this technique requires that an aspect of the theme be left incomplete in its earlier appearances in the parent movement. Beethoven could no more introduce such a technique into cadenzas written for the already fourteen-year-old C major Concerto than he could into the pair which he wrote for Mozart's D minor Concerto, neither work having been written with such a process in mind. This may partly account for the failure of some of Beethoven's ad libitum cadenzas to satisfy certain observers, Tovey in particular. The fugal treatment of the theme in cadenza 4 and the grandiose scoring of the opening bars of the Op. 61 Concerto in bars 96 ff. of cadenza 12 could both be interpreted as attempts at something akin to 'thematic completion' of themes which were already sufficiently complete in themselves. In both outer movements of the G major Concerto there occurs an example of thematic completion in the codas, where the slightly unstable or ambiguous main ideas are presented over unmistakeably tonic harmony in bars 356–70 and 594–600 respectively, and it is significant that this occurs at the very end of the movement, after the ad libitum cadenza in each case. One of the instances of thematic completion quoted by Kerman occurs in bars 261–7 of the first movement of the 'Waldstein' Sonata, during the 'quasi-cadenza'. Clearly there is nothing to prevent Beethoven from using the opportunity provided by an obbligato cadenza for practising thematic completion of this kind, but in the nature of the case an ad libitum cadenza does not offer comparable opportunities.

Kerman is anxious that the term 'second development' be avoided in discussion of Beethoven's codas, since the function of a coda is resolution rather than exploration, however many apparently developmental techniques may be used in the process. One of the faults of Beethoven's ad libitum cadenzas is that they do in fact resemble second development sections, and that they do explore new tonal and developmental possibilities at the expense of clear resolution. Mies has shown that they are frequently comparable in

---

[21] Even some of his examples of 'explicit cadenzas' are not sufficiently articulated to warrant the label 'cadenza' according to the definitions used here. See e.g. the passage starting in bar 335 of the first movement of the Quintet for Piano and Wind, Op. 16.

[22] Examples are found in bars 284–94 of the first movement of the 'Waldstein' Sonata, and bars 33–5 of cadenza 7.

length with the real development section, sometimes even longer. The same is true of some codas, but since resolution of tonal and thematic tensions is such a marked characteristic of Beethoven's codas, no confusion results. Beethoven's obbligato cadenzas, on the other hand, never resemble second developments.

Cadenzas or Eingänge?

Consideration of what follows the cadenza raises another issue, namely the difference between cadenzas and *Eingänge*.

  The difficulty concerns those hybrid cases which have been labelled here as 'rondo cadenzas'. Mies, in his discussion of Mozart's cadenzas, calls such passages *Eingänge* on the grounds that they lead into a thematic statement. Cadenzas by contrast, he says, serve not to decorate transitions, but to intensify and resolve the tensions of the movement, to hold up the flow of the movement, and articulate the cadence into an orchestral ritornello. What he does not take into account is that 'rondo cadenzas' do all these things except the last, and thus combine features of the cadenza and of the *Eingang*. In describing cadenza 8 as an *Eingang* with the function of a cadenza[23] Mies seems to contradict himself, since it is primarily by function that he distinguishes between the two. What he means is that this 'cadenza' is so short that it resembles an *Eingang*. Cadenza 11, which lasts only five bars, is even shorter; in fact it is the shortest as well as the only non-thematic ad libitum cadenza, but in these respects it resembles most of Beethoven's obbligato cadenzas; these are usually considerably shorter than the ad libitum cadenzas, and only one is thematically derived, namely that found in the first movement of the 'Emperor' Concerto.[24]

  In the interests of consistency of definition, the two phenomena should be distinguished by function rather than by content. The term *Eingang* is here reserved for those improvisatory passages which articulate a local event, such as the return of a rondo theme (G major Concerto finale, bar 415), or a transition to a new movement or section (between the second and third movements of the Violin Concerto, or bar 407 of the C minor Concerto finale). The primary function of a cadenza is harmonic resolution of the preceding paragraph, section, or movement. If it happens also to be followed by a thematic statement, as is for example the obbligato cadenza in the first movement of the Sonata for Cello and Piano, Op. 5 No. 1, then it possesses as a secondary function what for a genuine *Eingang* is the primary function —that of pointing ahead to a new event. The cadenza/*Eingang* problem, like the cadenza/coda problem mentioned above and the cadenza/capriccio prob-

[23] Mies, *Krise*, p. 19.
[24] It is true that the orchestral parts from the slow-movement cadenza to the B flat Concerto use the opening idea of the movement, but the solo part is not thematically derived.

lem of almost a century earlier, is an instance of the overlap in function which at times existed between the cadenza and other related phenomena. It is important to be able to distinguish between different traditions of improvisation; this is not to deny that different traditions sometimes converge.

The Content of Beethoven's Cadenzas

The cadenza volume of the new complete edition of Beethoven's works[25] contains seventeen 'cadenzas', although three of these are actually *Eingänge*.[26] In other words there are fourteen genuine ad libitum cadenzas by Beethoven, and apart from the pair which were composed for use in Mozart's D minor Concerto, they are all intended for use in his own concertos. These cadenzas are listed in Table 7, together with an indication of their length, and of the movement to which they belong. The numbering of the *Beethoven Werke* edition is used here and throughout the ensuing discussion. All are thought to have been written *c.* 1809.

Of the three cadenzas provided for the first movement of the C major Concerto, the first is incomplete, the second is relatively short, and the third, which is the one most often played, is the only ad libitum cadenza by

Table 7. *Cadenzas by Beethoven*

Cadenza	Length in bars*	Concerto movement
1	60+	no. 1/i
2	32	no. 1/i
3	126+	no. 1/i
4	79+	no. 2/i
5	65+	no. 3/i
6	100+	no. 4/i
7	51+	no. 4/i
8	11+	no. 4/i
9	35	no. 4/iii
11	5+	no. 4/iii
12	125+	Violin Concerto arrangement, i
15	15+	Violin Concerto arrangement, iii
16	66+	Mozart, K. 466/i
17	44+	Mozart, K. 466/iii

  * In most cases cadenzas are longer than the given no. of bars might suggest, since the more or less extended unbarred passages are counted as a single bar in the figure quoted. Hence the use of +.

[25] *BW* VII: 7.

[26] No. 10 is intended for use in bar 415 of the finale of the G major Concerto, no. 13 for the transition into the finale of the Violin Concerto arrangement, and no. 14 for bar 92 of the finale of the latter.

Beethoven which Tovey[27] considers to be completely successful. Mies[28] has shown how all three follow a broadly similar pattern, beginning with a version of the main theme, and moving on to develop not only this theme but also the main secondary theme of the movement.

Development is a key word here; there is nothing in Mozart's cadenzas to correspond to the type of extensive developmental treatment which occurs for example in bars 72–99 of Beethoven's cadenza 3, in which the opening idea of the C major Concerto is presented in quite new harmonic guises and subjected to imitation, diminution, and fragmentation for a stretch of over twenty bars. Whereas Mozart relies mainly on quotation, unfamiliar juxtaposition, and at the most a new continuation of thematic ideas, fragmenting the endings so as to lead forward and avoid regular cadences, Beethoven treats the cadenza as an opportunity to return to the techniques practised in the development section. Mozart maintains 'dominant tension' throughout his cadenzas: while never cadencing strongly in the home key, he never actually leaves it.[29] According to Swain it is on account of the close association of the main theme of the movement with tonic stability that Mozart makes relatively little use of it in his cadenzas,[30] although it should be pointed out that in his rondo cadenzas Mozart does make extensive use of the rondo theme. Beethoven, on the other hand, explores a wide range of keys in his cadenzas, and often establishes them clearly by quoting material of marked tonal stability. He tends to rely principally on the main theme of the movement; low-register dominants are no more prominent than other bass-notes, so the 'dominant tension' characteristic of Mozart's cadenzas is not clearly maintained.[31] Beethoven expands the tonal range far beyond the modest recommendations of Türk (see Chapter 2). Cadenza 1 quotes the second theme of the C major Concerto in E flat, F minor, and G minor, cadenza 5 approaches the G major statement of the second theme of the C minor Concerto via D major harmonies, reached through an enharmonic change from G flat to F sharp, while cadenza 16 digresses into B major and minor in a cadenza for a D minor movement! This tonal exploration, combined with further developmental treatment of the main themes, is what makes his cadenzas seem to resemble second developments. Perhaps the most obvious difference from conventional development sections, apart from the absence of orchestral accompaniment, is the use of rhapsodic bravura material to separate the sections devoted to different thematic ideas; these help to achieve an improvisatory, fantasia-like style.

---

[27] 'Prefaces', p. 316.

[28] *Krise*, p. 19.

[29] Swain, 'Form and Function', pp. 36 ff. Hence the prominence of low-register dominant harmony notes in his cadenzas.

[30] Ibid. 40. Relatively little use at the beginning of the cadenza, that is. Swain discusses a few instances of harmonic reinterpretation of the main theme later in the cadenza, but in comparison with Beethoven's extensive developmental treatment this still constitutes relatively little use.

[31] This is doubtless because his ad libitum cadenzas are often integrated into a larger section in which the 'cadential' context is present only at a deeper level of structure.

Towards the end of cadenza 3 is a good example of the use made by Beethoven of the trill in his cadenzas. As the Badura-Skodas have observed, double trills are most unusual in Mozart's solo cadenzas:[32] in Beethoven's they are fairly common. In his cadenzas he frequently sustains trills for long periods while motivic references are made above or below. Mozart too uses trills in this way, as for example at the end of cadenza 60, but Beethoven frequently applies this practice to double trills, and, as has been seen, he often delays or even avoids a conventional resolution of the trills, unlike Mozart.

Mention might also be made of the fact that the resolution of the trills towards the end of Beethoven's cadenza 3 is delayed for several lines of partly rhapsodic passage-work. When it arrives, the ending of the cadenza is unconventional. Not only does the trill stop, to be replaced at the end of the cadenza by detached dominant seventh chords, but there is a surprise 'piano' marking on the chord immediately preceding the re-entry of the orchestra.

A still more unconventional conclusion is found in cadenza 4, which seems to have been influenced by the surging codas of the later piano concertos, particularly the G major. The last eleven bars of cadenza 4 take place over a tonic pedal, and when the tutti re-enters it is with the effect not of resolving the cadence but of forming the peak of a huge crescendo built up over sweeping piano scales of B flat major. The cadenza does not contain a trill, nor is there any clearly articulated dominant harmony to resolve the cadential 6–4 and prepare the return of the tonic, which arrives remarkably unobtrusively and then simply remains. This is the cadenza which Tovey described as a joke, since the pompous 'fugato' with which it opens is so grotesquely out of keeping with the context. The concealment of the resolution may be seen as another aspect of the humour of the cadenza. If any of Beethoven's cadenzas deserves the epithet 'cadenza ma senza cadere', it is this one, not on account of its context in the concerto movement, but because of the lack of an articulated cadential resolution within the cadenza itself.

It should be remembered that the unconventional endings of these two cadenzas postdate the experiments with 'unresolved' cadential trills in the C major, C minor, G major, and Violin Concertos. They may be interpreted as attempts to disguise the articulation of the endings in spite of the conventional surroundings of the inserted cadences in the scores of the concertos.

Cadenza 5 provides a further illustration of many of the features observed in the discussion of cadenzas 1–3, namely the developmental treatment of the main theme of the concerto, the use of bravura material to articulate the different sections, quotation of the secondary theme, and use of long trills, including double trills with motivic work above and below. One distinctive feature of this cadenza is its slightly odd beginning with an echo of the bass progression A flat–G–F sharp which had preceded the cadential fermata. This has led Mies to the hypothesis that these first two bars were meant to be played

[32] *Interpreting Mozart*, p. 227.

during the last two bars of the tutti, and that the cadenza really only begins in bar 3, without any interruption in the solo part.[33] There are in fact many separately preserved sources of ad libitum cadenzas from the classical period which begin with the last few orchestral chords before the fermata.[34] In this instance, however, such an interpretation will not do, for the harmony of the first bar of the cadenza does not fit that of bar 414 in the cadential approach. A similar echo of the orchestral approach was to occur at the beginning of cadenza 12, written for the Violin Concerto arrangement (see below). It may be seen as an extension of the common practice of basing the opening of the cadenza on the motivic idea heard during the approach bars; here, however, it virtually amounts to a quotation.

Cadenzas 6 and 7 for the first movement of the G major Concerto both involve changes of metre. The first, which is the longer and more frequently played of the two, begins with a version of the main theme of the movement in 6/8, representing a rhythmic intensification. When the main secondary theme of the movement is quoted in bar 21, the music returns to common time. One of the most exciting moments in the cadenza occurs when these two metres are juxtaposed in bars 74–80, in preparation for a third thematic idea in bars 81 ff., which in turn leads to the 6–4 that signals the approaching end of the cadenza.

Much of this cadenza explores the tonic minor and related flat key areas. The second theme in bar 21, for example, is in B flat major, and the frenzied developmental section that begins with the return of 6/8 time in bar 36 explores these key areas further. Not inappropriately, the 6–4 harmony which arrives in bar 92 is actually the tonic minor, and the long trill on the supertonic which follows from bar 93 is a semitone trill. When the metre is suspended yet again seven bars later, the harmony underneath having eventually resolved onto the dominant in bar 99, the trill opens out beautifully into a tone trill with a B natural. An expressive flourish working up to a top C and back again leads into the trill on A which Beethoven included in the original score, and there follows what has been described above as the second, accompanied section of the cadenza—effectively a continuation and coda.

The second cadenza written for this movement is considerably shorter and rather more disjointed, in the manner of a wild and disorderly improvisation. Within the space of a few bars it works its way from the 6–4 on D to a 'presto' episode in 2/4 in C minor, utilizing the shape of the main theme in order to get there. The C minor episode is thematically unrelated to the movement, and comes to an end almost as abruptly as it had begun, when the Neapolitan D flat is reinterpreted enharmonically as C sharp, enabling Beethoven to move unexpectedly to A major for some expressive meanderings up and down the arpeggio and scale which lead to a statement of the opening theme in this

[33] *Krise*, p. 25.
[34] e.g. the cadenzas by Giordani discussed in Ch. 10, and cadenzas G and K from K⁶ 626a II.

astonishingly remote key. Having briefly established one very flat key and one very sharp key,[35] Beethoven leaps off once again into wild improvisatory passage-work, moving via some diminished seventh arpeggios to a series of double trills, each of which is accompanied by imitation of the main idea of the movement in both direct and inverted forms in the outer parts. The third such double trill is harmonized as the dominant of G major, and is prolonged in a passage which explores the highest notes available on the six-octave keyboard, before returning to Beethoven's score.

The third cadenza provided for this movement is even shorter, in fact it is very short indeed, lasting only eleven bars. It contains a few references to the opening theme, and its harmonic range is limited.

These three cadenzas are very different from one another, much more so in fact than the three for the C major Concerto first movement. It seems as if Beethoven was deliberately trying three very different solutions to the problem of supplying a cadenza to this movement. The first is probably the most successful, viewed outside its context. The 6/8 treatment of the main idea is inspired, and the thematic development is handled with the mastery of Beethoven's greatest middle-period works, achieving an immensely exciting sweep through to the trill. The second cadenza, being less coherent, lacks the assurance and dynamism of the first, but Beethoven was probably aiming here at a cadenza which sounded more like an improvisation and less like a composed coda/development section. The third cadenza seems intended to be as brief as possible, in order not to hold up the progress of the movement, nor to weaken the drama of what is still to come. In this respect it resembles the cadenza to the 'Emperor' Concerto more than either of the others. Magnificent and exciting though the first of these cadenzas for the G major Concerto is, it might be thought too big and too dramatic for its context, given that it is only a part of the coda. The most prophetic of the three, strangely enough, is the third, since it is this one which merges most successfully with the concluding section, whereas the two larger cadenzas tend to draw too much attention to themselves as if they were independent entities.

Beethoven supplies two cadenzas for the third movement of the G major Concerto, which were written as 'second cadenzas' to be paired with cadenzas 6 and 8 respectively. The first, no. 9, is the longer of the two, and it corresponds in excitement and forward thrust to no. 6, whereas the second, no. 11, is only five bars long and does no more than outline the G major arpeggio in preparation for a trill on the supertonic—the minimum requirement for a cadenza. Cadenza 9 opens with a dramatic treatment of the idea heard immediately before the cadential fermata, which is then extended for ten bars, to be followed by a more relaxed passage devoted to the second main

---

[35] Such is the tonal irregularity of this cadenza that Swain interprets the humorous heading given to it in the autograph, 'cadenza ma senza cadere', to refer to the lack of tonal stability within the cadenza ('Form and Function', p. 51). The interpretation adopted here, however, is that this heading refers to the context in the concerto.

theme of the movement. After this the semiquavers return and carry the music forward to the two dramatic chromatic harmonies which usher in the trill. Harmonically the cadenza ranges no further than C major, the subdominant—a particularly prominent key in this movement, which actually begins on the subdominant chord. Cadenza 9 is therefore much more concise than most of Beethoven's first-movement cadenzas. The shorter alternative, however, is so concise as to be virtually an unembellished cadence, and it lacks the tautness of no. 9. Beethoven seems to have been attempting to make cadenzas 8 and 11 as short as possible.

Of the four remaining cadenzas, nos. 12 and 15 were written for Beethoven's arrangement of his Violin Concerto, while nos. 16 and 17 are intended for use in the D minor Concerto, K. 466, by Mozart. No. 12 is one of Beethoven's longest cadenzas, and it is particularly remarkable for its use of a timpani solo to accompany the piano during the Marcia section (bars 36–54) and thereafter. The principal thematic idea of this concerto, stated by the timpanist in the opening bar of the movement, returns during this section of the cadenza in its original scoring. Indeed it permeates the texture, especially that of the development section, throughout the concerto. Mies draws attention to the frequent use of march-like, military rhythms in Beethoven's middle-period music,[36] and it seems to make sense to link this Marcia section with that particular strand in Beethoven's music. Its phraseology is entirely regular, making it unlike any other passage in a Beethoven cadenza: there are two eight-bar phrases, each repeated—a perfect miniature binary form! It seems a remarkably trite passage; the reason for this is that it serves as a relief to the intensity of the surrounding improvisatory passages, in the way that lyrical secondary themes in cadenzas normally do, but the (deliberate) effect here is not so much of relaxation as of bathos. (Such sudden changes in mood from great intensity to triviality were to become a feature of the late style; see for example the 'alla marcia' which follows the 'Heiliger Dankgesang' in the A minor Quartet, Op. 132.)

The first eight bars of the cadenza are a literal quotation of the first eight bars of the preceding tutti (which are in turn a transposed quotation of bars 28–35 of the opening ritornello). As was found to be the case in cadenza 5, however, this passage cannot possibly be intended to be played during the tutti since from bar 11 onwards it would not match the harmony of the orchestra. Its 'orchestral' style and its surprise harmony of B flat major immediately after the cadential fermata are unusual. In view of the repetition of so much of the preceding tutti, the unpianistic writing and the harmonic discontinuity with the penultimate, this opening does not appear particularly successful.

The climax of the cadenza is surely the moment when the material of the

---

[36] Mies, *Krise*, pp. 31 f. Other examples are the funeral marches in the Eroica Symphony and the A flat Sonata, Op. 26, and the first movement of the 'Emperor' Concerto.

first thirteen bars of the concerto is quoted with thick piano chords in bars 96–108; the virtuoso continuation leads directly to the trill, under which the ubiquitous drum-beat figure makes its appearance once again in left hand and kettle-drum.

The finale cadenza, by contrast, is an unambitious and more successful piece both in terms of its constant momentum and its modest scale, which enables it to fit more comfortably into its surroundings; the semiquaver figuration is maintained from start to finish—the material is either neutral bravura passage-work, or else quotation in 'orchestral' style of bars 273–6 from the cadential preparation, themselves derived from bars 46–7 of the movement. A series of double trills leaping through three octaves leads into the irregular resolution which is written into the score.

This cadenza is not particularly idiomatic. Quasi-orchestral textures are not uncommon in cadenzas (see Mozart, cadenza 64, bars [11]–[21], Beethoven, cadenza 2, bars 20–3), but here the cadenza seems to consist of very little else. The reason may be that Beethoven again feels the need to incorporate the passage within the coda, not allowing it to weaken the impact of the substantial amount of music still to be heard. 'La cadenza sia corta' seems once again to have been Beethoven's policy, and this could be seen as a natural step on the way to his adoption of the more ruthless policy 'non si fa una cadenza'.

The pair of cadenzas written for inclusion in Mozart's D minor Concerto, K. 466, offer a good illustration of the kind of stylistic discrepancy with the parent movement that was to become a feature of all ad libitum cadenzas written for the concertos of earlier composers for well over a century. At sixty-six bars, the first movement cadenza is longer than any Mozart cadenza, and it has already been observed that the tonal range, touching on B minor and major, far exceeds that of any Mozart example. Three themes from the movement are used—that of the opening, the first piano entry, and the piano's second subject. The opening idea in particular is subjected to a degree of developmental treatment rarely encountered in Mozart's cadenzas. Mies has pointed out how in the opening bars of the cadenza the three constituent parts of this first idea are presented successively rather than simultaneously as in Mozart's original—the triplet scale in the bass, the melodic outline of the upper part, and the syncopations of the upper parts. The concluding trill, while not as brilliant as those of some of Beethoven's other cadenzas, is nevertheless extended considerably and a number of thematic references are made underneath it, as is so often the case during Beethoven's cadential trills.

The finale cadenza is rather shorter, and also more brilliant—the concluding chain of trills and double trills is thoroughly characteristic of Beethoven's cadenza style and quite foreign to Mozart's. Two thematic ideas are treated in succession, the opening two bars of the rondo theme and the main second subject. The intensive preoccupation with the first of these in the earlier part of the cadenza is typical of Beethoven, although it should be remembered that it is also characteristic of Mozart's rondo cadenzas.

Why Did Beethoven Write Ad Libitum Cadenzas?

It is on the basis of the six-octave range employed in these cadenzas that they are currently assumed to have been written c.1809.[37] This is the date given (with a question mark) for all the above cadenzas in the work-list in *Grove*, and it was this dating which Mies used in his discussion of Beethoven's cadenzas in 1970. Sketches for cadenzas survive from the time of composition of the C major and B flat Concertos (mid 1790s),[38] but it was apparently more than a decade later that Beethoven first wrote complete cadenzas for use in any of his concertos. The reason for writing them is unclear. There is no evidence that he ever intended to publish them, and although it has been suggested that they might have been written for the Archduke Rudolph, or for some other pupil,[39] no proof exists. It is particularly interesting that Beethoven should have made sketches for cadenzas. He was perfectly capable of improvising them, and had he simply been writing down an improvisation it is unlikely that it would have taken the form of a sketch. He seems to have regarded the cadenza as a compositional problem even at the time of composition of the two concertos mentioned.

It seems that 1809 was a year of intensive preoccupation with cadenzas, and that Beethoven never returned to them or used them again in his music. As Mies points out, this was also the year of the fantasias Opp. 77 and 80 (the last instances of the use of this word in Beethoven's music) and of Beethoven's last concerto, the 'Emperor' Concerto, in which an obbligato cadenza merges imperceptibly with the coda. As Mies suggests, there may have been some internal motivation for the composition of so many improvisatory works in such a short space of time; his theory is that the compositional difficulty which Beethoven was trying to solve was the problem of reconciling the ad libitum tradition with his increasing tendency towards compositional control and integration.

As late as 1804, Beethoven is known to have approved the use of ad libitum cadenzas written by soloists other than himself in performances of his concertos. Ferdinand Ries recounts in *Biographische Notizen* how he sought Beethoven's advice over the provision of a cadenza for a performance of the C minor Concerto: 'I had asked Beethoven to compose a cadenza for me, which he refused, and instructing me to write one myself, said he would correct it.'[40]

---

[37] See G. Kinsky, *Das Werk Beethovens: Thematisch-bibliographisches Verzeichnis seiner sämtlichen vollendeten Kompositionen*, rev. H. Halm (Munich, 1955), 47 f.

[38] See G. Nottebohm, *Zweite Beethoveniana* (Leipzig, 1887), 66 ff.

[39] Kinsky, rev. Halm, *Verzeichnis*, pp. 36, 47 f., 94, 138.

[40] F. G. Wegeler and F. Ries, *Biographische Notizen über Ludwig van Beethoven* (Koblenz, 1838; rev. A. C. Kalischer, 1906; repr. 1972), 114; trans. F. Noonan, *Remembering Beethoven* (London, 1988), 101.

He goes on to relate how Beethoven recommended the revision of one particular passage, but that in the actual performance, Ries disregarded Beethoven's advice and performed his own version. He brought it off well, and Beethoven was apparently delighted. While there is no good reason to suppose that after 1809 Beethoven would have objected to the interpolation of an ad libitum cadenza written by the performer in the first four piano concertos,[41] it does seem that he took a decision at around this time not to invite ad libitum interpolations from the performer in subsequent works.

Tovey quotes a remark of Beethoven's to the effect that no artist deserved the title of 'virtuoso' unless his improvisations could pass for written compositions.[42] Traditionally, didactic texts on the improvisation of cadenzas had always proclaimed the reverse, namely that cadenzas, even if they had been prepared in advance, should always sound as if they were being improvised in performance. How is this apparent contradiction to be explained?

It should be made clear, first of all, that Beethoven's remark applied principally to the improvisation of entire pieces—it was common practice at this time for a virtuoso performer to include a certain amount of improvisation in a concert, perhaps of variations or a rondo or fantasia. These should, according to Beethoven, sound like previously composed music, that is to say they should, as far as possible, possess a logical structure, obey the rules of composition, and achieve the effect of a carefully planned work.

These, then, are the qualities of a composed work that improvisations should seek to make their own. The qualities of improvisation that 'prepared' cadenzas should attempt to imitate, however, are rather different. In this case it is the spontaneity, the rhetorical perfection, the absence of a studied, mechanical effect that is sought. In Beethoven's view, good music ought to combine the spontaneity and naturalness of improvisation with the assurance and finely balanced structure of composition. Thus it is that each strives to imitate the other, without losing its identity.

Tovey regards Beethoven's ad libitum cadenzas as attempts to combine 'the rhetorical perfection of an extemporization'[43] with a high degree of compositional control. Beethoven's practice of merging the cadenza with the coda indicates that he was also keen to incorporate the rhetorical perfection of improvisation into his compositions. Three clear stages in this process may be identified: the first, 'cadenza, ma senza cadere'—deceptive resolution of the trills resulting in ambiguity over the point at which the cadenza ends; the second, 'la cadenza sia corta'—abbreviation of the ad libitum section in recognition of the fact that it is merely a part of a larger entity, namely the

---

[41] L. Misch, 'Non si fa una cadenza', *Beethoven-Studien* (Berlin, 1950), 141, assumes that Beethoven would in fact have objected, but this assumption seems to be based on nothing more solid than Misch's personal distaste for cadenzas.

[42] Tovey, 'Prefaces', p. 315.

[43] Ibid. 316.

coda; and the third, 'non si fa una cadenza'—no more ad libitum insertions from the performer, the composer assumes complete control over the text.

Mies argues that after abandoning the ad libitum cadenza and the fantasia Beethoven achieved a new synthesis of improvisatory freedom with compositional control in his so-called 'third-period' style. Instrumental recitatives, rhapsodic passages, expressive trills, sharp contrasts in mood, intense concentration of idea, blurring of structural divisions—all these things have been observed in Beethoven's cadenzas, and all were to be incorporated into his late style. There is a sense in which Beethoven's last quartets and piano sonatas represent the final chapter in the history of the classical cadenza; it would be an incomplete history, however, which ignored Beethoven's contemporaries.

13

The Virtuoso Concerto

IT is now widely held that the sources of Beethoven's keyboard style are to be found not only in the works of Viennese composers of the last few decades of the eighteenth century, but also, and perhaps more significantly, in the works of non-English composers resident in London and writing in the 1790s, known as the 'London Pianoforte School'. A. L. Ringer[1] points out many parallels between Beethoven's piano music and that of Clementi and Dussek in particular, but he also mentions John Field and Johann Baptist Cramer.[2] All four composers wrote at least one piano concerto, but it was Dussek who produced the greatest number.

Jan Ladislav Dussek

Dussek ranks alongside Viotti as one of the finest composers of concertos in the 1790s. Indeed, both composers deserve more attention than they receive.

Table 8.   *Craw's List of Piano Concertos by Dussek*

Craw no.	Key	Opus no.	Date
1	B flat	—	1779 (inaccessible)
2	C	Op. 1 No. 1	before 1783
3	E flat	Op. 1 No. 2	before 1783
4	G	Op. 1 No. 3	before 1783
33	E flat	Op. 3	1787
53	E flat	Op. 15/26	1789
77	F	Op. 14	1791?
78	F	Op. 17	c.1792
97	B flat	Op. 22	1793
104	F	Op. 27	1794
125	C	Op. 29	1795
129	C	Op. 30	1795
153	B flat	Op. 40	1798
158	F	—	1798?
187	G minor	Op. 49/50	1801
206	B flat	Op. 63 (2 pianos)	1805–6
238	E flat	Op. 70	1810

* Information from thematic catalogue of Dussek's works in H. A. Craw, 'A Biography and Thematic Catalog of the Works of J. L. Dussek (1760–1812)' (diss., Univ. of Southern California, 1964).

[1] 'Beethoven and the London Pianoforte School', *MQ* 56 (1970), 742 ff.   [2] Ibid. 743.

A list of Dussek's seventeen piano concertos is supplied in Table 8. Cadential fermatas are commonly found in the earlier concertos, up to and including Op. 17, C. 78, but seldom thereafter. We know from an eye-witness account that Dussek's cadenzas used to impress audiences in London on his arrival there:

Near the end of the first movement [in a concerto] there was always a 'cadenza', which gave the performer an opportunity of displaying his powers in *bravura*, or to show off any peculiar merit that he possessed. In this instance Dussek finished his cadence with a long shake and a turn that led in the 'Tutti' to finish the movement, and he was rapturously applauded.[3]

Half of Dussek's concertos, though, do not require cadenzas at all, and these concertos are concentrated in the latter part of his career, suggesting a preference in his later work for an integrated coda rather than an articulated cadenza. Nevertheless, to deduce with Harold Truscott that Dussek 'found out how to rid the concerto of the *cadenza*-pest, and did so'[4] is to assume a degree of dissatisfaction with the whole notion of ad libitum cadenzas that is not borne out by the evidence.

An interesting case to consider in this connection is that of the finale of the F major Concerto, Op. 27, C. 104, composed in 1794. Truscott omits to mention this concerto when listing those concertos by Dussek which contain

Ex. 57. *J. L. Dussek, Piano Concerto, Op. 27, C. 104, finale cadenza (from 1st edn.)*

---

[3] Mrs Charlotte Papendiek, *Court and Private Life in the Time of Queen Charlotte*, ed. Mrs V. D. Broughton, 2 vols. (London, 1837), ii. 184 f. This account seems to refer to a performance in Feb. 1793, although the context suggests that it was Dussek's first appearance in England, which occurred in 1789. See Craw, 'A Biography and Thematic Catalog of the works of J. L. Dussek (1760–1812)' (diss., Univ. of Southern California, 1964), 69.

[4] H. Truscott, 'Dussek and the Concerto', *The Music Review*, 16 (1955), 52.

cadenzas,[5] perhaps because the 'cadenza' (a rondo cadenza in fact) is supplied in the first edition,[6] and thus appears to be obbligato (it is reproduced in Ex. 57). Truscott claims that 'in all the rest [of Dussek's concertos] the *coda* is so contrived as to give the effect of a *cadenza* without being one or holding up the flow of the music'.[7] Yet this passage is clearly a cadenza, and as far as Dussek was concerned it is an ad libitum cadenza, for he supplied alternatives in later performances, some of which found their way into later editions.

In 1808 Breitkopf and Härtel published a piano concerto in F by Dussek as Op. 66.[8] The concerto in question is not in fact a new work, but a combination of the outer movements of Op. 27 with the slow movement from Op. 22. The finale cadenza appears in a greatly expanded version, lasting over three pages. It is likely that this version is identical to the revision of Dussek's 'lively and difficult piano concerto in F major, in which he had included a new, imaginative, tasteful and very attractively designed finale',[9] which the composer had performed at a concert in Leipzig the previous year. This concert occurred shortly after the death in 1806 of Dussek's great friend, pupil, and patron, Prince Louis Ferdinand of Prussia, in whose service Dussek had spent two years;[10] it may be supposed that Dussek was keen to regain for himself a reputation as a performer among the wider public. Thus he agreed to appear in Romberg's concert in Leipzig and took the opportunity of enlarging the cadenza in order to make a startling impression.

The following year in Paris, he tried the same trick again with even greater success. Craw quotes the following account of his performance of the Op. 27 concerto:

In the rondo, which is the most spirited caprice one could imagine, each return of the delightful motive transported the audience: but the enthusiasm reached a peak when he improvised a cadenza (an entire fantasia) in which all his ideas were reproduced with the most startling harmonic effects. The following morning the publisher Imbault visited Dussek and bought that cadenza from him for a hundred louis—it was engraved in a new edition of the concerto.[11]

No edition by Imbault of this concerto has been located.[12] However it is probable that the cadenza referred to here is identical to the one which appeared in three different Parisian editions of the concerto in the course of

---

[5] He mentions the three concertos, Op. 1, C. 2–4, the concertos Op. 3, C. 33, and Op. 15, C. 53, in 'Dussek', p. 42. Cadenzas are also required, in fact, in the concertos Op. 14, C. 77, and Op. 17, C. 78, in addition to the concerto under consideration here.

[6] Corri and Dussek, London, 1794. The cadenza is labelled.

[7] Truscott, 'Dussek', p. 42.

[8] Advertised in *AMZ* 10 (Mar. 1808), facing col. 416.

[9] *AMZ* 9 (May 1807), col. 544.

[10] *Grove*, v. 755.

[11] Craw, 'Biography', p. 170. The passage referred to is found in Amédée Méreaux, *Les Clavecinistes de 1637 à 1790: Histoire du clavecin, portraits et biographies des célèbres clavecinistes* (Paris, 1867), 80.

[12] Craw, 'Biography', p. 272.

the nineteenth century,[13] and which appears to be a later reworking of the Breitkopf cadenza. It omits a lyrical D flat major episode, maintaining greater tension by proceeding directly with thematic fragmentation and development after the initial flourish. With this one exception, all other sections of the cadenza occur in expanded form in the French version.[14]

The replacement of the passage quoted in Ex. 57 with an extended improvisation by the soloist was clearly not only sanctioned but practised by Dussek as late as 1808. So it can hardly be claimed that he regarded the cadenza as an intolerable convention needing to be expunged from the concerto.

Further evidence of a favourable disposition towards the ad libitum cadenza is found in some of the arrangements which Dussek made of violin concertos by Viotti as keyboard concertos (see Chapter 11). At least two such arrangements contain extensive slow-movement cadenzas by Dussek. Had he disapproved of the cadenza as much as Truscott suggests, he could have omitted cadenzas from his performances of such concertos (omitting also, of course, the cadential preparation).

The fact that the relatively few classical concertos in the standard concert repertoire today almost invariably contain cadenzas often gives rise to the false impression that this is true of virtually all classical concertos. Consequently, many commentators are misled into interpreting the absence of cadential fermatas as a bold rejection of convention by a composer anxious to champion the cause of good taste against the tyranny of virtuoso performers and demanding audiences.

Muzio Clementi

Only a single keyboard concerto by Muzio Clementi has survived. The concerto in question, which is in C major, also exists in a transcription as a solo piano sonata.[15] It is possible that other sonatas are transcriptions of lost concertos.[16] The first-movement cadenza, which is written out in the sole source of the concerto,[17] is retained in the sonata version, as is the cadential

---

[13] Craw mentions ('Biography', p. 272) that the Pleyel edn. (1816) of the concerto is probably a copy of the (lost) Imbault edn. The same finale cadenza is included in the 1815 reissue of the Sieber edn. (GB-Lbl g. 452m. (4)), and also, contrary to Craw's statement on p. 272 of 'Biography', in the Richault edn. (1841). In each of the three cases different plates are used.

[14] A further alternative cadenza to this finale, though not by Dussek himself, is contained in a manuscript in GB-Lcm, MS 195. It is by a certain Thomas Field, jun., and is dated 1802. It seems that it was not only Dussek who felt at liberty to replace the 'cadenza' from the original version.

[15] The sonata is listed in A. Tyson, *Thematic Catalogue of the Works of Muzio Clementi* (Tutzing, 1967), 72, as Op. 33 No. 3. Some edns. of these sonatas were published with different opus numbers.

[16] See L. Plantinga, *Clementi: His Life and Music* (London, etc., 1977), 158, 162 f.

[17] A-Wgm, Autograph Giov. Schenk.

fermata in the second movement. If not an especially distinguished cadenza (Philip Radcliffe describes it as 'otiose')[18] it is conventional mainly on account of its rather commonplace material—numerous allusions are made to the rising scale of 8–3 chords which constitutes the opening theme of the movement.

There is a certain resemblance between this opening theme and that of the finale of Beethoven's C major Sonata, Op. 2 No. 3, written soon after the publication in 1794 of Clementi's sonata. The Beethoven work has other points in common with the Clementi sonata, suggesting a connection that is more than fortuitous. It too contains a cadenza, and the strong bravura element and abundance of material have led a number of commentators to suggest the influence of concerto style.

Even though there is only one extant concerto by Clementi, there are several other cadenzas in existence, in the first instance because he sometimes included cadenzas in sonatas, such as the duet Op. 14 No. 3. His best-known examples are the parodies of the cadenza style of Mozart, Haydn, Vanhal, Kozeluch, Sterkel, and himself contained in *Musical Characteristics*, Op. 19, published in 1787.[19] With an average length of around twenty bars, these cadenzas are long enough to display some individuality, and Clementi takes the opportunity to exploit different and 'characteristic' types of figuration and elaboration in each. The middle part of the 'Cadenza alla Haydn' works insistently on a tiny rhythmic motive (Ex. 58), and the 'Cadenza alla Vanhall' exploits quasi-orchestral figurations.

The 'Cadenza alla Clementi' contains an amusing passage in which the remote key of A minor is reached during an E flat major cadenza, via an enharmonic modulation. The return to the tonic 6–4 is achieved via a 'finger-drill' figure of the kind which later became familiar in manuals of keyboard technique, in which a standard semitonal modulation is used to take the exercise through all twelve tonalities[20] (see Ex. 59). For present purposes the chief interest of the cadenzas lies in the fact of their existence. Clearly by 1787 it was taken for granted that performers would express their individuality in the cadenzas that they performed. If at an earlier stage the most important matter to consider in composing or improvising a cadenza was unity of *Affekt* with the rest of the movement, by now there was scope not simply to match the movement, but to add to it a new and to some extent

---

[18] *NOHM* viii. 328.

[19] A more detailed discussion of these cadenzas, and of the preludes which were included in the publication with them, is given in E. Badura-Skoda, 'Clementi's "Musical Characteristics" Opus 19', in H. C. Robbins Landon and R. E. Chapman (eds.), *Studies in Eighteenth-Century Music: A Tribute to Karl Geiringer on his Seventieth Birthday* (London, 1970), 53 ff.

[20] Such chain modulations are not found, however, in Clementi's own principal didactic work, the *Gradus ad Parnassum*, with the exception of no. 17, and even this proceeds up a tone at a time instead of a semitone. Perhaps Clementi used the semitonal modulating chain in his teaching without committing it to paper, or perhaps the passage in this cadenza is no more than an intriguing anticipation of the finger-drills of Béranger, etc.

Ex. 58.   *M. Clementi, 'Cadenza alla Haydn', Op. 19*

Ex. 59.   *M. Clementi, 'Cadenza alla Clementi', Op. 19*

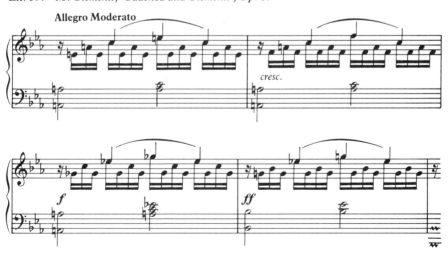

foreign element, involving the idiosyncrasies of the performer. There is no suggestion that these cadenzas belong to any particular concerto, and one has to assume that they were not written with specific concertos in mind. Rather they could be used in any concerto of the appropriate key and tempo (all are suitable for fast movements). In this respect they look backwards to the interchangeable, thematically unconnected cadenzas of the mid-century, while their independence of style from that of the movement looks ahead to the cadenzas used in nineteenth- and twentieth-century performances of the concertos from the classical repertoire.

John Field

Composed between 1799 and 1832, John Field's seven piano concertos show signs of an incipient romanticism in their delicate chromatic colourings, and the frequent nocturne-like writing. Considerable virtuosity is required in places, particularly in the fifth concerto, known as 'L'Incendie par l'orage' on account of the 'storm' passage inserted into the first movement. Daniel Steibelt had scored a great success on his arrival in London in 1798 with a concerto containing a storm passage, and the present work was clearly intended by Field to match the impact of Steibelt's popular work, which it exceeds both in technical brilliance and musical quality. The first movement of 'L'Incendie par l'orage', composed in 1815, contains not only the storm passage itself, but also an obbligato cadenza—the only instance in Field's work of a genuine cadenza (the word itself appears not infrequently in his scores referring to a rhapsodic flourish of some kind). Accompanied by pizzicato strings, it starts in an exceptionally high register, with the left hand above the right. In the course of the cadenza the left hand gradually works its way down the keyboard, only reaching a true bass register a little over half-way through. It is a cadenza in tempo. While the 'Emperor' Concerto might conceivably have served as a stimulus, there are precedents in the work of Viotti and others, and this passage is not quite so innovative as Patrick Piggott suggests in his study of Field's music.[21] None of the piano concertos requires an ad libitum cadenza.

Johann Baptist Cramer

Johann Baptist Cramer contributed rather more than either Clementi or Field to the cadenza repertory. Out of nine concertos three contain cadenzas, each of which is obbligato. The first of these, from the third concerto, Op. 26, appeared in 1801, in other words well before Field's 'L'Incendie' and

---

[21] P. Piggott, *The Life and Music of John Field (1782–1837)* (London, 1973), 169.

Beethoven's 'Emperor' Concerto. Both this and the following example, found in the fourth concerto, Op. 38 (*c*.1806), occur in rondo finales and function as rondo cadenzas, whereas the third example, the longest of the three, filling almost four pages in the piano part, occurs in the slow movement of the eighth concerto, Op. 70 (1822). While these cadenzas make some use, in the earlier stages, of motivic fragments of a commonplace character, bearing no particular relation to the material of the parent movements, and while they include a certain amount of recitative-like writing, they are perhaps most notable for their slightly mechanical exploitation of technically difficult figuration in the manner of the piano studies for which Cramer is best known. For their date these cadenzas are surprisingly limited in harmonic range.

Cramer was one of a great many composers of lightweight virtuoso display pieces for solo piano in the early years of the nineteenth century—sets of variations, rondos, fantasias, etc. He seems to have made more use of the cadenza in these works than did the majority of his contemporaries. While in some instances the 'cadenza' is little more than a brief rhapsodic elaboration of the 6–4 harmony, in other works the cadential preparation is quite orchestral in character, and is followed by fairly extended, if rather mechanical bravura figurations.[22]

Other Virtuosi

It is impossible here to single out more than a handful of the many other virtuoso pianist-composers who performed their own concertos during the 1790s and the first decades of the nineteenth century. Typical among them were Daniel Steibelt and Joseph Wölfl. Their reputation has suffered on account of their tendency towards superficial virtuosity and liking for special effects. Both in fact have had the misfortune that a particularly ostentatious work of theirs has directly inspired (or provoked!) a work of greater quality by another composer. In Steibelt's case, the storm interlude in the Third Piano Concerto known as 'L'Orage' was the inspiration for John Field's 'L'Incendie par l'orage', while Wölfl's virtuoso piano sonata, 'Non plus ultra', Op. 41, gave rise to Dussek's 'Plus ultra' sonata, C. 221. Philip Radcliffe describes Wölfl as a 'fluent but undistinguished composer of piano music'.[23]

There are no cadenzas in any of Steibelt's eight piano concertos, although they are supplied with plentiful rhapsodic embellishments to articulate such moments as the arrival of a second subject, or of the recapitulation, or the refrain of a rondo, and these passages are not infrequently labelled 'cadenza'. Wölfl, on the other hand, places inserted cadential fermatas in the first movements of each of his first two concertos,[24] and he supplies obbligato cadenzas in tempo in the third concerto and in 'Le Calme'.[25]

[22] See e.g. Cramer's arrangement of *Kreutzer's Favorite Rondo* (London, 1817).
[23] *NOHM* viii. 335. [24] Op. 20 in G major and Op. 26 in E major.
[25] Op. 32 in F major and Op. 36 in G major.

Like many contemporary composers Johann Nepomuk Hummel made only limited use of the cadenza, but written-out *Eingänge* occupy a prominent place in his concertos. A boy-pupil of Mozart, he often performed Mozart's concertos, and wrote his own cadenzas for certain of them.[26] His earliest printed original concerto is a Double Concerto for Piano and Violin in G, Op. 17 (1805). The first movement contains an extended obbligato double cadenza, lasting seventy bars. It is based on the tripartite scheme so commonly used by Mozart, although the pace is slackened and there is a great deal of virtuoso filler material. The dominant seventh harmony preceding the second section, for example, occupies eight bars. A minimum of thematic material is spun out at length with empty figurations and overlong sequences. The harmony, unusually for such a long cadenza, remains quite firmly in one place, with very little chromaticism. The concluding trill lasts for approximately eight bars—a virtuoso prolongation also common at other points in Hummel's concerto movements. (The trill at the final solo cadence in the first movement of his B minor Piano Concerto Op. 89 lasts for twenty-two bars!)

The Disappearance of the Cadenza

A number of documentary sources from this period can shed further light on the decline of the ad libitum cadenza. In addition to the comments of Hummel discussed in Chapter 4, it may be useful to consider those of one or two other writers.

A surprisingly early reference comes in Spohr's autobiography, in a passage describing a performance given in 1803 in St Petersburg by the mad violinist Tietz of a concerto of his own composition. 'In all three movements he introduced rather attractive cadenzas in the old manner . . . They were evidently improvised, for they were quite different the second time round.'[27] Admittedly the remark is ambiguous; the 'old manner' could refer to the content of the cadenzas, to the use of cadenzas in all three movements, to the practice of improvising them, or to the very fact of their appearance. If the latter, though, then the remark seems to indicate that cadenzas for melody instruments were already becoming a thing of the past. Vocal cadenzas certainly were—it has been seen how both Mozart and Haydn made less use of them in their later years—and the impossibility of performing on melody instruments cadenzas comparable in scale with the huge keyboard cadenzas found in the virtuoso concertos of the early nineteenth century may have been responsible for the earlier decline of melody instrument cadenzas. Viotti's solution—the use of orchestral accompaniment—had the effect of integrating

---

[26] GB-Lbl Add. Ms. 32222 fol. 89b ff. Others are included in printed edns. of Hummel's arrangements of various piano concertos by Mozart.

[27] Trans. directly from the German version, as it appears in Spohr, *Lebenserinnerungen*, i. 43.

the cadenza more closely with the parent movement, and this led inevitably to the loss of clear articulation and the disappearance of the cadenza.

A writer from the 1820s, F. H. J. Castil-Blaze, makes some further comments on the decline of the cadenza in his *Dictionnaire*.[28] Under the article 'Ad libitum' he says the following:

One frequently finds 'ad libitum' underneath highly complicated 'points d'orgue', rapid runs, chromatic scales; the inexperienced musician passes the 'points d'orgue' over in silence, and substitutes for the runs and flourishes the large notes painstakingly added below in order to help him simplify the awkward passage.

Castil-Blaze seems to be reviving an older usage of the phrase 'ad libitum' here, applying it not simply to the manner of performance, but to the option over inclusion or omission of a passage (the sense in which Locatelli described the capriccios from his Op. 3 violin concertos as 'ad libitum'). Large-scale cadenzas, it seems, were sometimes omitted.

Under 'point d'orgue', Castil-Blaze has this to say:

The bravura arias of the Italian school used to conclude with a 'point d'orgue' or cadenza; this custom has gradually disappeared. It is no longer found even at the end of the first allegro in concertos and symphonies concertantes; the silence used to distance (*refroidir*) the listeners, and the 'point d'orgue', even if difficult and rendered well, did not awaken as much admiration and enthusiasm as the simple trill following immediately after a rapid, vehement passage.

This may not be the most significant explanation for the decline of the cadenza; if it is true, however, that the taste of the public had turned away from elaborate cadenzas as Castil-Blaze suggests, then it would seem that the last nail in the coffin of the classical cadenza had been firmly driven home.

[28] F. H. J. Castil-Blaze, *Dictionnaire de musique moderne*, 2nd edn. (Paris, 1825).

Bibliography

◇◇◇

Agricola, Johann Friedrich, *Anleitung zur Singkunst* (Berlin, 1757).

Algarotti, Francesco, 'Saggio sopra l'opera in musica' [1755]; trans. anon. as *An Essay on the Opera* (London, 1767).

Bach, Carl Philipp Emanuel, *Versuch über die wahre Art das Clavier zu spielen*, 2 vols. (Berlin, 1753–62); facs. repr., ed. L. Hoffmann-Erbrecht (Leipzig, 1957); trans. W. J. Mitchell as *Essay on the True Art of Playing Keyboard Instruments* (New York and London, 1949).

Badura-Skoda, Eva, 'Cadenza', *Grove*, iii. 586 ff.

——'Clementi's "Musical Characteristics" Opus 19', in H. C. Robbins Landon and R. E. Chapman (eds.), *Studies in Eighteenth-Century Music: A Tribute to Karl Geiringer on his Seventieth Birthday* (London, 1970), 53 ff.

——and Paul, *Mozart-Interpretation* (Vienna and Stuttgart, 1957); trans. Leo Black as *Interpreting Mozart on the Keyboard* (London, 1962).

Boyden, David D., *The History of Violin Playing from its Origins to 1761* (London, etc., 1965).

——'The Corelli "Solo" Sonatas and Their Ornamental Additions by Corelli, Geminiani, Dubourg, Tartini and the "Walsh Anonymous"', *Musica Antiqua Europae Orientalis*, iii (Bydgoszcz, 1972), 591 ff.

Brossard, Sébastien de, *Dictionnaire de Musique* (Paris, 1703); trans. and ed. A. Gruber as *Sébastien de Brossard: Dictionary of Music* (Henryville, etc., 1982).

Brown, A. Peter, *Joseph Haydn's Keyboard Music: Sources and Style* (Bloomington, 1986).

Burney, Charles, 'Sketch of the Life of Handel', *An Account of the Musical Performances in Westminster Abbey . . . in Commemoration of Handel* (London, 1785).

——*A General History of Music*, 4 vols. (London, 1776–89); ed. F. Mercer in 2 vols. (London, 1935).

——*Dr. Burney's Musical Tours in Europe*, ed. P. Scholes, 2 vols. (London, etc., 1959).

Castil-Blaze, François Henri Joseph, *Dictionnaire de musique moderne*, 2nd edn. (Paris, 1825).

Cooper, Barry, 'The Evolution of the First Movement of Beethoven's "Waldstein" Sonata', *Music and Letters*, 58 (1977), 170 ff.

Craw, Howard Allen, 'A Biography and Thematic Catalog of the Works of J. L. Dussek (1760–1812)' (diss., Univ. of Southern California, 1964).

Crickmore, Leon, 'C. P. E. Bach's Harpsichord Concertos', *Music and Letters*, 39 (1958), 227 ff.

Cudworth, Charles, 'The English Organ Concerto', *The Score*, 8 (1953), 51 ff.

Daffner, Hugo, *Die Entwicklung des Klavierkonzerts bis Mozart* (Leipzig, 1906).

Dittersdorf, Carl Ditters von, *Autobiography*, trans. A. D. Coleridge (London, 1896; repr. 1970); original work, *Lebensbeschreibung* (Leipzig, 1801).

Dounias, Minos, *Die Violinkonzerte Giuseppe Tartinis* (Wolfenbüttel, 1935).

Drummond, Pippa, *The German Concerto: Five Eighteenth-Century Studies* (Oxford, 1980).

Edwards, Owain, 'The Cadenza in Eighteenth-Century English Concerto Fugues', *The Music Review*, 36 (1975), 92 ff.

Encyclopédie ou dictionnaire raisonné des sciences des arts et des métiers . . . , ed. D. Diderot and J. d'Alembert, 17 vols. (Paris, 1751–65; Suppléments, 4 vols., Amsterdam, 1776–7).

Encyclopédie méthodique: Musique, ed. N.-É. Framery and P. L. Ginguené, 2 vols. (Paris, 1791–1818).

Engel, Hans, *Die Entwicklung des deutschen Klavierkonzerts von Mozart bis Liszt* (Leipzig, 1927; repr. 1970).

——*Das Instrumentalkonzert*, 2 vols. (Wiesbaden, 1971–4).

Feder, Georg, 'Wieviele Orgelkonzerte hat Haydn geschrieben?', *Die Musikforschung*, 23 (1970), 440 ff.

Ferand, Ernest T., *Die Improvisation in der Musik* (Zurich, 1939).

——*Improvisation in Nine Centuries of Western Music* (Cologne, 1966).

Fischer, Wilhelm, 'Wiener Instrumentalmusik vor und um 1750', *DTÖ* xix/2, vol. 39 (Vienna, 1912; repr. Graz, 1959), pp. xxv ff.

Fleischer, H., *Christlieb Siegmund Binder (1723–89)* (Regensburg, 1941).

Freeman, Daniel E., 'The Earliest Italian Keyboard Concertos', *Journal of Musicology*, 4/2 (1985–6), 121 ff.

Giegling, Franz, *Giuseppe Torelli: Ein Beitrag zur Entwicklungsgeschichte des italienischen Konzerts* (Kassel and Basle, 1949).

Goldschmidt, Hugo, *Die Lehre von der vokalen Ornamentik* (Berlin, 1907).

Haas, Robert, *Aufführungspraxis der Musik* (Potsdam, 1931).

Haböck, F., *Die Gesangskunst der Kastraten* (Vienna, 1923).

Helm, E. Eugene, *Thematic Catalogue of the Works of Carl Philipp Emanuel Bach* (New Haven and London, 1989).

Hess, Willy, 'Die Originalkadenzen zu Beethovens Klavierkonzerten', *Schweizerische Musikzeitung*, 112 (1972), 271 ff.

Heussner, Horst, 'Zur Musizierpraxis der Klavierkonzerte im 18. Jahrhundert', *M-Jb* (1967), 165 ff.

Hiller, Johann Adam, *Anweisung zum musikalisch-zierlichen Gesang* (Leipzig, 1780).

Hoffmann-Erbrecht, Lothar, 'Klavierkonzert und Affektgestaltung: Bemerkungen zu einigen d-Moll Klavierkonzerten des 18. Jahrhunderts', *Deutsches Jahrbuch der Musikwissenschaft für 1971*, 16 (1973), 86 ff.

Hummel, Johann Nepomuk, *Ausführliche theoretisch-practische Anweisung zum Piano-Forte-Spiel* (Vienna, 1828); trans. as *A Complete Theoretical and Practical Course of Instructions on the Art of Playing the Piano Forte* (London, 1828).

Hutchings, Arthur, 'The English Concerto With or For Organ', *MQ* 47 (1961), 195 ff.

Johansen, Unni, *The Instrumental Cadenza of the Period c.1700–c.1770* (diss., Univ. of Uppsala, 1983).

Katzenberger, Günter, *Die Kadenz im Instrumentalkonzert bei Beethoven und das*

Stilproblem der nichtoriginalen Kadenzen zu Beethovens Konzerten (diss., Univ. of Innsbruck, 1963).

Kerman, Joseph, 'Notes on Beethoven's Codas', in A. Tyson (ed.), *Beethoven Studies*, iii (Cambridge, 1982), 141 ff.

Knödt, Heinrich, *Die Konzertkadenz* (diss., Univ. of Vienna, 1911).

—— 'Zur Entwicklungsgeschichte der Kadenzen im Instrumentalkonzert', *SIMG* 15 (1913–14), 375 ff.

Lee, Douglas A., 'Some Embellished Versions of Sonatas by Franz Benda', *MQ* 62 (1976), 58 ff.

Marcello, Benedetto, 'Il teatro alla moda', written *c.*1720; trans. R. G. Pauly, *MQ* 34 (1948), 371 ff. and 35 (1949), 85 ff.

Matthews, Denis, 'Adrian Boult Lecture: Cadenzas in Piano Concertos', *Recorded Sound*, 68 (1978), 724 ff.

Mersmann, Hans, 'Beiträge zur Aufführungspraxis der vorklassischen Kammermusik', *Archiv für Musikwissenschaft*, 2 (1919–20), 99 ff.

Mies, Paul, *Die Krise der Konzertkadenz bei Beethoven* (Bonn, 1970).

Misch, Ludwig, 'Non si fa una cadenza', in L. Misch (ed.), *Beethoven-Studien* (Berlin, 1950), 135 ff.

Neumann, Frederick, *Ornamentation and Improvisation in Mozart* (Princeton, 1986).

Newman, William S., *The Sonata in the Classic Era*, 2nd edn. (New York, 1972).

Petrobelli, Pierluigi, *Giuseppe Tartini: Le fonti biografiche* (Venice, 1968).

Pierre, Constant, *Histoire du Concert Spirituel 1725–1790* (Paris, 1975).

Piggott, Patrick, *The Life and Music of John Field (1782–1837)* (London, 1973).

Plantinga, Leon, *Clementi: His Life and Music* (London, etc., 1977).

Quantz, Johann Joachim, *Versuch einer Anweisung die Flöte traversiere zu spielen* (Berlin, 1752); facs. repr. of 3rd edn., 1789, ed. H.-P. Schmitz (Kassel and Basle, 1953); trans. E. R. Reilly as *On Playing the Flute* (London, 1966; 2nd edn., 1985).

Reinecke, Carl, *Zur Wiederbelebung der Mozartschen Clavierconcerte* (Leipzig, 1891).

Riepel, Joseph, *Erläuterung der betrüglichen Tonordnung* (Augsburg, 1765), vol. iv of *Anfangsgründe zur musikalischen Setzkunst*, 5 vols. (1752–68).

Ringer, Alexander L., 'Beethoven and the London Pianoforte School', *MQ* 56 (1970), 742 ff.

Rousseau, Jean-Jacques, *Dictionnaire de musique* (Paris, 1768).

Ryom, Peter, 'La Comparaison entre les versions différentes d'un concerto d'Antonio Vivaldi transcrit par J. S. Bach', *DAM* (1966–7), 91 ff.

Schering, Arnold, *Geschichte des Instrumentalkonzerts* (Leipzig, 1905).

—— 'Die freie Kadenz im Instrumentalkonzert des 18. Jahrhunderts', *International Musical Society Congress Report*, ii (Basle, 1906), 204 ff.

Schmid, Ernst Fritz, 'Schicksale einer Mozart-Handschrift', *M-Jb* (1957), 43 ff.

—— 'Haydn's Oratorium "Il Ritorno di Tobia", seine Entstehung und seine Schicksale', *Archiv für Musikwissenschaft*, 16 (1959), 292 ff.

Schmitz, Hans-Peter, *Die Kunst der Verzierung im 18. Jahrhundert* (Berlin, 1953; 2nd edn., 1965).

Scholz-Michelitsch, Helga, *Das Orchester- und Kammermusikwerk von G. C. Wagenseil: Thematischer Katalog* (Vienna, 1972).

Schünemann, Georg, 'Johann Christoph Friedrich Bach', *B-Jb* 11 (1914), 45 ff.

Schwarz, Boris, 'Beethoven and the French Violin School', *MQ* 44 (1958), 431 ff.

Spitzer, John, 'Improvised Ornamentation in a Handel Aria with Obbligato Wind Accompaniment', *Early Music*, 16/4 (November, 1988), 514 ff.

——and Zaslaw, Neal, 'Improvised Ornamentation in Eighteenth-Century Orchestras', *JAMS* 39/3 (1986), 524 ff.

Spohr, Louis, *Lebenserinnerungen*, ed. F. Göthel, 2 vols. (Tutzing, 1968); trans. anon. as *Louis Spohr's Autobiography*, 2 vols. (London, 1865).

Stevens, Jane R., 'The "Piano Climax" in the Eighteenth-Century Concerto: An Operatic Gesture?', in S. L. Clark (ed.), *C. P. E. Bach Studies* (Oxford, 1988), 245 ff.

Stockhammer, R. *Die Kadenzen zu den Klavierkonzerten der Wiener Klassiker* (diss., Univ. of Vienna, 1936).

Swain, Joseph P., 'Form and Function of the Classical Cadenza', *The Journal of Musicology*, 6/1 (Winter 1988), 27 ff.

Tartini, Giuseppe, *Traité des agrémens de la musique* (Paris, 1771); trans. and ed. E. Jacobi (Celle and New York, 1961).

Tosi, Pier Francesco, *Opinioni de' cantori antichi e moderni, o sieno Osservazioni sopra il canto figurato* (Bologna, 1723; repr. 1968); trans. J. E. Galliard as *Observations on the Florid Song* (London, 1742); ed. M. Pilkington (London, 1987).

Tovey, Donald Francis, 'Prefaces to Cadenzas for Classical Concertos', *Essays and Lectures on Music* (London, etc., 1949), 315 ff.

Truscott, Harold, 'Dussek and the Concerto', *The Music Review*, 16 (1955), 29 ff.

Türk, Daniel Gottlob, *Klavierschule* (Leipzig and Halle, 1789); facs. repr. ed. E. Jacobi (Kassel, etc., 1962); trans. R. H. Haggh as *School of Clavier Playing* (Lincoln, Nebr., and London, 1982).

Uldall, Hans, *Das Klavierkonzert der Berliner Schule* (Leipzig, 1928).

Ursin, F., *Die Klavierkonzerte Joseph Haydns* (diss., Univ. of Vienna, 1929).

Wade, Rachel W., *The Keyboard Concertos of Carl Philipp Emanuel Bach: Sources and Style* (Ann Arbor, 1981).

Walter, Horst, 'Haydns Klavierkonzerte aus textkritischer Sicht', in E. Badura-Skoda (ed.) *Bericht über den Internationalen Joseph Haydn Kongress Wien 1982* (Munich, 1986), 444 ff.

Ward Jones, Peter, 'The Concerto at Mannheim, *c*.1740–1780', *Proceedings of the Royal Musical Association*, 96 (1969–70), 129 ff.

Warren, Charles W., 'Punctus Organi and Cantus Coronatus in the Music of Dufay', in A. W. Atlas (ed.), *Dufay Quincentenary Conference* (Brooklyn, 1976), 128 ff.

Wegeler, Franz Gerhard, and Ries, Ferdinand, *Biographische Notizen über Ludwig van Beethoven* (Koblenz, 1838); rev. A. C. Kalischer, 1906; repr. 1972; trans. F. Noonan, *Remembering Beethoven* (London, 1988).

White, Chappell, 'Did Viotti Write any Original Piano Concertos?', *JAMS* 22 (1969), 275 ff.

——'Viotti's Revision of his 19th Violin Concerto', in R. Weaver (ed.), *Essays on the Music of J. S. Bach and Other Divers Subjects: A Tribute to Gerhard Herz* (Louisville, 1982), 223 ff.

——*Giovanni Battista Viotti (1755–1824): A Thematic Catalogue of His Works* (New York, 1985).

Whitmore, Philip, 'The Cadenza in the Classical Keyboard Concerto' (diss., Univ. of Oxford, 1986).

——'Towards an Understanding of the Capriccio', *JRMA* 113/1 (1988), 47 ff.

Winter, Robert, 'Performing Beethoven's Early Piano Concertos', *Early Music*, 16/2 (May 1988), 214 ff.

Wohlfahrt, Hannsdieter, *Johann Christoph Friedrich Bach* (Berne, 1971).

Wolff, Christoph, 'Zur Chronologie der Klavierkonzert-Kadenzen Mozarts', *M-Jb* (1978–9), 235 ff.

Wotquenne, Alfred, *Thematisches Verzeichnis der Werke von Carl Philipp Emanuel Bach (1714–88)* (Leipzig, 1905; repr. 1964).

Glossary of Terms

ad libitum cadenza: a cadenza which might equally well be replaced by another, with the composer's blessing.

cadential fermata: the sign ⌒ used to indicate the beginning of a cadenza; this may be either the point at which an ad libitum cadenza could be introduced, or else the point at which an obbligato cadenza begins.

cadential trill: the trill marking the end of a cadenza.

cadenza: an improvisation, or a passage intended to sound like one, inserted within a structural cadence, thereby causing it to be audibly prolonged.

cadenza fiorita: a cadence ornamented by divisions which do not add to its length.

cadenza in tempo: a cadenza that is measured and barred throughout—often an ensemble cadenza or an accompanied solo cadenza.

capriccio: an extremely brilliant and quite extended solo passage often terminating in a cadenza, and found in certain violin concertos by Locatelli, Vivaldi, and Tartini; some eighteenth-century keyboard music contains examples of bravura passages which seem to belong to the same tradition.

composed fermata: the effect of a held note or chord at the beginning of an obbligato cadenza in the absence of a fermata sign, the full duration of the note or chord being written out.

deceptive cadenza: an improvisatory cadential prolongation, metrical at least at the beginning, which merges seamlessly with what has gone before; in the absence of any clear articulation of the opening it cannot strictly be called a cadenza.

divisions: a type of ornamentation in which longer notes are divided up into many short ones.

Eingang: a fermata embellishment which leads into a new section, especially common in rondos before restatements of the theme.

embellished fermata: improvisatory ornamentation of any type of pause chord.

ensemble cadenza: a cadenza for more than one soloist.

extended cadence: the extension of a soloist's cadence by means of a brief passage preparing for the introduction of a cadenza; the extension is clearly a linking passage and could not be interpreted as the beginning of a ritornello (see 'inserted cadenza').

false-start cadenza: a passage in which the composer makes as if to introduce a cadenza, but does not in fact do so, thereby thwarting the listener's expectations.

final cadenza: a cadenza introduced at a tonic cadence at or towards the end of a piece.

final solo cadence: in a ritornello movement the cadence leading from the final solo section into the final ritornello.

halbe Kadenz: an embellished Phrygian cadence, common in baroque music.

hidden cadenza: an obbligato cadenza with no indication in the score that it is a cadenza at all.

inserted cadenza: a cadenza introduced during an orchestral ritornello or similar passage, over a cadence which is inserted there expressly for the purpose of accommodating the cadenza.

integrated cadenza: a cadenza related to its parent movement by common material, and consequently suitable for use only in that particular parent movement.

interchangeable cadenza: a cadenza which may be used in any context given the appropriate key and *Affekt*, because it is not based on material borrowed from any parent movement.

multiple cadenza: a cadenza in two or more real parts throughout.

obbligato cadenza: a cadenza supplied by the composer in the score of the parent movement, which may neither be replaced by another nor omitted.

parent movement: the movement of a concerto or other work for which a particular cadenza is intended.

penultimate: the note or chord from which a cadenza is launched—usually a unison dominant or a tonic 6–4.

perfidia: either (*a*) one of three short passages by Torelli scored for two violins over a bass pedal, or (*b*) an extended passage of dominant preparation, usually over a bass pedal, common towards important cadences in late baroque Italian violin music; named because of its resemblance in style to the three Torelli passages.

pre-tutti cadenza: a cadenza introduced at a cadence leading from a solo section into a tutti.

rallentando cadenza: an improvisatory cadential embellishment in which the music begins to slow down before the arrival of the pausing bass-note; in the absence of clear articulation of the opening it cannot strictly be classed as a cadenza.

rondo cadenza: a cadenza which terminates by leading into a solo restatement of a rondo theme, thereby combining the functions of cadenza and *Eingang*.

simple cadenza: a cadenza written as a single part over a stationary bass.

subsidiary cadenza: a cadenza introduced at a cadence, usually in a foreign key, in the middle of a movement (i.e. not at or towards the end).

General Index

∽⧓∾

Italicized references indicate musical examples.

Abel, Carl Friedrich 159, 160
Affekt 25, 37, 48, 89, 110, 192, 208
Agricola, Johann Friedrich 20, 22, 23, 30, 31, 47
Alberti bass 99, 108
Alembert, Jean le Rond d' 162
amateurs 5, 11, 49, 92–3, 97, 102, 104, 107, 142, 153
Archduke Rudolph 201
Arne, Thomas Augustine 161
ars combinatoria 27
August, Peter 102–3

Babell, William 66
Bach, Carl Philipp Emanuel 9 n., 20, 28–30, 31, 33, 36–7, 48, 61, 76, 77–97, 98, 99, 100, 103, 105, 133, 134–5, 147, 150, 174 n., 178, 189
  La Boehmer, H. 81 (Wq. 117 No. 26) 135 n.
  keyboard cadenzas, H. 264 (Wq. 120) 47, 80, 83–93, 96, 97
    no. 1 89–91
    no. 2 92 n.
    no. 3 92 n.
    no. 9 91
    no. 15 30 n.
    no. 18 *89*
    no. 20, 'Einfall' 87–8
    no. 24 91, 92 n.
    no. 26 91
    no. 28 92 n.
    no. 33 *92*
    no. 34 92 n.
    no. 46 91 n.
    no. 48 92 n.
    no. 49 92 n.
    no. 54 92 n.
    no. 60 30 n.
    no. 74 92 n.
  keyboard concertos 77 n., 79–97, 123
    H. 407 (Wq. 5) 92 n.
    H. 408 (Wq. 46) 91, 92 n.
    H. 409 (Wq. 6) 92 n.
    H. 411 (Wq. 8) 80 n.
    H. 414 (Wq. 11) 30 n., 91

H. 416 (Wq. 13) 81 n.
H. 417 (Wq. 14) 91
H. 419 (Wq. 16) 82
H. 424 (Wq. 21) 91
H. 427 (Wq. 23) 91 n.
H. 428 (Wq. 24) 80, 88
H. 429 (Wq. 25) 80 n., 92 n.
H. 430 (Wq. 26) 79 n., *81*, 89
H. 433 (Wq. 27) 55
H. 434 (Wq. 28) 79 n., 87, 88
H. 437 (Wq. 29) 79 n.
H. 441 (Wq. 31) *81*, 89
H. 442 (Wq. 32) 91
H. 444 (Wq. 34) 79 n., 87 n., 88
H. 446 (Wq. 35) 79 n.
H. 447 (Wq. 36) 88
H. 465 (Wq. 39) 79 n.
H. 467 (Wq. 40) 79 n.
H. 471–6 (Wq. 43) 5, 83, 92, 93–7
  H. 471 (Wq. 43 No. 1) 82 n., 94
  H. 472 (Wq. 43 No. 2) 80 n., 94
  H. 473 (Wq. 43 No. 3) 94, 95–6, 189 n.
  H. 474 (Wq. 43 No. 4) 29 n., 93, 94, 96–7
  H. 475 (Wq. 43 No. 5) 94, 95–6, 189 n.
  H. 476 (Wq. 43 No. 6) 82, 94, *95*, 96
H. 478 (Wq. 45) 84, 89
H. 479 (Wq. 47) 80 n., 97
keyboard fantasias 67, 135
keyboard sonatas 58, 77–9, 83–4, 150
  H. 25 (Wq. 48 No. 2) 77
  Probestücke, H. 70–5 (Wq. 63 Nos. 1–6) 21, 78
    H. 71 (Wq. 63 No. 2) 78
    H. 73 (Wq. 63 No. 4) 33, 78
    H. 75 (Wq. 63 No. 6) 33, 78
  Sonaten mit veränderten Reprisen, H. 136–40 and 126 (Wq. 50) 92
  H. 204–7 and 184–5 (Wq. 54) 79
  H. 208 (Wq. 57 No. 4) 32 n.
  Württemberg Sonatas, H. 30–4 and 36 (Wq. 49) 79
    H. 33 (Wq. 49 No. 3) 79 n.
    H. 36 (Wq. 49 No. 6) 78 n.

Bach, Carl Philipp Emanuel (*cont.*)
  Miscellanea Musica 88
  ornaments to keyboard works, H. 164
    (Wq. 68) 93
  Sonatina, H. 449 (Wq. 96) 87
  *Versuch über die wahre Art das Clavier zu
    spielen* 9 n., 20, 28–30, 33, 37, 54,
    78–9, 80, 85 n., 89
Bach, Johanna Maria 84
Bach, Johann Christian 103–5, 106, 159, 160
  keyboard concertos:
    Concerto No. 6 in F minor 100 n.
    Five early works 103, 105
    Six concertos Op. 1 104, 106, 159
    Six concertos Op. 7 104
    Six concertos Op. 13 104–5, 159
Bach, Johann Christoph Friedrich 105–6
Bach, Johann Sebastian 47, 65, 68–73, 99, 100
  Concertos:
    Brandenburg Concerto No. 5,
      BWV 1050 70, 72 n., 73, 100
    Concerto in C for 2 Harpsichords and
      Strings, BWV 1061 68 n.
    Harpsichord Concerto in D minor,
      BWV 1052 70, 73
    Harpsichord Concerto in D major,
      BWV 1054 47, 71–2
    Organ Concerto, BWV 594 69–70
    Triple Concerto, BWV 1044 73
    Violin Concerto in E major,
      BWV 1042 47, 71–2
  Fugue in A minor, BWV 543 12 n.
  Fugue in A minor, BWV 894 73
Bach, Wilhelm Friedemann 61 n., 100
Badura-Skoda, Eva and Paul 12, 18 n., 61,
  119, 123, 129–32, 135, 137, 138, 144,
  196
Balbastre, Claude-Bénigne 157, 163, 164, 165
Beauvarlet-Charpentier, Jean-Jacques 164
Beecke, Ignaz von 133
Beethoven, Ludwig van 12, 59, 61, 88 n., 107,
  142–3, 180, 181–203, 204
  cadenzas 48, 54, 148; (*Beethoven Werke*
    VII: 7)
    no. 1 194–5, 196, 198
    no. 2 194–5, 196, 198, 200
    no. 3 194–6, 198
    no. 4 192, 196
    no. 5 195, 196–7, 199
    no. 6 197, 198
    no. 7 185 n., 192 n., 197–8
    no. 8 193, 198
    no. 9 198–9
    no. 10 194 n.
    no. 11 188 n., 193, 198–9
    no. 12 192, 197, 199–200
    no. 13 194 n.
    no. 14 194 n.

    no. 15 199, 200
    no. 16 194, 195, 199, 200
    no. 17 194, 199, 200–1
    codas 188–93, 196, 198, 201, 202–3
  concertos
    Piano Concerto in E flat, WoO 4 181, 182
    Piano Concerto No. 1, Op. 15 181,
      185–6, 192, 194–5, 196, 201
    Piano Concerto No. 2, Op. 19 182–3,
      187, 193 n., 201
    Piano Concerto No. 3, Op. 37 182, 183,
      187–8, 193, 195, 196, 201
    Piano Concerto No. 4, Op. 58 15 n., 61,
      182, 183–5, 186, 187, 189, 191, 192,
      193, 194 n., 196, 197, 198
    Piano Concerto No. 5, 'Emperor',
      Op. 73 12, 36 n., 176, 180, 181, 186–7,
      191, 193, 198, 199 n., 201, 210, 211
    Triple Concerto, Op. 56 181, 188, 189
    Violin Concerto, Op. 61 82, 185, 187,
      189, 196
    arranged as a piano concerto 181, 192,
      193, 194 n., 197, 199
  Concert Rondo in B flat for piano and
    orchestra, WoO 6 187 n.
  fantasias 181, 203
    Choral Fantasy, Op. 80 201
    for piano, Op. 77 201
  march-rhythms 199
  Quartet in B flat, Op. 18 No. 6 186 n.
  Quartet in A minor, Op. 132 199
  Quintet for piano and wind, Op. 16 192 n.
  sketches for cadenzas 201
  sonatas:
    for cello and piano, Op. 5 No. 1 58,
      190 n., 193
    for piano in C, Op. 2 No. 3 190–1, 208
    for piano in A flat, Op. 26 199 n.
    for piano in C, Op. 53,
      'Waldstein' 186 n., 189–90, 192
  symphonies:
    No. 1 in C 191
    No. 3 in E flat, 'Eroica' 191, 199 n.
    No. 4 in B flat 186 n.
    No. 9 in D minor, 'Choral' 96
  trills 185, 186, 187, 188, 190, 196, 198, 200,
    202, 203
Benda, Georg Anton 55, 99
Béranger, Oscar 208 n.
Berlin 79, 84, 88, 98–9, 101, 103, 105, 108
Best, William Thomas 68
Binder, Christlieb Siegmund 101, 102, 103
Boccherini, Luigi 155 n.
Boucher, Alexandre-Jean 34
Boyton, William 161
Brahms, Johannes 60, 119, 172, 185
  Piano Concerto in D minor 60–1, 185
  Violin Concerto 60, 61

Broschi, Riccardo 74 n., 75
Brossard, Sébastien de 7 n.
Brosses, Charles de 162
Burgess, Henry 157
Burney, Charles 3 n., 52, 65, 74, 75 n., 98, 102, 104, 157, 163

cadenzas:
  cadenza fiorita 7, 21, 23, 52, 53
  cadenza in tempo 6, 48, 82, 96, 125 n., 144, 151, 174, 180, 210, 211
  deceptive 15, 61, 70, 156, 183 n., 185
  duet 11, 20 n., 23, 32–3, 48, 75, 79, 149
  ensemble 11, 14, 47, 48, 107, 126, 137, 144, 145, 146, 147, 164, 169, 174, 180, 190 n.
  false-start 15, 57 n., 58 n., 185
  hidden 16, 18, 82, 96, 151, 176 n., 182
  integrated 23, 30–1, 48, 49, 127, 148, 171, 180, 188
  interchangeable 23, 31, 49
  rallentando 9, 16, 21
  rondo 38, 60, 107, 114, 123 n., 124, 137, 143, 144, 146, 147, 172, 193, 195, 201, 206, 211; *see also* rondo
  subsidiary 6, 7, 22, 80, 108 n., 110, 150, 158
caesura 16, 18, 38, 54, 59, 70, 91, 123
Cambini, Giuseppe Maria 168–9
Cannabich, Christian 106
capriccio 10 n., 38, 40, 41–6, 68, 69–70, 100, 105, 147, 155, 165, 193, 213
Castil-Blaze, François Henri Joseph 213
castrato 74, 162
Charlotte, Queen 104
Clementi, Muzio 162, 204, 207–10
  Concerto for piano in C 207
  Gradus ad Parnassum 208 n.
  Musical Characteristics, Op. 19 118, 128, 153, 208–10
  Sonata for piano, Op. 33 No. 3 207 n.
  Sonata for piano, 4 hands, Op. 14 No. 3 208
coda 205, 206
  see also Beethoven, codas
Concert Spirituel 65 n., 163, 164–5, 171
Corelli, Arcangelo 39, 157
  Sonatas, Op. 5 8, 9
  Op. 5 No. 3 39, *40*
  Op. 5 No. 11 8
Corrette, Michel 165
Cramer, Johann Baptist 162, 177, 178–9, 180 n., 204, 210–11
  concertos for piano:
    No. 3, Op. 26 210
    No. 4, Op. 38 211
    No. 8, Op. 70 211
  Kreutzer's Favorite Rondo (arr.) 211 n.
  studies 211
Czerny, Carl 187 n.

Dale, Joseph 161
Damoreau, Jean-François 164
Davaux, Jean-Baptiste 166–8, 169
Diderot, Denis 162
Dittersdorf, Carl Ditters von 28 n., 49 n., 111
divertimento concerto 108, 109–10
division 7
Dresden 101–3, 108
Dublin 33
Dubourg, Matthew 33–4
Duphly, Jacques 163
Dupuis, Thomas Sanders 156–7
Dussek, Jan Ladislav 162, 177, 178–9, 180 n., 204–7
  piano concertos 204–7
    Op. 1, C. 2–4 206 n.
    Op. 3, C. 33 206 n.
    Op. 14, C. 77 206 n.
    Op. 15, C. 53 206 n.
    Op. 17, C. 78 205, 206 n.
    Op. 22, C. 97 206
    Op. 27, C. 104 205–7
    Op. 66 206
  Piano Sonata 'Plus ultra', Op. 64, C. 221 211
dynamics 77, 81, 94, 106, 136, 160, 183, 188, 189, 190, 196

Eichner, Ernst 106, 165
Eingang 4, 35, 37–8, 72, 106, 110, 114, 119 n., 121, 122 n., 124, 128, 143, 160, 178, 181, 185, 193–4, 212
Eisenstadt 149, 150
empfindsamer Stil 100, 105, 110
Encyclopédie 162
England 68, 103–4, 155–62, 170
Enlightenment 98
Esterházy family 149

Farinelli 74–6
Faustina Bordoni 52, 101
Felici, Alessandro 155
Felton, William 157, 158
Field, John 58, 204, 210
  Piano Concerto No. 5, 'L' Incendie par l'Orage' 210, 211
Fischer, Johann Christian 159
Framery, Nicolas-Étienne 164 n.
France 3–4, 74, 162–70, 180
Frederick the Great 30, 98, 99, 101
Frederick William I of Prussia 98
French Revolution 162, 171
Frescobaldi, Girolamo 9
Friedrich August III of Saxony 101–2
Friedrich Christian, Elector of Saxony 101
Frischmuth, Léonard-Louis 47 n.

galant 99, 105, 108, 149, 155, 159–61
Galuppi, Baldassare 154, 155
   Sonata, Op. 1 No. 2 155
   Sonata, Op. 2 No. 3 155
Gaviniès, Pierre 165 n.
Gazzaniga, Giuseppe 155
Geminiani, Francesco 157
Giacomelli, Geminiano 75
Giordani, Tommaso 159, 160
   cadenzas 160, 161–2, 197 n.
Gluck, Christoph Willibald 126, 147
Graun, Carl Heinrich 98, 99
Guerre des Bouffons 162

Haigh, Thomas 161
halbe Kadenz 35, *36*, 37
Hamburg 80, 82 n., 83, 84, 92, 93
Handel, George Frideric 33, 50, 52, 65–8, 76,
   155, 157, 158, 160, 161
   Alessandro 52
   Messiah 51
   organ concertos 65–8, 160
      Op. 4 65, 66–8
         No. 1 68
         No. 2 66–8
         No. 4 66–8
      Op. 7 65–6
         No. 6 65
   Poro 75, 76
   Rinaldo 66
harp 168
Hasse, Johann Adolf 101
   Alessandro nell' Indie 52 n.
   Artaserse 52 n., 75
Hawdon, Matthias 157, 161
Haydn, Joseph 128, 149–53, 154, 185, 186,
   208, 212
   arias 150–1
   concertos:
      in D for corno di caccia 151
      for *lira organizzata* 151
      for keyboard instruments,
         Hob. XVIII 151
         No. 1 152
         No. 2 152 n., 154 n.
         No. 3 151
         No. 4 16–18, 151
         No. 6 152
         No. 11 56, 151, 152
   The Creation 150
   keyboard cadenzas (attrib.) 149, 152
   quartets 102, 150
      Op. 9 150
      Op. 33 No. 6 150
   Il ritorno di Tobia 58 n., 150–1
   sonatas for keyboard 150
   symphonies 102, 149–50
      Nos. 6–8 149
      No. 7 149
      No. 24 149
      No. 45 150 n.
      No. 54 149–50
      No. 68 15 n.
      No. 87 150
      No. 96 150
      No. 102 149
   trios, for baryton 150
   Variations in F minor for piano 127
Hayes, Philip 160–1
Hayes, William 157–8
Heinichen 101
Herbst 7 n., 21
Hiller, Johann Adam 20, 21, 25–6, 37
Hoffmeister, Franz Anton 111
Hofmann, Leopold 110 n., 149
Hook, James 160
Hummel, Johann Nepomuk 58, 59, 212
   cadenzas for Mozart's concertos 119, 212
   Concerto for piano and violin, Op. 17 212
   Concerto in B minor for piano, Op. 89 212

Italy 154–5, 162

Jommelli, Nicolò 155
Josef Maria Benedikt of
   Donaueschingen 142

Kellner, Johann Peter 69, 70
Kerman, Joseph 191–2
Knödt, Heinrich 4 n., 12, 39–40, 84, 190 n.
Kozeluch, Leopold 114–18, 128, 208
Krebs, Johann Ludwig 100
Krumpholtz, Johann Baptist 168 n.
Kunzen, Adolph Carl 100 n.

Leipzig 101, 206
Levy, Sarah 84
Liszt, Franz 119
Locatelli, Pietro Antonio 10 n., 41–6,
   100 n., 155, 163, 165, 213
   Violin Concertos, Op. 3, 'L' Arte del
      Violino' 41–6, 213
      No. 8 *41–3*
      No. 9 45 n.
   Violin Sonatas, Op. 6 43 n.
Lodron, Countess 122
London 104, 105, 108, 154, 162, 171, 204, 210
London Pianoforte School 204
Louis Ferdinand, Prince of Prussia 206

Mannheim 106–8, 128, 135
Marcello, Benedetto 10
Maria Theresa, Empress 75
Martini, Padre Giovanni Battista 154
Matteis, Nicola 9
Mattheson, Johann 22

Medieval polyphony 10
Mendelssohn, Felix 60
mensuration 48
messa di voce 36
Metastasio, Pietro 101, 147
Meyer, Leonard 175
Michel 82 n., 83, 88, 91 n., 92
Mies, Paul 142–3, 185 n., 188, 190 n.,
    192–3, 195, 196–7, 199, 200, 201,
    203
Monn, Matthias Georg 108 n.
Moscheles, Ignaz 119
Mozart, Konstanze 128, 133
Mozart, Leopold 128, 134
Mozart, Nannerl 128
Mozart, Wolfgang Amadeus 4, 5, 13, 24, 31,
    37, 38, 48, 61, 83, 106, 111, 114, 118,
    119–48, 150, 153, 160, 172, 174–5, 181,
    185, 189, 193, 195, 196, 200–1, 208,
    212
  arias 110, 124, 125–6
  cadenzas, K[6] 626a I 133, 136–44
    no. 1 143
    no. 2 143
    nos. 5–7 135, 137
    no. 8 128, 138
    no. 9 138
    no. 10 138
    no. 11 128, 138
    no. 12 138
    no. 14 138
    no. 15 139
    no. 16 135, 139
    no. 17 123, 133, 139–40, 143
    no. 18 133, 135, 139–40, 143
    no. 24 143, 146–7
    no. 27 141
    no. 32 121
    no. 33 121
    no. 43 174 n.
    no. 47 143
    no. 49 123 n.
    no. 51 123 n.
    no. 52 140
    no. 53 140
    no. 54 123, 140
    no. 57 143
    no. 58 123
    no. 60 143, 196
    no. 61 140–2, 144, 146
    no. 62 *130–2*
    no. 63 143 n.
    no. 64 143, 200
    deest (K. 242) 136–7, 144, 146
  cadenzas, K[6] 626a II 133–6, 138
    A 135
    B 135
    C 133, 134

D 135–6
F 135–6
G 135–6, 197 n.
H 135–6
K 133, 134, 197 n.
N 136
O 136
deest (K. 40?) 134
La clemenza di Tito 125, 147
concertos 110
  for clarinet, K. 622 122
  for horn, K. 412 (386b) and 417 122
  for piano:
    K. 175 124, 133
    K. 238 137
    K. 246 128, 138
    K. 271 122 n., 134, 139, 140, 143
    K. 414 (385p) 141
    K. 450 36, 128, 174 n.
    K. 451 128, 143
    K. 453 82, 124, 189 n.
    K. 456 140, 143
    K. 459 24, 122–3, 128, 143
    K. 466 119, 124, 192, 194, 199, 200
    K. 467 58 n., 119 n., 124
    K. 482 119 n., 124
    K. 488 122, 140–2
    K. 491 119 n., 123 n., 124, 187–8
    K. 503 119 n.
    K. 537 119 n.
    K. 595 122, 128, 132, 143
  for two pianos, K. 365 (316a) 128, 143,
    146–7
  for three pianos, K. 242 122, 128, 136,
    146
  for violin, K. 219 36
concerto arrangements 120 n., 124
  K. 37 124
  K. 40 133, 134, 135
  K. 41 124
  K. 107 124 n.
    No. 1 124, 135
    No. 2 57
Concertone, K. 190 (186E) 126, 144
Concert Rondo in D, K. 382 124, 146
Davide penitente, K. 469
La finta semplice 125
Idomeneo 125
Mass in C minor, K. 427 (417a) 125, 126,
    145, 146
Mitridate 125
Musical Joke, K. 522 126, *127*
Oboe Quartet, K. 370 (368b) 126
Posthorn Serenade, K. 320 126, 144, 146,
    147
Quintet for piano and wind, K. 452 6 n.,
    126, 144, 145
Rondo in F, K. 494 18, 69 n.

Mozart, Wolfgang Amadeus (*cont.*)
  Die Schuldigkeit des ersten Gebots 125
  sonatas:
    for organ, K. 336 (336d) 126
    for piano
      K. 332 (300k) 14
      K. 333 (315c) 127, 146
      K. 533 12, *13*, 16, 40
    for violin and piano, K. 306 (3001) 127,
      134, 145
  string quartets 102
  symphonies 102
  trills 123, 146, 147
  variations for piano on
    'Ein Weib ist das herrlichste Ding',
      K. 613 127 n.
    'Lison dormait', K. 264 (315d) 127 n.,
      145
    'Salve tu Domine', K. 398 (416e) 127 n.,
      145, 147
    'Unser dummer Pöbel meint',
      K. 455 127 n., 145
  Die Zauberflöte 125 n.
Müthel, Johann Gottfried 100

Nachlassverzeichnis 84, 85
Naumann, Johann Gottlieb 101, 102
Navoigille, Guillaume 165
noëls 165

opera buffa 162
opera, comic 125, 126, 147

Paganini, Nicolò 46
Pagin, André-Noël 163, 165
Paisiello, Giovanni 155
Paradis, Maria-Theresia 111, 114
parenthesis 175, 188
Paris 47, 106–7, 108, 135, 145, 154, 157, 163,
  164, 165, 166, 168, 171, 174, 206
Pellegrino, Ferdinando 155
perfidia 12 n., 38–41, 68, 69, 70, 99 n., 158,
  161 n.
Petrini, Franz 168 n.
Philip V of Spain 75
Pierron, Therese 128, 138
Pisendel, Johann Georg 10, 101
Pleyel, Ignaz Joseph 111
point d'orgue 3 n., 12 n., 163, 213
Pokorny, Franz Xaver 155 n.
Pollet, Jean-Joseph-Benoît 168 n.
Porpora, Nicola:
  Eomene 74 n.
  Mitridate 52 n.
  Siface 52 n.
Potsdam 98
Prague 101
Pugnani, Gaetano 171

Quantz, Johann Joachim 3–11, 12, 20, 22, 23,
  24–5, 26, 27, 30, 31, 32–3, 35–6, 47–8,
  49, 53, 61, 72, 75, 89, 98, 101, 158
  Versuch einer Anweisung die Flöte traversiere
    zu spielen 3–11, 20

Rachmaninov, Sergei 60
Ramm, Friedrich 106
recitative 133, 139, 149, 182, 203, 211
Reichardt, Johann Friedrich 100–1
Reinecke, Carl 119
Rheinsberg 98
rhetoric 22, 80, 110, 202
Riemann, Hugo 61 n.
Riepel, Joseph 20, 22, 23, 24, 27–8, 47
Ries, Ferdinand 201–2
Rigel, Henri-Joseph 145, 165, 169–70
ritornello form 10, 54, 58, 68, 99, 108, 110,
  123–4, 126, 147, 150
Romberg, Bernhard 206
Rome 74
rondo 4, 37, 38, 99, 104, 108, 110, 124, 144,
  146, 160, 172–7, 185–6, 193, 202, 206,
  211; *see also* cadenzas, rondo
Rossini, Gioacchino 12
Rousseau, Jean-Jacques 3, 162
  Dictionnaire de Musique 3 n., 4 n., 163,
    164 n., 165
Rudolph, Archduke *see* Archduke
Ruppin 98
Rutini, Giovanni Marco 155

St Petersburg 212
St Roch 165
Salieri, Antonio 111, *112–14*
Sammartini, Giuseppe 32 n.
Sanssouci 98
Scarlatti, Alessandro
  Griselda *51*, 52 n.
Schaffrath, Christoph 99
Schale, Christian Friedrich 99
Schenker, Heinrich 57 n.
Schering, Arnold 72
Schobert, Johann 165
Schroeter, Johann Samuel 135–6, 159, 160,
  161
  Concertos Op. 3 135–6
Schumann, Robert 59, *60*
Schwerin 69–70, 84
Second World War 61
Séjan, Nicolas 164
Seven Years War 101
Spohr, Louis 34, 212
Stamitz family 106
Stanley, John 157, 158–9, 161
  Concertos, Op. 2 161
  Concertos, Op. 10 161
  Organ Voluntaries, Op. 5 158

Organ Voluntaries, Op. 6 158, 161
Organ Voluntaries, Op. 7 158–9
Steibelt, Daniel Gottlieb 58, 162, 177, 178,
    210, 211
    Piano Concerto No. 3, 'L'Orage' 210, 211
Steinbacher, Johann Michael 108, *109*
Sterkel, Johann Franz Xaver 111, 118, 128,
    208
Sturm und Drang 100
symphonie concertante 47, 48, 104 n., 106–7,
    126 n., 164, 165, 166, 168, 169, 170,
    180, 213

Tartini, Giuseppe 33, 44–6, 47 n., 52–3, 70,
    99, 105, 160, 163
    Traité des agrémens de la Musique 20, 26–7,
    29 n., 45
    Violin Concerto, D. 103 45–6
Tessarini, Carlo 160
Tomasini, Alois Luigi 150
Torelli, Giuseppe 38–40
Tosi, Pier Francesco 10, 20, 21–4, 52–3
Tovey, Sir Donald Francis 188, 190 n., 191,
    192, 195, 196, 202
transcription 47, 48, 68, 69–70, 147, 207
Türk, Daniel Gottlob 21, 22, 23, 30–1, 33, 48,
    49, 79, 195

Übergang 37

Vanhal, Johann Baptist 56, 118, 128, 208
variations 99, 104, 110, 124, 127, 145–6, 159,
    202, 211
Vauxhall Gardens 160
Vienna 108–18, 124, 132, 144, 146, 150
Viotti, Giovanni Battista 59, 148, 162, 164,
    171–80, 204, 210, 212
    violin concertos 59, 144, 171–7
    No. 19 171 n., 178

Nos. 22–9 172
No. 22 172–6, 177
No. 23 178
No. 24 177 n.
No. 25 178, 179
No. 27 172 n., 176–7, 179, 186
No. 28 171
No. 29 177
arranged as piano concertos 171, 177–80,
    189 n., 207
Wh. Ia: 1 177 n.
Wh. Ia: 3 180 n.
Wh. Ia: 5 180 n.
Wh. Ia: 7 177 n., 178, 180 n.
Wh. Ia: 8 177 n., 178
Wh. Ia: 9 178
Wh. Ia: 10 178, 179, 180 n.
Wh. Ia: 11 178
Wh. Ia: 12 178
Wh. Ia: 13 178, 179, 180 n.
Wh. Ia: 14 177 n., 178
Vivaldi, Antonio 10, 39–41, 44, 45, 46, 68–70,
    73, 99, 100 n., 101, 155, 163
    violin concertos 10, 73
    RV 208 69
    RV 208a 44 n., 69
    RV 581 44 n.
    RV 583 44 n.
Vogler, Abbé Georg Joseph 107–8

Wagenseil, Georg Christoph 109–10, 149,
    165
Wendling, Johann Baptist 106
Westphal, Johann Jacob Heinrich 83–4
Wolff, Christoph 120, 128, 138, 140
Wölfl, Joseph 211
Wotquenne, Alfred 83

Xaver, Prince 101